Nov, 14th 2021

To: Mr. James B. Patterson
New Beginnings!
A. J. Taajwar

Against All Odds

My personal experiences
of living the street life
… and the price I paid

Goldsboro, NC

ISBN: 979-8-55-631937-0

For teaching me how to free my heart to love, for accepting me as I was and believing in me when no one else did, I dedicate *Against All Odds* to Katherine R. Naland.

Table of Contents

Introduction

Against All Odds is an uncannily true story of being tried, convicted, and sentenced to prison at age 15, as an adult, and the man that prison experience would eventually produce. This story has very long legs, covers many unexplored dimensions, and provides a rare bird's-eye view of growing up behind prison walls, living the street life to survive, and being caught up in the revolving doors of recidivism for over 40 years.

"Except for the Grace of God, there go I."

From personal experience, *Against All Odds* takes the reader deeper into the world of crime and punishment than any book on the market today. A story of true resilience and raw determination, the reader will witness the evolution of how one man faced life's adversities on his journey to finding the better man within.

1. Wake Up to This

May 1974, I woke up to the sounds of metal gears turning and grinding, followed by steel clashing against steel. It was a distinct and unmistakable sound; so distinct that once heard, you would never forget. It was the sound of a jail-cell door being opened and closed. It took me several moments to emerge from the thick fog of my deep sleep, only to come face to face with the reality and gravity of my situation. I was a 15-year-old juvenile being held at the Gary, Indiana, city jail on two counts of murder—Count One Murder, Count Two Murder—during the perpetration of a robbery. Both offenses carried either life imprisonment upon conviction or death: the electric chair if the death sentence was sought.

I sat up suddenly, taking in my surroundings. The entire cell was made of steel: the walls, the sink, and the toilet, the bunk beds, and of course the bars and doorway that served as an entrance. Looking out of the cell, one could see the common area where prisoners ate their meals, should the jailer on duty feel inclined to let us out. Here were two steel picnic tables securely fastened to the floor. Steel bars ran the length of the common area from floor to ceiling. You could see out the windows, yet these steel bars were actually a partition, keeping prisoners approximately four feet or so from access to the windows themselves.

Sitting on the edge of the steel bunk bed, my elbows resting on my knees and both hands holding my head, I looked down at my feet and noticed I had on no shoes. Then a flood of memories hit me in a sudden rush and it dawned on me that, in an instant, my life would never be the same again—not ever! While I had been held at the Gary City Jail on three prior occasions for juvenile-delinquency offenses, this time I had completely crossed the line of no return.

Where were my shoes, coat, belt, and the worn-out blanket the jailer gave me during booking? They were stacked on one of the steel picnic tables in the common area, out of reach. Before crying myself to sleep, I had stopped one of the jailers while he made his routine rounds for head count. I asked him if I could go home for Mother's Day, which was only a day or two away. I promised him I would return. The officer looked down at me and without saying a word, walked away. The next thing I knew, my cell door was grinding open with its metallic sound. The officer reappeared and ordered me to come out. Taking my shoes, belt, coat, and the ragged blanket, he ordered me back into my cell. I stood there looking at the closed cell door bars dumbfounded, trying to figure out what had just taken place. It would be the last thing I remembered before folding up like a tent and crying myself to sleep.

I imagine I probably went into a state of shock, a sudden and disturbing effect on the emotions of a 15-year-old, because I recall very little of my remaining stay at the Gary City Jail from that point on. The actions of the jailer knocked me off balance, mentally and emotionally, because my young adolescent mind could not conceive why he treated me as he did. I felt he was punishing me by taking my property and clothes. It would be years later that I realized how ridiculous and crazy I must have sounded, asking if I could go home on Mother's Day, under the circumstances. The officer actually took those possessions from me thinking that I might harm myself; at least that's what I came to believe and accept.

Perhaps two or three days later, my cell door was opened and the jailer ordered me to grab all my belongings because I was being transferred to the Lake County Jail in Crown Point, Indiana. My four codefendants were downstairs already waiting when I arrived, and we were placed in the transport holding tank altogether. I had not seen them since our arrest and remember looking at my codefendants, Spann and Gamble, with open contempt and disgust. In my presence, both had informed the police that I had been the trigger man during the robbery-murder, a blatant violation of the code of silence.

There was very little talk among us, as I recall, and once at the Lake County Jail, the five of us were split up again. Clifford, who was only 16 at the time, and I were assigned to the juvenile section, located on the third floor. Spann, who was 28, and Gamble, 22, were placed together in one of the rough adult sections. From the stories I heard, neither of them had an easy life in jail. Jessie, who was 18 at the time, was housed in another adult section on the second floor; he too faced some rough times. For the next year and a half, while awaiting trial, we only saw each other during court hearings.

The old Lake County Jail in Crown Point, Indiana, was an old condemned building when I was incarcerated there in 1974. The windows were all broken out and covered with plastic. The bricks for the exterior wall were so loose, I once used a spoon to dig one out. The juvenile section consisted of three cells and a day-room area. Although each cell had its own toilet, only one was usable. All three constantly leaked water and the overall conditions were quite deplorable. The new county jail was still under construction and behind schedule by a couple of years and would not be open until January the following year. It was under these conditions that I got my first real taste of incarceration.

Today, the old Lake County Jail is a town landmark. The building is now a museum; at least that's what I've been told. The jail was made famous in the 1930s when the notorious bank robber, John Dillinger, escaped from the jail using a fake gun carved from a bar of lye soap, colored black with shoe polish. Rumors say I was held in the very same section from which Dillinger escaped. I can't say this is a fact. I do know for a fact that in 1974, some 40 years later, the county jail was still passing out lye soap for prisoners to wash and bathe.

Clifford and I were housed in the juvenile section. Two other prisoners awaiting trial were in the section already; neither were juveniles. France, 18 years, was considered an adult who could not survive the adult section. I came to learn he had been beaten, sodomized, and made to dress like a female. Rudy, 24, could not survive the adult section because he killed a street guy who had many friends incarcerated in the jail system. Although Rudy was quiet and mostly kept to himself and wanted no trouble, France was a loud mouth and always on some personal mischief. It didn't take me long to discern from where his malfunction derived. He wanted others to suffer the same fate and mistreatment to which he had been subjected. He would try me almost immediately, only to quickly get put in his place.

Being a little big man all my life and having the courage of a true warrior, France made the mistake of underestimating me and called me out for some rough play—chest boxing—where boys exchanged punches to the chest and body. This little game was actually a ploy used to determine one's level of superiority over the opponent. One day, he simply hit me in the chest with a soft sucker punch and said, "let's box." I returned the favor by hitting him back as hard as I could, knocking him backwards two or three feet, and said, "I will fight your ass for real and not for play." I was instantly mad and stood there looking him straight in the eyes, waiting for him to make the next move. I was never one to play those types of games because I could not stand for anyone to put their hands on me or grab and wrestle with me.

Clifford, in contrast, was big for his age, about six feet and well over 200 pounds. Clifford would attach himself to me and become a loyal soldier. Locked up together, we got to know one another rather well and being codefendants created a bond between us that made Clifford and myself a formidable combination in the juvenile section. I became the thinker—the brain and planner—taking on the leadership role between us to impose my personal will and influence in the section. Turning Clifford into my enforcer, I transformed him from being a gentle giant into an aggressive big man who respected me, fed on my confidence, and followed my lead without question. Prior to our incarceration, Clifford knew of me from my bad-boy days at school. We both had attended Pulaski Junior High School where my reputation was well known; although I didn't know of Clifford, he knew of me.

It did not take me long to realize that France possessed a deviousness and wickedness that, if allowed to go unchecked, posed a potential threat. It was almost like I could see straight through him. He attempted to set the tone in the section. He wanted to run things, be the cell boss, and implement the same type of jailhouse system used to violate him in the adult sections. France was weak beneath a fake tough-boy persona and I saw it. He was also full of anger and hate as a direct result of his own jailhouse experiences. I became his nemesis, his game spoiler, and an open adversary. On a mental level, France was absolutely no match for me and my dealings with him only served as a catalyst to sharpening my future survival skills.

Perhaps the most important aspect of my early days in the old Lake County Jail was my discovery of how illiterate I was and my vow to do something about it. Reading my criminal indictment and hardly understanding a word served as a double-edged sword of sorts: one edge cutting me down, causing a sense of embarrassment, and the other edge a motivational tool to engage in self-improvement. Barely able to read or write, I started habits and practices I would engage in for many years to come, consciously deciding to undertake a self-betterment plan.

My real first reading came from the King James version of the New Testament. It would become the first book of substance I would read cover to cover. In those early days, I needed a crutch and, like many prisoners before me, when in trouble and facing the yoke of incarceration, we turned to God. I was no exception. During that first couple of months, I read the Bible and the little Daily Bread booklet faithfully every day, and I prayed for a miracle that never came. Although religion had always been in my life, turning to God in jail was purely a selfish act with selfish intentions. Yet, as fate would have it, nothing miraculous occurred to free me from incarceration, but I would live to never regret turning to God in those darker moments and troubled times.

I got in the habit of writing words down, looking them up in the dictionary, using my new vocabulary when talking and when writing letters home. Initially, I was drawn to the big expensive-sounding words and my interest grew into a true fascination with how words could draw a vivid picture of my inner thoughts and feelings. I developed a passion for reading and writing. I read every day. Eventually I got to where I could read a book each day, sometimes two! My reading selections were often limited so it got to the point where it did not matter what the material contents were. I read for the pure pleasure of reading and self-education, and the more I read, the more my writing skills improved and my intellect grew.

Although France did not remain in the juvenile section for very long, he consistently created mischief and a bad atmosphere. Whenever a new young prisoner arrived, France put on his bully show. I allowed the scenes to play out until things got completely out of hand. During this time, I was on my little spiritual journey and refused to let France take undue advantage of the young boys who were in and out of jail in a matter of days, sometimes hours. If not for me intervening, France would have brutalized and sodomized every kid that came into our section.

France would be transferred back into one of the adult sections. Rudy would be sentenced and sent to prison after negotiating a plea agreement for a lesser offense. Clifford and I were moved into the day room of an adult section, which was on indefinite lockdown for disciplinary reasons. I believe the lockdown was due to a planned escape attempt. Several months later, the section would be placed under ever more stringent disciplinary sanctions after I picked the lock to the dayroom and opened the cell doors where the adults were housed.

The adult section dayroom, converted into a juvenile holding unit after the conditions in our section were deemed unlivable, was no more than a boxed-in area with two solid walls of concrete and two walls made of steel bars that ran from floor to ceiling. The back wall had a door opening that led into the bathroom and the shower area. There was a single steel picnic table in the middle of the room and a bench approximately four feet long built into the side wall. We had no other accommodations and slept on the floor. About six or seven four-men cells were located in the back of the unit that housed the adult prisoners and, by law, juveniles are not allowed to be incarcerated with adult criminals while awaiting trial. But the officials at the Lake County Jail adhered to the rules of law seemingly when it best served their purposes.

Normally, the cell doors for the sections were opened early in the morning, prior to breakfast, and left open all day until night head count, usually about 10 o'clock. Because the unit was on lockdown, the adults were only allowed access to the dayroom once a week for visits. They were permitted to shower, shave, and wait for a visit from family, friends, or loved ones in the dayroom, along with the juveniles. Visiting hours lasted only four hours and was no doubt the weekly biggest event, as prisoners made preparations for visits that may or may not come. These were heartbreaking days for those of us who did not receive visitors and I was no exception.

I was incarcerated for perhaps six months or so when the juvenile section was moved, and by this time I had grown much more callous. For the sake of survival, I was developing and growing into a true product of my environment. Already being a tough streetwise kid with the heart of a gunfighter and possessing a hair-trigger temper, I became hardened and considerably more ruthless. Adopting the age-old jailhouse philosophy, "survival of the fittest." I grew less concerned regarding the plight of those who came and went overnight. Most juveniles were only locked up for petty delinquency offenses and never stayed in jail more than 72 hours. I had a murder beef hanging over my head and faced a life prison term. With no outside assistance, I practically stood alone and on my own. I gradually grew more and more nonchalant and my attitude changed with the passing of time until "only the strong survived" became the law of the land. If you did not have what it took to stand up and defend yourself, you got no help from me, and that's all there was to it. Should you defend yourself—even in a losing effort—your stay may not be an easy one, but at least it would not be a horrific experience that left life-long scars.

The first time the adult criminals were allowed out of their cells into the dayroom with the juveniles, I had no idea as to how things would proceed. This was an all-White section after all, and the racial climate had yet to be determined. Most sections were either all-White or all-Black, and, for the most part, whenever the two were integrated, racial tensions followed, and a violent outcome inevitably ensued. But things would go smoothly in the dayroom from Day One and everyone coexisted harmoniously.

Big Al Cross and his brother were the shot callers to a large extent and pretty much carried the weight and influence in the section. Big Al was in his forties at the time: a seasoned old convict who had been in and out of prison for most of his life. I could see the toil of the years etched into his face as if every line represented the hardships of a life of crime and his years of incarceration. Al Cross was a tall lanky fellow, top heavy in the chest and bony legs, a common sign among prison body builders who worked the upper body and neglected the lower. Al would be the first convict I got to know and our friendship would last for years. He was one of those exceptional White boys who got along easily with Blacks and, for some reason, he liked me. As a matter of fact, most adult prisoners gravitated to me and showed love and also got rather protective, especially Big Al Cross.

From Al, I learned the fundamentals of doing prison time: how to carry and conduct myself, and how to command respect on all levels from fellow prisoners and from my jailers. Big Al Cross taught me how to play solitaire too, a game I would literally come to play for hours while thinking about life in general or contemplating my situation. He also taught me a jailhouse workout exercise routine consisting of calisthenics and isometrics, all geared toward working the upper body, of course. Indirectly, I learn from Al how to embrace the next man, based on the true nature of individual character, skin color being a mute factor, and to always pay close attention to my surroundings, staying alert and aware at all times. I would further learn from this old convict how to get favors and preferential treatment from my jailers. Just watching Big Al in action, I learned his mannerisms when interacting with the jail officers, how he talked to them, the firmness in his tone of speech and his man-to-man approach. From mere observation I too learned how to get my share of perks and favoritism using proven convict tactics.

Like a stray alley cat you decide to feed one day, you look up and see you've got an unwanted freeloader on your hands, showing up unannounced and at any given time. That was France. I looked up one day and there he was again, walking through the door on weak legs. I immediately noticed his awkward walk and asked him what was wrong. France claimed boys in the other section held him down and punched his legs repeatedly, beating them so badly he could hardly walk afterwards. I accepted the explanation without question and thought no more about the matter. Days later, I came to learn through the jailhouse grapevine that France had ran out of his previous section when the officer opened the section door to collect the breakfast eating utensils, trays, and spoons. No one beat his legs. The awkward walk was due to anus penetration following a gang rape.

The jailhouse grapevine is a reliable and very dependable means of communicating. Throughout the prison system, the network consisted of private or confidential note passing, better known as kites. There are absolutely no limits to the ingenious ways convicts come up with to fly those kites to their intended destination, no matter the distance. The jailers passed pertinent information and prisoners used word-of-mouth exchanges when all prisoners from a different section were held in the same holding tank for court appearances, and in some cases, messages were passed through the ventilation system from one section to the next. Messages passed through the jailhouse ventilation unit often meant very bad news for someone. You could not commit a violation in one section and flee to another, intending to escape jailhouse justice, because the venting system would track you down like a wanted man.

Thus, the jail grapevine eventually had France's story on the air waves. Beaten and broken from the inside out and in a way that defied the human soul and spirit, France came back into the juvenile section with a humble and submissive attitude. Yet, as he recuperated and grew stronger, so did his brazen behaviors, only now France was worse than before. He did not know how to live with his shame and the only way to see himself as not being a victim was to victimize others. I would see many young boys and grown men experience similar demoralizing encounters and that person was never ever the same again.

After a couple of weeks, physically stronger and feeling a sense of defiance and boldness, France decided it was time to try me once again. Having stayed up late the night before, I woke up at breakfast to catch France eating my food tray. Usually, Clifford would get my tray and bring it to me every morning and mostly every meal during the day. On this particular occasion, Clifford was persuaded to think it was all in fun and games, with no malicious intent involved, and did not wake me up for breakfast as usual. I saw the matter as another attempt by France to establish dominance and impose his influence.

I mildly expressed my disapproval, pulled Clifford to the side, and verbally chastised him before laying back down. Breakfast was served so early we often went right back to sleep after breakfast. I couldn't sleep. My mind was working overtime, plotting and planning how best to deal with France. Suddenly, around lunch, I had a bullish idea that would leave no doubt in France's mind as to who ran things and just where I stood. A firm believer that actions speak louder than words, I waited until lunch was being served and got in the very front of the line. Three trays came into the section. I took the first and passed it to Clifford. Taking the other two, I looked France up and down with a lot of contempt and open hostility, straight out taking his tray: no hiding, no sneaking, and no bluffing.

I stood at the picnic table with one foot propped up on the bench and proceeded to eat. France came over and asked for his tray. I just mean mugged him and quietly said between clenched teeth, "Pay back is a bitch, ain't it?" Clifford was instantly on point and closed in on France from behind. Cliff knew I was in combat mode and did not hesitate to make his presence felt. France tried to laugh the whole thing off and accept it gracefully, but I saw the total defeat in his eyes and he never challenged me again.

Eric would become the next long-term juvenile locked up with us. With an extensive juvenile record, Eric was charged with robbery and robbery while inflicting bodily harm: offenses that carried a life prison sentence. Waived over from juvenile court to adult court to stand trial, he was unable to make bond and therefore remained in jail. Not like the one and two nighters, Eric knew very well what he was up against, and understood the chances were that he was prison bound. Eric was a friendly stand-up guy, and although he did not possess the ruthless mentality of a hardened prisoner, he would fight to defend himself to the bitter end, win or lose. Being man enough to defend yourself and being willing to do so dictated how you lived and survived in the county jail.

Two youths came in a couple of days after Eric, both too weak for the Lake County juvenile section. By the time day turned into night, France had them fighting each other. The loser would lose his manhood, probably in the exact same way France lost his manhood. I did not stop this from taking place because by now my attitude was simply, represent yourself when called out or deal with the consequences, whatever they may be. If you stood up for yourself and showed the heart to fight, you got my support, but I absolutely would not fight your battles. For personal reasons, I do not wish to speak in great detail regarding this incident because some things are best left buried in the past. Let's suffice it to say things went really nightmarishly bad for both combatants.

The picnic table was situated in the center of the dayroom and both boys took turns running from each other around the table, neither throwing a single blow. One would chase the other until he stopped and put his hands up to fight, then the chaser became the runner. The scene played out hilariously for about 10 or 15 minutes before any real fighting starting. The fighting proved just as comical as the initial chase scene. Jailhouse laws prevailed that night and I truly regret not maintaining more control over the situation when I had the power to do so. The one thing I learned from that night was, play tough on the streets, act tough when with your boys, but you better really be tough behind bars.

Having befriended me on a little-brother status, Big Al schooled me every chance we talked. His convict wisdom groomed me, his advice directed me, and his actions showed me the path I was about to travel. The golden rule he preached most often was "mind your own fucking business." He would say this with such force and seriousness until I responded in kind with the same aggressiveness saying, "I fucking understand what you mean, Al" or "OK, OK, O fucking K, man!" Big Al was really teaching me the proven and tested code of prison conduct and the golden rules would prove golden, as promised. Mind your own fucking business and 50 percent of all potential problems are instantly solved.

My first real test regarding minding my own business was unplanned and unscripted, with the entire incident including multiple and very valuable lessons. France, the constant loudmouth and agitator, had some harsh words with Big Al. The mildly heated verbal exchange took place while Al was locked up in his cell on the adult end and France was in the dayroom on the juvenile end. I recall Al saying what he had to say and nothing more. France continued on with a hollow grandstand act, perhaps misreading Big Al's silence as a sign of having talked the man down. The following visiting day, when the adults were allowed in the dayroom area with the juveniles, the record would be set straight.

Being a streetwise youngster, I already possessed the uncanny ability to observe and be aware and read the signs of things going on around me. I saw Big Al the moment he walked into the dayroom on visiting day, shirtless and wearing an expressionless look. He headed over to where France stood and asked if they could talk privately in the bath/shower room, which was the only blind spot in the whole section. I heard a thump and more thumps followed by the sound of someone crashing into a wall. Then I saw France briefly appear in the doorway of the bathroom, only to disappear just as quickly. France had attempted to make a mad dash in a futile effort to escape Big Al and Al simply snatched him right back into the bathroom and proceeded to pound him further. A couple of days later, France was once again transferred to another section of the jail. I would not see him anymore until we landed in the same prison, perhaps a year later. By this time, France had turned fully to homosexuality and willingly engaged in gay relationships as his new way of life.

You must understand that I was just a kid in a foreign and unnatural environmental, compelled to adjust accordingly. I had to decide how I was going to live and survive my situation and not become a victim. From the very beginning, I told myself I would rather die on my feet than live on my knees, and that position was non-negotiable. At this point, I had only an outline in mind as to the kind of man I wanted to become. What happened between Big Al and France no doubt became the single greatest influence shaping and molding my future character as a man, foreshadowing the manner I would carry and conduct myself while incarcerated. Perhaps in that particular instance, I saw clearly the man I would be and the man I refused to be.

Really, everything about how Big Al confronted and dealt with France demonstrated a first-hand textbook convict move. Al was a stand-up guy who commanded respect. I too wanted to be a stand-up guy who commanded respect so I copied and personalized every convict move Big Al made. For example, with France, Al did not participate in the back-and-forth dialog often associated with the buildup to a jail-house fight. I learned to say very little and allow my actions to speak for me, something that seemed to become second nature. But pulling a guy aside to confront him man to man became a signature move of mine over the years to come. You take the crowd and friends out of play and you take away the spotlight. Then you truly get a chance to see what kind of man you're up against and clearly demonstrate the kind of man you represent, man to man. Perhaps the most important thing I discovered through my friendship with Big Al was the first major step in learning to respect and embrace a man: to respect a man based on his very own merits as an individual.

When the winter months arrived, the old Lake County Jail proved it was unfit for human habitation and the living conditions were outright deplorable. Cardboard and plastic covered the windows against the winter chill. Day and night, we stayed fully dressed to keep warm and we all slept in the dayroom on the floor. Our mats were a yellow piece of foam, although more black than yellow and covered with assorted stains and cigarette burns. Our meals were served in a metal pan the size of a pound cake with everything mixed right in together. I got a tooth pulled and believe it or not, they used a pair of pliers to extract that tooth. I would emerge from it standing on my feet because my die had been cast and my direction seemed predetermined.

2. G.I.

I was in the streets at an early age, out there trying to be grown before my time. I was not really a bad kid, not in the sense that I was always into mischief, being irresponsible, or engaging in criminal behavior. For the most part, I was a loner and an adventurer, never affiliated with any of the numerous gangs that roam the busy streets of Gary, Indiana. Perhaps being neutral is what enabled me to travel in and out of what others would consider forbidden territories. Although I knew and associated with members of different cliques and gangs, for some reason I never had an interest in being made a member. I liked my independence and not being limited by anything or anyone. I had a different idea about things and wanted to march to the beat of my own drum.

I actually loved running the streets and, during the course of a day, there is no telling where I would end up. As a youngster growing up on the streets of Gary, every day was an exciting adventure. I can vividly recall the summer of 1970 when my mother, along with my brother David, my sister Mary, and I arrived in Gary, Indiana. From the moment we got off the Greyhound bus, I fell in love with the bright lights and fast-paced activity of city life. The change from living in the deep South with my grandparents in North Carolina to the city life of Gary, Indiana, was a fascination and like a homecoming of sorts.

My mother had lived in Gary about six months or so with my five other brothers and sisters. She had finally gotten up enough strength and resolve to leave my physically abusive stepfather. Perhaps it was a homecoming of sorts for her as well because my mother was reuniting

15

with her three oldest children. My brother David and I had lived with our grandparents for the previous five years and my sister Mary came two or three years later to live with us. With my stepfather out of the picture, my mother came south for us; I can still hear my grandmother verbally chastising my mom for making the trip from Indiana to North Carolina alone in a broken-down station wagon with my two-year-old baby brother. Truly, God was with her because that station wagon pulled into my grandparents' front yard and died, never to move again except for a trip to the junkyard.

It was late at night when we arrived in Gary and made the short trip from the bus station to our new little two-bedroom apartment we would share with my Aunt Dorothy and her two kids. It was a very humble beginning for our family: ten kids and two adults living in a two-bed-room ghetto apartment. My aunt would move into her own apartment a few blocks away a couple of months later and my mother would be on her own with her eight children. Now, when I reflect on the circum-stances of those days, I am compelled to acknowledge the fantastic job my mother did in providing for us and getting the family through the difficult times. My mother proved to be a woman who put her kids first in every regard, going without for the sake of taking care of her off-spring. To this day, I can't think of a single person who could stretch a five-dollar bill as well as my mother. Give her a twenty-dollar bill and she made it last until the end of the month, with change left over. The woman was absolutely incredible in money management and got the most for her buck. We still tease mom about her money-management skills today. She wasn't a tightwad or what you would call a stingy per-son by far; to the contrary, she was a very giving woman. She simply had an uncanny ability to get the most out of a dollar.

I can clearly recall the night we arrived in Gary and mom took David and me out for a walk to the store, a 24-hour spot located on Broadway. It was a beautiful summer night and it was really late, perhaps past mid-night, but my mother didn't care. We lived in the red-light district and the nightly activities were just getting into full swing. I remember the life and energy that seemed to fill the air. I felt alive and happy. I re-member the prideful stride and the extra pep in my mother's steps as the three of us walked along. She was truly beaming with the joy of having her two sons walking at her side. Here we were, walking fearlessly through no doubt the roughest and toughest neighborhood in the entire city, and without a care in the world. For that brief moment, our togetherness would overshadow everything of the past and the negative elements of our surroundings.

David and I would always get the business about how we talked because we were the new kids on the block. It didn't take long for someone to try one of us because of our southern drawl, thinking we were country bumpkins. Living in North Carolina for five years had washed out the New England accent that Dave and I got teased about as kids in the South. Now we sounded real country, and learning the Midwestern lingo would start with fighting for Dave and myself. Although I had already witnessed Dave put in work on several occasions, my first confrontation came when a boy from the basement apartment in our building started teasing me about my country grammar. The boy was about my age and came from one of those large families already hardened by the rough neighborhood.

I don't recall the details of how the incident unfolded. There was an exchange of hostile words, then his sister told him to kick my ass. The other proceeded to follow his sister's instructions to beat me up and took a wild swing at me. I easily ducked the punch and in one smooth motion, slid in under the blow, grabbing the kid, lifting him into the air, and body slamming him like a rag doll. He lay on the ground looking at me dumbfounded and dazed, as if he couldn't quite figure out what had just happened. At least two or three of his brothers and sisters were present. The sister instigating the fight was the oldest, a teenager already scarred and battle tested. This was a family that stuck together. They fought others as hard as they fought amongst themselves and I half expected them to gang up on me. Instead, the big sister broke out in a fit of laughter upon seeing what happened to her kid brother and, as if on cue, the others joined in. I never figured that one out. Perhaps it was due to the expression of bewilderment painted on her brothers' face as he lay there on the ground that produced the laughter. Or perhaps she possessed a childish mischievous nature and found her own sense of humor in instigating the scuffle. Either way, I stood my ground for a brief moment before quickly walking away to my comfort zone at the front end of the apartment building. By no means was I inclined to learn if the laughter was a momentary thing that would eventually give way to becoming an all-out mob attack.

I was a mild-mannered, polite, and very quiet kid, but someone you did not want to back into a corner because I had a strong will for self-preservation. My mother always said I had a bad temper, yet it took a lot to really piss me off. But once angry, I held an unforgiving grudge for a long time. A gentle storm lay beneath my surface that would erupt into a full-scale disaster once provoked.

My brother David, who was far more physical than me, was kicking some ass on a regular basis in the early days of our move to Gary. Dave was far more outgoing, quicker to cultivate friendships, and got into far more street activities than I did. In a short time, he had joined a gang—the 18th Avenue Gangsters—and started building his bad-boy reputation. David earned his respect on the block and in the neighborhood by beating up boys older and bigger than him. We were both much stronger and healthier than the other kids as a direct result of our country living. The five years we spent in North Carolina made us true country boys. Dave and I were used to working the fields, feeding the hogs, taking care of the horses, and chopping wood. Most everything we ate was fresh and grown by us: potatoes right out of the ground, corn straight from stalks, and peas and string beans freshly picked. I mean, as kids, we could access every kind of farm-grown produce you can imagine. We ate off the land and never went hungry. During the winter months, my grandma would have a hog slaughtered and pack her big deep freezer to the brim. We had pecan trees, apple trees, pear trees, and fields of strawberries, watermelons, and cantaloupes. Many days I chased chickens off their nests to get my breakfast eggs.

So of course, our healthy eating and country-boy work ethic gave us a physical advantage over most adversaries we faced. I can still recall David and his friends horse playing and wrestling in the grass on the baseball field directly across the street from our apartment building. He would be laughing and tossing the other boys with ease and they would jokingly comment about him being cock strong and saying he needed some sex in his life. As for me, I never played like that. I was too serious minded and couldn't stand for people to grab me or get physical with me, playing or no playing. Even when my brother David used to wrestle me down when we were kids, he realized how mad it made me. Then he would do it only on those occasions when he wanted to get under my skin and run off laughing, often with me chasing him, usually with a weapon of sorts in hand.

David was a good big brother and was the first one I ever recall telling me he loved me: words I had rarely heard before. Dave moved faster and further into the street life of Gary than I did. As the days turned to weeks and weeks turned into months, he tried to protect me from falling into the dark holds of ghetto living, which led to a short-lived life. Those who were members of his gang liked me and often invited me to hang out with them, but Dave wasn't having it. When they would be hanging out on the street corner drinking wine and doing their thing and I happened to bump into them, the bottle of wine would be passed to me and after a couple of sips, David would send me off like I had no business being among his gang. Of course, it didn't take much persuasion and I went about my merry way, putting up no resistance because I wasn't into the street-corner hang-out activities, being a loner and very independent. I did hang out with the gang on several occasions and, true to form, I picked up my share of bad habits and mischievous ways from them. Shoplifting was the one money-making influence the gang passed on to me and I readily embraced because it proved to be a harmless hustle from my perspective at the time.

The gang would go into stores in large numbers and steal cigarettes, wine, and clothes to dress up with or other merchandise to get pocket money. Once I learned the ropes, I took things to a different level; shoplifting became a side hustle for me when proven necessary. In some cases, shoplifting showed my patience and raw determination because if I saw something in a store downtown, I often got it by one means or another. For example, I remember seeing a pair of black and white patent-leather boots in a J.C. Penney store that I liked on sight. These boots got my attention and I was determined to get them. Whenever I made my rounds downtown, going in and out of the many department stores, I always made it my business to stop at Penney's to visit my black and white boots, case the store, and look for the opportunity to get them. It took me about six months to finally get those boots. They would be in different locations most every time I went into the store. One day, while skipping school, I found my chance. Believe it or not, the boots were now on a mannequin that I undressed for the boots and quickly made my exit from the store.

Also, while hanging out with the 18th Avenue Gangsters, I was involved in my first shoot-out with a rival street gang in the immediate area. To my knowledge, the two had been feuding for weeks and then one night, while about ten of us were walking down an alley, the feud climaxed with gunfire. I don't recall how I came to be with them on this occasion, but there I was in the middle of my very first shoot-out at age 12. The gang was either looking for trouble or anticipating it because the crew were packing three weapons: two sawed-off 12-gauge shotguns and a sawed-off 32-caliber carbine rifle. You could tell the group of teenagers had been drinking and partying elsewhere before I ran into them, evidenced by their loud talking and drunken behavior.

As the gang walked down the alley en route to the gang's clubhouse, one of the boys stopped to take a leak as the rest of us continued on. Suddenly we heard the gang's distress whistle and the group of boys turned in unison in the direction of the whistle, everyone on full alert. A little over halfway down the alley stood the boy taking a leak, confronted by approximately six or seven members of the opposing gang. We all turned and marched back down the alley to assist the boy who had strayed from the pack and now found himself cornered by rival gang members. Our approach distracted the other gang long enough for the straggler to sprint down the alley to rejoin our group. The two teenage gangs squared off, tossing the usual exchange of belligerent words back and forth. Then I heard someone from our group say, "Let's shoot," yet no one took immediate action to follow through on the suggestion. Kenny, who was the leader of the gang, took the single-barrel sawed-off shotgun from one of the other boys who appeared too afraid to use it and fired the miniature cannon. The blast was tremendous. A big ball of fire exploded from the weapon and, for a brief moment, it seemingly lingered at the open end of the shotgun barrel before gathering itself and rushing in the direction where the other boys stood. The explosion itself was enough to scare the hell out of me; however, in reality, this weapon—at the distance we were apart—was mostly bark, with very little bite. The sawed-off shotgun is a weapon that is very menacing and quite deadly only up close and personal.

Both gangs instantly dispersed, running in opposite directions following the shotgun blast. My brother David and Kenny urged me to follow them as we dashed down the alley and side streets at a full gallop. This incident occurred a little before midnight and I remember turning some corners that practically left us in total darkness. But this was Kenny and David's stomping ground and they knew the back streets better than me; all I had to do was keep up with them. My adrenaline was pumping and the excitement of the moment had me light on my feet as if I could run full speed for miles and not be exhausted. Back at the gang's clubhouse, the gang gathered as one boy after another trickled in until everyone was accounted for. Exhilarated with excitement from the night's action of gunplay, everyone wanted to talk all at once, expounding on how they saw the scene unfold. Later, David, Kenny, and I would walk home together out of paranoia, conscious of everything that moved on the streets. By this time Kenny, who was 16 or 17 and already considered family, was staying with us when he needed a place to stay because his mother had put him out. As a matter of fact, my mother's phone number was the only information found on Kenny when he was murdered in 1989, which led to identifying his body. Kenny would be gunned down in the streets almost 20 years after this shootout and only two blocks from where it had occurred. His killers would be shot to death two days later by one of the very boys who were with us that night: a long-time friend and member of the 18th Avenue Gangsters from the old days.

I falsified my age shortly after moving to Gary, raising it from 12 to 13 years old to get a job as a paperboy. I met a guy name Bobo in my gym class when school started that year and we became good friends. Bobo was a fat chubby fellow who often got teased by the other boys in our gym class. Being something of an outsider myself, I befriended him. Bobo was the youngest of four brothers and although he was teased in class at school, he had no problems in the neighborhood due to his brothers and their reputation in the hood. This would prove important because Bobo's paper route was in the red-light district of the border where we lived and where you didn't have to look for trouble, because trouble could easily find you. By approval of the mayor and city officials of Gary, the border was a crime-infested safe haven for any and all illegal activities; therefore, it was rather difficult for the *Gary Post Tribune* to keep paperboys on these border paper routes. Paperboys would get bullied, beat up, and robbed if they didn't have backup or strong connections in the neighborhood, and later I would learn I was no exception. I would be tried until my brothers and the 18th Avenue Gangsters made it clear that my troubles would be their troubles.

My paperboy hustle started with helping Bobo deliver his papers after school, and from Bobo I learned the tricks of the trade. Then, one day, a paperboy quit and Bobo took me in to see the district manager; suddenly, I was a paperboy. My first paper route actually ran through the heart of Gary's red-light district, this being the main stripe for the primps, hustlers, prostitutes, drug dealers, gamblers and the like. None of this activity bothered me in the least. Rather, I found myself totally infatuated by it all. The pimps and players drove nice new cars, dressed to impress, and had deep pockets bulging with the almighty dollar. The prostitutes were some of the most beautiful females my young eyes had ever seen. These women were movie-star beautiful and were far from being the crackhead rock stars and drug addicts who primarily work the streets today.

To me, I had the most prestigious and lucrative route in the district. Yet in reality, my route was all flash and dash with the ghetto glitter of ephemeral success. Each day I would look forward to delivering my newspapers because my route provided me the opportunity to come into direct contact with the real movers and shakers on the border: the players who seemingly had it all or were getting their fair share of the cash that made the world revolve. In less than a month, I took on the responsibilities of a second route, which was also on the border and in the red-light district. I acquired a third paper route a short time later. Although most paperboys only carry two routes, I would eventually end up taking over four paper routes, nearly covering the entire border area. I even took over Bobo's route.

Working with who would become a life-long friend, Bobo and I had learned how to manipulate the paper-route business and turn it into a hustle, one that produced a great deal of pocket change. I mean real pocket change: nickels, dimes, and quarters. While making our regular deliveries, individuals on the streets would often ask if we had an extra paper for sale. Of course, we sold as many newspapers as we could, and in this manner, made a dollar or two for ourselves, which was significant pocket money at the time. To solve the problem of not having enough papers for our remaining customers, we simply went to the district manager and claimed our bundle was short. Sometimes we arrived early at the drop-off location where several boys in the area would pick up their newspapers and take a few papers from those bundles. Rarely, but occasionally, we didn't bother with those to whom we failed to deliver newspapers. If that customer was a serious paper reader, they would call the *Post Tribune* and the *Tribune* would get a paper to them. The Sunday newspaper especially was in high demand among my street-life clientele.

We were up and out delivering the Sunday paper before dawn and at a time when the old pimps, players, and other hustlers were still out plying their individual trades or wrapping up their game from the long night before. These guys would buy papers and give very generous tips. If three were present, all three would buy; if six, all six would buy, as if competing or trying to maintain a certain image, one following the lead of the other. Because my business was so good on Sundays, I always got out early on Sunday mornings, making it to the drop-off location long before the other boys and hitting the other bundles of papers for 15 to 20 extra newspapers for my side hustle to get my day started.

Collection time also proved to be one of my better days; on these occasions, I got the chance to go inside the apartments or houses where the prostitutes worked. During regular deliveries, I simply dropped off the paper at the door of my customers and kept on stepping. But on collection day, I had to knock on doors to collect my fees and would get invited inside these illegal sex havens to receive my pay. There were brothel-type houses in which five to ten girls worked and a Madame functioned as an overseer. Then you had your solo or freelance working girls operating from their apartments. All up and down my routes, I had houses of pleasure and I loved it. At the brothel-type set ups, the girls would be laying around on couches or walking about the room wearing skimpy and very sexy lingerie while I stood there, shy and half nervous, admiring the beauty of these women all at once. The solo workers and freelancers always seemed to be more teasing, whereas the brothel girls were somewhat flirtatious but more serious and business minded. It was also the solo workers and freelancers who gave me kisses on the cheek, put an arm around me, or touched me in a nonsexual way. These women also sent me on different little errands for them, usually to the store for cigarettes or soda.

The one experience that stands out foremost for me as a paperboy is a trip I won to New York City. The *Gary Post Tribune* often sponsored contests as incentives to encourage paperboys to solicit new customers. A certain number of new customers would earn whatever prizes were up for grabs at the time. The criterion for winning the trip to New York revolved around who could solicit the most new customers over a 90-day period. Two boys from each district who produced the highest numbers were designated the winners. When the contest was first announced, I remember saying to myself right on the spot, "I'm gonna win this New York trip." It's hard to explain the feeling that came over me in that moment, but I never doubted I would win that trip. Once I had mentally locked in on winning the trip to New York, I would pursue my objective in a relentless manner. Years later, when reflecting on the energy and the diligence I exerted in accomplishing my set goal, I would realize that possessing such an attitude is the golden key to succeeding in whatever one chooses to do in life. I will always remember the drive and confidence that moved me like a force that knew exactly where to go and just what to do at every juncture in winning the trip to New York.

My paper route served another, more meaningful purpose in addition to providing me with a ghetto boy hustle. I was a bread winner as well in the family. Raising eight children on her own was no easy task for my mother and when her measly welfare check and food stamps ran out toward the end of each month, my paper route money kept us going. My collection days would fall during the last week of each month and at a time when it was hard living in our household. Mom would be down to her very last dollar. The food stamps would be long gone and the cupboards were fast approaching empty. It was on these occasions that all the money I could collect from my paper route customers went straight to my mother. The two of us had a standing agreement: she used my paper route money and we would pay my *Post Tribune* debt once she received her welfare check. My mother could always depend on me and she knew it, and when called upon, I responded accordingly. Being there for my mother and my family under these circumstances, regardless of how small my contributions were, still gave me a profound sense of significance and purpose.

Things gradually began to change when we moved from the red-light district and the border district to a newly built low-income housing development on the far east side of town. I had already acquired a number of bad habits by this time, a year older and much more street wise and savvy. My paper route enterprise had gotten both old and too time consuming for the payout. Because our family moved from the red-light district on the upper west side of town to the far east side, it became too much of a hassle to maintain my paper routes. This was during the summer of 1971. I will always remember the move because our address was 1971 Iowa Street. The housing community was one of the first such low-income prefabricated government houses built under then Mayor Richard Hatcher, who was Gary's first African American mayor. These houses were supposed to be an attempt to shift from project-style living to a more community environment, only it was a half-hearted effort on the mayor's part to boost his public image. We were the first to move into our new government-sponsored residence and one of the first families to settle in the new neighborhood.

Just like when we initially came to Gary, Indiana, it was necessary to prove myself among the would-be tough boys in the surrounding area and their gangs. Only by this time I was more seasoned and knew how to handle myself in the streets; I was no longer the naïve little country boy. It didn't take long at all for the boys my age to recognize I was no pushover. My brother David, Kenny, and the 18th Avenue Gangsters had already prepared me with a bad-boy disposition. Later, when I started school at Bethune Elementary, located directly at the end of our street, my own reputation would begin taking form. Several school yard fights and my nonchalant attitude in class and on the playground set the tone for what would eventually become the end of my school days. Soon I had my own little following of boys who wanted to hang with me because I represented the new rebel. Having already beaten up one of the boys considered a school-yard bully and engaging in verbal confrontations with one or two of the others, I let it be known I had no fear and my feet did not know how to run from a fight. I would get my respect the old-fashioned way—by earning it—and many who opposed me in the beginning befriended me later.

It was during my sixth-grade year at Bethune Elementary School that I began to lose interest in school altogether. I picked up the habit of skipping school from my brother David and stepbrother Kenny, along with the 18th Avenue Gangsters. This practice began the previous school year when living on the border and attending Gary Froebel High. Froebel, which held classes from the fifth through the ninth grades at the time. David, Kenny, and most of the Gangsters attended Froebel and were always into some form of mischief. I was in the fifth grade and would see them hanging out during both lunch periods, flirting with the girls or shaking down some poor soul for whatever pocket change he had. Following their lead, I started taking the two lunch breaks myself and hung out with the gang. I would also see them leaving the school grounds, mob deep, knowing they were not going to return. I didn't envy these guys, but I did admire what I thought was the big boy way of doing things; deep inside, I wanted to be a real big boy too.

I only hung out with these guys during lunch hours, but when they left the school grounds with no intention of returning for the rest of the day, I stayed behind and went to my remaining classes. David wouldn't allow me to run with them, nor was I quite ready to start playing hooky all day. One incident clearly stands out in my mind while hanging out with the gang and my brothers during lunch hour. One day, we were in the corridor of the band-room area, perhaps the most secluded spot in the school, where very few teachers came during the lunch period. Naturally, the students made this their cigarette-smoking corner. You could usually find a crowd of students gathered along this corridor, mostly of the delinquent sort, girls and boys alike.

David, Kenny, and I, along with several other members of the 18th Avenue Gangsters, were hanging out in the band-room corridor smoking cigarettes and indulging in idle conversation. Suddenly a boy appeared who easily could have passed as an adult. The boy stood over six feet and had to weight over two hundred pounds. He had a rich dark black complexion and the facial features of a Zulu tribesman. I didn't pay much attention to him at first, but the gang zeroed in on him immediately. After some discussion among the gang members in which I could only hear my name being repeated, they all gathered around me having come up with a plan to launch an assault on the big boy, with me initiating the contact. The plan was for me to approach the boy who towered over me like a giant and sucker punch him. Without giving the idea a second thought and wanting to impress the gang, I agreed and proceeded to do exactly as instructed. The gang moved into position, inconspicuously posting up around the much bigger boy, waiting for me to make my move. I calmly walked over to where the boy stood and punched him as hard as I could in the face. For a brief moment I thought I was about to be crushed, as the boy turned to me with surprise and anger curved into his dark features. Uttering words of my promised annihilation by his hands, the boy advanced toward me with blood in his eyes: a grave mistake. Before you could blink, the gang was all over him like a wolf pack beating the giant to his knees. I have no idea why this boy was targeted and I didn't ask questions, then or later.

Shaking kids down for their lunch money, picking fights, and skipping school were three of many bad habits I picked up from my brothers Kenny and David and their gang. By the time I reached junior high school, I had developed into a real bad boy. In two years, city life had completed changed my personality and perspective on life in general. I started smoking cigarettes when I was 12 years old, around the same time I smoked my first joint of marijuana. I also started drinking cheap wine and beer at the age of 12. By the time I was 13, I found myself embarking on a totally new and different lifestyle from the country-boy living I had grown used to while living with my grandparents. It's strange how environments can influence the behavior and thinking of a young person. Although I refuse to place blame somewhere else, it's very true—at least very true to me—that my move to Gary, Indiana, had a great deal to do with how my life evolved to me growing into the man I became. Still, I'm quick to admit that I willingly drank from the poisonous cup of crime, corruption, and mischief that eventually became my chosen way of life for almost 40 years.

By the time I reached junior high school, I had completely lost all interest in school. I rarely attended classes and when I did go to school, it was due mostly because I had little else to do. My first year at Pulaski Junior High School, I initially began skipping classes just to hang out for both lunch periods. From there, I went on to attending my morning classes and after both lunch periods, my school day was over. It got to the point that I fell so far behind that I became too embarrassed to participate in classroom activities and therefore made fewer and fewer classroom appearances. Before long, the only time I went near the school was during lunch period to play my bully-boy role and shake down other students or flirt with young girls. Toward the end of the school year, my reputation had fully developed. Students, teachers, and school security officials all knew me. I made regular visits to the principal's office and neither his lectures nor his suspensions deterred my delinquent and bad-boy conduct. The male gym teachers attempted to counsel me and encourage a change in my behavior, to no avail. One wood shop teacher tried disciplining me with a paddle he made from a piece of 2x4 lumber. That shop teacher got his paddle taken and knocked over his desk for his efforts.

It's difficult to express or explain what I was going through at that point in my life. Without putting undue blame on my father, I tend to feel and strongly believe that a father figure in my life at that time would have made all the difference. My junior high school year at Pulaski no doubt saw the full emergence of my delinquent behavior. For a teenager,

I was well on the path of no return, and those who tried to reach me failed. I had no one I could look up to or respect enough to get my attention, and I had to find a reason to respect a person before I could listen to a word any man had to say. So I became my own man and the only way I knew how to approach life was the way I was learning from the streets. Male figures would come later, trying to give advice after I had become street tough. By this time, I had my own way of thinking and could only see the world through my young teenage eyes.

I had a small following of Pulaski boys who transferred from elementary school with me, and this became my school yard mob whenever I did attend school. Of course, I was designated the unspoken leader of the pack and my little crew was influenced by what I did or said. A brother named Ant was my main partner and he too was on the bad-boy fast track; he would also end up in prison with me on a murder charge at age 16. Another brother named Mansy fit right in with us. The rest of the guys ran with us mainly because it was much safer. The boys that rolled with my little mob did not have to worry about being pressured or being bullied, and for the most part, they seemingly drew strength and courage from how I carried myself. We did not represent ourselves as a gang. Rather, we were just a group of tough boys going to a tough inner-city school who hung out together, mostly out of self-preservation. Although I was a loner by nature, I still found myself in the middle of everything that happened at Pulaski and my guys always came running to me when there was trouble.

One day during lunch hour, one of my guys came running to me, excited and out of breath. He explained that a security officer working in the school cafeteria was in the dining room physically manhandling one of our crew members. Needless to say, being the glory seeker, I lived for moments such as this. Without hesitation, I took off in the direction of the school cafeteria, pumped up with a false sense of self-importance. Upon entering the dining room, I saw a crowd of students surrounding the security officer, who had Mansy pinned against a wall with a hand gripping him by the throat. The students were screaming and angrily yelling at the security officer to let Mansy go, but the man appeared totally possessed with unhealthy intentions. The mere sight of the situation pissed me off. Yet the fact that three or four other members of our mob were just standing there, rendering no assistance, infuriated me even further. Granted, the security officer was a mammoth of a fellow and represented an authority figure; still, we had to protect our own from such abuse, regardless of the odds or the circumstances or consequences.

I pushed my way through the crowd, coming up on the security officer from his blind side. With all my might, I swung a haymaker of a punch, catching him just below his right jawbone. The rest of my guys standing idly around seemed to move into action immediately, as if given a green light that the security officer was fair game. Suddenly, the scene looked like a pack of hyenas attacking a water buffalo, or a bunch of pygmies trying to bring down an elephant. The action could not have lasted much longer than ten or fifteen seconds. We pounced on the security officer, striking him from all directions until he released his grip on Mansy and started swinging back at us. Other students got into the action too, because no one had any special love for this guy. He was often on one of his power trips with the students. After exchanging more blows with the security officer, we all dispersed. That was only Phase One of the chaos about to erupt throughout the school.

Instead of disappearing into the crowd like my boys, I stopped to look for my hat, which I had lost during the altercation. While in search of my hat, the security officer came up behind me and, looping his belt around my neck, began slinging me around like a rag doll. Some students tried to warn me of his approach, but I couldn't or wouldn't run. With his belt around my neck, he swung me in a full circle. Somehow, I managed to get my feet between his legs and tripped him. We hit the floor with me landing on top and I commenced to punch him in the face before we even settled from the fall. I was angry as hell by now and all I saw was red rage, the need to defend myself prevailing over all sense of reasoning. Several girls who hung out with me and my little crew rushed over and began kicking the security officer as I continued to pound him with my fist. The next thing I knew, the principal and other teachers were pulling me off him. I remember taking one last kick at his testicles as I was being pulled away, my anger still completely out of control. We were seventh and eighth grade students and there was no issue regarding right or wrong or who was at fault or not at fault. Things simply unfolded as they did.

The security officer had a sister who also went to Pulaski, and later I learned that she, along with one of her friends, had gotten beaten up too. There were also those who were overheard making negative comments about us being troublemakers and how we should be kicked out of school. These comments only led to more fighting, and before all the drama was over, the entire school was in chaos and classes were cancelled for the remainder of the day. I received a one-week suspension for my involvement in this incident, which I wore as though it was a badge of honor. Seven students got suspensions: five boys and two girls. The security officer got fired.

3. The Crime

When starting my second year at Pulaski, going to the eighth grade, I recall the principal summoning me to his office the very first day. His inquiry concerned my previous-year conduct and behavior and whether he should anticipate the same during the current school year. He asked me a great many questions regarding my home life, what I wanted to do or be in life, and other general questions along those lines. Then he asked why I behaved so indifferent and radical at school. The question caught me completely off guard and my answer even surprised me. I told him that, in the first grade, I was held back a year, and now seeing myself a grade behind the other students my age caused me to resent the school system. My reply came off the top of my head as though the thought had really existed. In fact, I had never given a second thought to being held back in the first grade, had practically forgotten the issue until that very moment, and had never entertained a negative view of the matter. But in that instant, it was the quickest reason that came to mind to justify my past conduct. Then, unexpectedly, the principal picked up the phone and called for my school records. Confirming my allegation about being held back a year, the principal picked up the phone a second time and suddenly I was given a double promotion to the ninth grade and transferred to Emerson High School the following day.

At Emerson, I don't recall spending a single whole day at school, and probably went to only one or two classes before dropping out entirely. I was out in the streets hustling and doing my street thing. Selling drugs while drinking and smoking weed all day quickly took the place of going to a boring classroom.

The classes I learned from on the streets of Gary, Indiana, proved more appealing and to my liking than public school. I was a great student and a fast learner on the streets. When it came to the street hustle, I was very much the entrepreneur and an equal opportunist. Having pledged no gang affiliation worked to my advantage and allowed me to move about the city to hustle wherever the paper chase led, and I had the courage to pursue. I sold marijuana, pills, and acid, which were the more common recreational drugs during the early '70s. When I had no drugs to push, I would literally spend the entire day downtown shoplifting. Yet, by the same token, when it came down to the hustle and the paper chase for the almighty dollar, I was never one dimensional. I had legitimate means of getting my hustle on, as well as illegitimate. I worked for anyone who would give me a job and actually held down three different jobs before I turned fifteen where my employer knew I should have been in school.

The major turning point in my life came in early May 1974. I made a decision that went against the grain on a promise I had made to myself. Soon after my fifteenth birthday, in January 1974, I pulled my first robbery with some guys I promised myself I would never deal with again. I was no professional stick-up man by far, yet I had enough sense to recognize when I was pulling a robbery with some straight idiots. But fate would deal me a very ugly hand and I would be left to play it out. That particular day, I could have decided to go north instead of south or turn left instead of right and perhaps my whole life would have turned out totally differently. But then again, predestination will seek you out and find you when certain things are deemed inevitable.

Skipping school one day as usual, I ran into Jessie, Spann, Gamble, and Clifford. They had just pulled a burglary, the one crime I never felt comfortable doing and shied away from. I was hanging out at Pulaski during the last lunch period, kicking it with my boys before slipping off into the rest of my day in the streets. They were walking past the school playground when I decided to join them; lunch hour was pretty much over and I had no real plans other than how I could get some money in my empty pockets. Jessie and I often hung out together and were close friends. I met Spann and Gamble through Jessie and his brother. These are the very guys I promised myself never to get involved with again when it came to street crimes. All these guys were much older than me, but petty, shallow, and really clueless and outside their league. As for myself, I had no idea what I was about to get myself into. Yet, for certain, my life would never be the same again as the next 24 hours unfolded.

I was rather glad to see Jessie because I had not seen him in the hood for several days. I would learn that he had been hanging out with and staying with Spann and Gamble, who had an apartment on the upper east side of Gary. Jessie, being the skillful manipulative brother that he was, saw how weak these two buffoons were and simply moved in and took over. Cliff was a good kid; he was a little slow but had a good heart and merely got caught up by getting in way over his head. Cliff knew of me by way of reputation from my bad-boy days at Pulaski. I first met Spann and Gamble through Jessie's brother. We hung out together one night, drinking cheap wine, and decided to perform a robbery.

Now, when reflecting back on how this whole episode unfolded, I realize my involvement was a direct result of me trying to impress these older brothers with my courage. Although all these guys were older than me—Jessie was 18, his brother was in his 20s, Spann was 28, and Gamble was 22—still, I felt more mature and more advanced in my thinking. Many will think I was being used and manipulated by them and they probably were thinking the same thing. But in reality, I knew precisely what I was doing every step of the way. That first robbery we pulled together came off so sloppy, clumsy, and incompetent that I vowed to never ride with them again. We robbed a barroom establishment. Gamble, Spann, and I went in to carry out the deed.

There were three or four customers in the bar as we entered and announced it was a stick-up. Spann, who I quickly learned was a certifiable alcoholic, proceeded to grab the first customer's half-finished beer and guzzle it down. Gamble had jumped over the bar counter and went for the cash register, which he fumbled with, unable to open. Spann continued to guzzle down his second beer. Me, I literally stood there perplexed and wondering what in the hell I had gotten myself into. Suddenly, I snapped and started issuing commands, telling Spann to leave those fucking drinks alone and ordering the bartender to open that cash register for Gamble. Why listen to the young 15-year-old wannabe stick-up kid? Because the wannabe stick-up kid was the only one with the gun in his hand. Yes, out of the five of us, I was the only one with a weapon. I was the only gunman and that decision was chosen by me. Not only was I very knowledgeable when it came to firearms, I loved guns. I was truly infatuated with them. My grandfather taught all his sons how to hunt and shoot. When living with granddaddy, the boys in the household learned about guns purely for the purpose of hunting and also to kill an occasional snake. In Gary, Indiana, I purchased my first gun at age 12. It was a 32-caliber stub nose and I had to wrap rubber bands around the hammer so it would have enough striking force to fire when the trigger was pulled. I took charge of the single weapon among us because I felt safer with the gun in my hands rather than in the hands of my partners in crime.

The holdup completed, we exited the tavern in haste, getting only the cash in the register. Jessie, who was supposed to be the lookout man, had already abandoned his post and was in the car with his brother, the designated get-away driver. Let the truth be known. Jessie and his brother were the type that wanted someone else to do the dirty work and heavy lifting while they stayed out of the direct line of fire. Everything about this amateurishly executed robbery caused me to give serious thought to my not-so-promising career as a potential stick-up kid, and the less than two hundred dollars get-away money split five ways would discourage me even further. Yet, the one thing that captivated my youthful egoism was the head rush of excitement that engulfed me immediately following the robbery. It was an adrenaline rush I had never experienced before and I enjoyed the moment, at least temporarily.

The second robbery I would eventually commit with Spann, Gamble, and Jessie after vowing to never deal with them on that level again proved to be the biggest mistake I've ever made in life. I remember leaving school that day with them and we ended up at Spann and Gamble's little apartment where, once again, the subject of pulling a robbery surfaced in the conversation. They had burglarized someone's house earlier before meeting up with me but obviously came up empty-handed. It seemed from the discussion that the group was already considering a robbery. I should have left right then. Instead, I stuck around and listened to them make their robbery plans. Off the top, I stated I wanted absolutely nothing to do with the planned stick-up. My first compromise came when I volunteered to let them use one of my guns, a 22-caliber carbine. My second mistake came when I agreed to act as the lookout man for the group, the role Jessie always wanted to play.

The initial plan was for Gamble, Spann, and Cliff to carry out the hold-up with Cliff, at age 16, being the gunman. I had to teach Cliff on the spot how to use the weapon because he was clueless. As a matter of fact, Spann and Gamble were also clueless as to how my 22 carbine worked. My ultimate compromise came that night when the robbery was to happen. The target, once again, was a barroom establishment located several blocks from Spann and Gamble's apartment. We were in an abandoned house next door to the tavern, making final preparations. I saw the struggle Cliff was having with the gun and, in that instant, a powerful thought overwhelmed me: a clear voice saying if Cliff went in with the gun, he would definitely be killed that night. Taking the gun from Cliff, I opened the door to my total commitment to participating in the hold-up.

From the very moment we entered the bar, things began to spiral out of control. Once again, I possessed the only weapon we had, the youngest of the group, and the one person who didn't want to have a thing to do with the crime from the start, yet there I was. I recall letting the others enter the tavern first with me right behind them, drawing my carbine, announcing it was a stick-up, and demanding everyone place their hands on the bar. Three patrons, along with the bartender, were present and all of them responded to my announcement as if it came as a surprise to them. This was a White folks' establishment deep in a Black neighborhood so those who frequented the bar knew bad things happened in this crime-infested area. The three White patrons would comply with my commands without hesitation, but the bartender instead placed his left hand on the bar and with his right, slowly began reaching for something beneath it. Again, I repeated my instructions for everyone to place their hands on the bar, this time, directing my every word to the bartender. Looking at me as though he defied both my purpose for being there and my very existence, he continued to reach for whatever it was beneath the bar.

Cliff stood a little to my right, Spann stood about midway of the bar, and Gamble had leaped over it, right where the cash register was located. Everyone and everything seemingly momentarily froze in time as the scene between the bartender and me played out. I repeated myself for the third time. The bartender continued to reach. I remember a peculiar expression on his face and a look in his eyes that said he knew something I didn't. Just as he grasped whatever he was reaching for and began to raise his right hand, I fired my weapon. The high-pitched crack of the 22 carbine echoed through the now quiet bar as I pulled the trigger. A single shot from the small-caliber firearm struck the bartender in the temple area of the head and he dropped to the floor. The sequence of events happened so fast that it was over as quickly as it began, although there were brief moments that seemed to play out in slow motion. I remember Gamble leaping over the bar counter and, as if he had spring in this shoes, jumped right back over, heading for the nearest exit. I heard the sound of racing footsteps and the tavern door opening and closing. I was momentarily numb with fear, totally confused, and perhaps, to some extent, in a mild state of shock. When I looked around, I discovered that I stood alone in the bar, my partners in crime having deserted me. I felt like I was actually living a bad dream that kept getting worse by the minute.

Finally, snapping out of the daze that befogged my mental facilities, I backed my way out of the tavern, leaving the three terrified patrons frozen stiff on their bar stools with open fear filling their eyes. Back out on the streets, I broke into a full-paced gallop. Hitting the nearest alley to avoid the main streets or drawing unwanted attention to myself, I ran as if possessed. My feet seemed to scarcely touch the ground at all! I ran as though I could out run the crime I had committed, as if I ran far enough and fast enough, I would escape the reality of what I had just done. By the time I reached the alley, I spotted two other figures running for their lives approximately a city block or more ahead of me. There was no doubt in my mind that the figures were my supposed partners in crime. I ran on with my surroundings being a mere passing blur as I dashed down the dark alley, my heart beating thunderously in my chest. Everything that was happening seemed so surreal. It appeared as though I was watching myself perform every act from the outside looking in. I couldn't believe what was happening or the role I had played in it all.

Back at the apartment, the group of would-be stick-up men reassembled, arriving within seconds of each other and coming in from different directions. No one spoke for several minutes, once the five of us gathered in Spann and Gamble's apartment following the failed robbery attempt. I don't recall who spoke first or what was said because, for the most part, I still remained numbed and despondent by the entire experience. I felt the utmost contempt toward my partners in crime and wanted to be anywhere but around them. Immediately upon returning to the apartment, I recall how everyone seemed to sit apart from one another, as if doing so would dissociate themselves from the next man and the crime we had committed. No one wanted to mention the shooting. We didn't know if the bartender was alive or dead, but I knew in my heart of hearts that the deed had, in fact, been done.

Jessie came over to sit beside me and asked what happened inside the bar that led to the shooting. I remember the others remaining at a distance on the far side of the room, talking among themselves. This was due mainly to the extremely hostile attitude I openly demonstrated toward my so-called partners in crime. The robbery and shooting had definitely shaken me, yet my anger and contempt regarding my crime partners superseded my rattled nerves. Jessie was the only one who could talk to me and he got that advantage on the strength of the bond and friendship that existed between us, because for the most part, I was half pissed with him also. As Jessie and I talked, the entire chain of events seemed to move from unreal to real. As we discussed the failed robbery, my every word spoken brought with it the focus of reality and I could find no comfort in thinking optimistically. The main question left unanswered was whether the single shot fired at the bartender was fatal. Each of us speculated and pondered the question silently and verbally. Although we were only four or five blocks from the tavern, no man was willing to risk returning to the crime scene for the purpose of ascertaining the true facts of the matter: was the bartender alive or dead?

After sitting there with them, lost in thought for what seemed like endless hours, I got up and left without saying a word. How I went from not wanting any involvement in this robbery to becoming the principal participant would haunt me for many years to come. I walked home alone that night. How I got there I do not recall, hearing and seeing nothing along the way. I lived more than a mile from where Spann and Gamble stayed and got home well after midnight. I do remember meeting up with one of my guys from the old gang I ran with at Pulaski once I reached my neighborhood. It was Mansy and he needed a place to crash for the night, so I agreed to let him spend the night with me. Making a blanket pallet on the living room floor, we bedded down for the night, talking and listening to the radio. I told Mansy about the shooting and attempted robbery and we were listening to the radio in hopes of receiving information about what happened. I slept very poorly that night, never falling into a deep sleep, restless and worried. Subconsciously, I knew I was in big trouble. The following morning, Mansy and I were up and on the move long before my younger brother and sisters were up preparing for school. I would never make it back home.

Being uncertain of my next course of action, I went back to Spann and Gamble's apartment, hoping against hope that the bartender had survived the shooting. Yet, upon my arrival, the first thing they did was inform me of the bartender's death. I tried to keep my composure and take the news in stride. Perhaps I projected the desired appearance on the outside; however, on the inside, I was a deeply troubled young man. I was 15 years old and I had killed a man, a felonious act unable to be corrected or undone, even if I commanded all the man-made power beneath the sun. I can't begin to express or explain what I was thinking and feeling. I found myself under attack by a barrage of conflicting emotions I couldn't run from or hide from. I reasoned with myself, saying the shooting was not my fault because the bartender forced my hand, leaving me little choice. For the rest of my life I would wrestle with the issue, never coming to a rational conclusion because there was no rational conclusion to reach.

Already in too deep, I found myself sitting around the apartment discussing plans for yet another robbery with these guys. Jessie and I decided to get out of town as soon as possible and needed get-away money to flee the city. Granted, I truly despised the idiots I found myself in cahoots with, but out of necessity, I felt I needed them to further my own personal objectives. We stayed around the apartment all that day, scheming and plotting about potential targets, once the cover of darkness came. Little did I know at the time, but Gamble and Spann had spread the word up and down their block about being involved in the robbery murder during the day. That night, Gamble and I went out to steal a car intended to be used for our planned robbery spree. Gamble claimed he had the talent and skill to steal cars. It took me less than 10 minutes in the streets, looking for a car to boost with him, to realize Gamble did not have a clue about what he was doing. Once again, my frustration and anger boiled over and I felt so stupid and foolish for getting involved with these uncouth individuals, because Gamble couldn't steal a car even if the keys were left in the vehicle waiting.

Totally discouraged, we headed back to the apartment, our mission a complete failure. Neither of us said a word as we made the trip. Upon reaching the block on which Spann and Gamble lived, I recalled immediately feeling something was amiss. Instinctively, my body became tense, ready for the unexpected. I scanned the streets and the surrounding buildings, seeing nothing out of place or alarming. I knew something was wrong and all I wanted to do was reach the security of the apartment as quickly as possible, where I thought I would be safe from the certain danger that surely lurked in the dark. I remember walking down the short flight of stairs leading to the basement apartment, still looking over my shoulder, a deep-rooted uncertainty gripping at my gut. I can distinctly remember how unusually quiet it was inside the apartment and on the streets, as Gamble knocked on the door. I could actually perceive the potential threat that lay ahead, as though the handwriting was written on the walls in bold bright letters.

Giving my undivided attention to the outside elements around me, I failed to consider any possible threat from inside the apartment. When the apartment door suddenly swung open, an arm reached out, seizing Gamble and me in a firm hold, snatching us both into the apartment all in one smooth motion. Taken by complete surprise, a veteran homicide detective had opened the door with his 45-caliber automatic pistol in one hand, pointed straight at my face, the other hand lashing out to grab Gamble, pulling us both into the apartment at the same time. The homicide detective's move was shrewdly calculated and perfect executed, and under any other circumstances, I probably would have applauded the move; it was very cleverly done. He had used the element of surprise to his advantage before it dawned on either of us what was happening. Once again, the chain of events unfolded so fast that we had absolutely no time to react.

Now in the hallway leading into the apartment and living room area, Gamble tried to talk tough and demanded to know what was going on, sort of pulling away from the detective. His action was met with a lightning fast blow from the homicide detective, striking him squarely on the jaw and knocking Gamble right off his feet. Inside the apartment, three more detectives stood waiting, guns drawn, and at the ready. These detectives had Spann and Jessie under close guard while adjusting their positions to cover the newcomers to the apprehend and arrest party. Once inside the apartment, one detective instructed me to face the wall and place my hands on my head. Spread eagle, I stood there with the barrel of a pistol resting against the back of my head while I was searched. Then, a detective ordered that I be taken into one room and Gamble into another. This would be the beginning of the brutal on-scene interrogation for which the Gary Police Department was notoriously known for.

Two Black detectives took me into a bedroom and immediately pounced on me. A blow knocked me onto the bed and I bounced back up like I wanted to fight. The two detectives commenced to pound, pistol whip, stomp, and beat me until a White detective came in to stop them. Leading me back into the living room, I was instructed to face the wall and put my hands on my head again. I was leaking blood from two head wound gashes due to the pistol whipping, and my face was already beginning to swell from the beating. Gamble laid on the living room floor, a tall lanky detective kneeling over him, striking Gamble repeatedly in the throat with judo chops and asking who the trigger man in the robbery was. At first, Gamble made a halfhearted attempt to deny any involvement or knowledge of the crime. As quiet as the detectives kept this knowledge, they already knew who the perpetrators were and the roles they played in the crime. They had already beaten confessions out of my other three codefendants during the short time Gamble and I were out looking for a car to steal.

The detective continued questioning Gamble until, suddenly, I heard the word "go on and tell him 'cause we already did." It was the voice of Spann and the words rolled off his trembling lips in such a matter-of-fact way that I couldn't believe my ears. Gamble was still laying on the floor receiving judo chops to the throat. Gasping between breaths, he mumbled to the detective, "I will show you." Getting up off the floor, Gamble, on shaky legs, walked over to where I stood facing the wall and tapped me on the shoulder. Gamble really did not know me or my name. As a matter of fact, Jessie, who was my old street-running partner, was the only one who truly knew me by name. Gamble would identify me as the trigger man in the robbery with his tap on the shoulder and the detective made him confirm what the tap meant by asking, "You mean the little man was the trigger man?" From that point on, I would be referenced to and known as the Little Man who was the Trigger Man.

Gamble, having identified me as the trigger man, earned a reprieve from any further brutal interrogation at the hands of the detectives, but immediately placed my life in imminent peril. Everyone was taken into custody and removed from the apartment except me. I was left alone with two Black street-toughened homicide detectives and had no idea what to expect next. Yet, I had a deep gut feeling that something mischievous was on the horizon. The detectives led me to a utility room and ordered me to kneel on the floor, facing the corner like a kid being given a time out, the harsh way. The utility room was a dimly lit area right off the kitchen, and I recall how uncomfortable I felt on my knees facing a corner. It was not my kneeling position that caused my discomfort; it was an internal feeling. The two detectives stood at the kitchen sink, washing my blood from their hands while whispering together, their weapons within easy reach. One detective kept glancing in my direction out of the corner of his eyes. Both men were pretending to pay little or no attention to me. I would overhear one of them say, "He's not going to go for it." Go for what, I asked myself. In that instant it dawned on me that the detectives were actually setting me up to make an escape attempt so they could gun me down in cold blood.

The utility room had a door that led outside into the alley, with about ten stairs leading up to the door and, seemingly by chance, the door was conveniently left wide open. I saw the open door and a detective, keeping a sly eye on me, took notice of my observation and whispered to his partner with a sense of excitement in his voice, "He see it, he see it!" In that moment, an overwhelming calmness enveloped me saying, "be still, be perfectly still and don't move, and everything would be okay." I would later learn that these two detectives were not only street toughened and hard core, but they were bigger crooks than I could ever be or would become. They were badge-wearing criminals. They killed in cold blood, robbed and stole from street hustlers, and committed practically every crime beneath the sun. During this moment, they were plotting, scheming, and deviously conspiring to murder a 15-year-old boy. These two detectives had nefarious reputations on the streets of Gary, Indiana, as gangster cops playing both sides of the fence. Both would eventually face criminal investigation by the federal government during their law-enforcement careers. And as the years passed, I became more and more aware of what the two arresting detectives on my case were truly capable of doing, and considered myself very lucky.

I would overhear the detectives whispering again, saying, "He ain't gonna go." We will never know how far these two detectives would have gone as my judge, jury, and self-proclaimed executioners, because any further plans would be spoiled. The White detective, who had already stopped the two from beating and pistol whipping me, would suddenly reappear, demanding to know what was going on. This White detective took charge of me from that point on, escorting me from the apartment and driving me to the Gary Police Station himself. Once at the police station and clearly seeing the damage his two fellow detectives had inflicted on me, this officer would also arrange for me to be taken to the hospital, where I received stitches for my two head wounds. I never told my mother what happened that night, but she would tell me how the White detective had confided in her, describing the spoiled plot to kill her son.

Once at the Gary Police Station located at 1301 Broadway, I was escorted to the detective division on the second floor. The four-story building itself and those at work seemed unorganized, unkempt, and very poorly managed. These were common conditions found in inner-city jails where Blacks were being housed: conditions that ranged from borderline to inhumane. As I entered the detective bureau, I saw an open area cluttered with desks and two or three individual small offices off to the side. I observed my partners in crime already present. Each of them sat beside one of the desks scattered throughout the detective bureau. A detective sat with each of them, typing out their statements and confessions. I received no more than a quick guilty glance from each of them as they continued to provide their confessions in a useless attempt to mitigate their roles in the crime. I kept hearing, "The Little Man was the Trigger Man," as if my confidants were trying desperately to distance themselves from me and their responsibility for the murder. I remember experiencing a feeling of betrayal and emptiness that left me thinking nothing mattered in life anymore. In my youthful ignorance, I believed in the street code of silence, and this would be the first indication that such a code was practically obsolete and soon would be nonexistent.

My mother was called and a uniformed policeman escorted her to the detective bureau when she arrived. I could hear mom long before I saw her. She was angry in such a way that I had never before heard; this soft-spoken and tender-hearted woman was turned into a loud and one very pissed off individual. Coming up the stairs leading to the detective bureau, she was talking major trash, consumed by the heat of the moment. Mom had it really hard raising eight kids on her own and although I engaged in a lot of juvenile delinquency behaviors, I was the one she could absolutely depend on. Having bailed me out of jail several times already, I believe my mother feared for me and the obvious path my life appeared to be taking. I heard her saying how tired she was of me constantly getting into trouble. At one point, she stated no longer being able to handle me and that she wanted me sent off to Boys School for Juvenile Delinquents. She would rage on until she was finally inside the interrogation office where I sat waiting. When my mother saw me, her entire attitude suddenly changed. Dried blood was all over my clothes and matted in my hair. My face also had begun to swell and I look disfigured.

Directing her question to no one in particular, my mother demanded to know what happened to her son. She was given no answer. In reply, instead, they threw a shocking curve ball at her, informing my mother that I was being charged with a very serious crime: two counts of murder. If my physical appearance disturbed and upset my mother, the news of the criminal charges leading to my arrest would be like throwing a rock through a glass window. Her composure seemed to unravel before my eyes as she processed my physical condition and the cause of my arrest. I had always known my mother to be a pillar of strength and a woman who held her emotions in check very well. But now she sat at my side, helpless to aid or assist her son, the hurt and pain self-evident in her tearing eyes. The degree of concern written on my mother's face and the intense distress reflected in her eyes were such things I had never seen before in this woman. Perhaps in this hour, I was really a kid: a kid dealing with all the conflicting emotions that came with the unfortunate situation I found myself up against.

4. Prison Bound

January 1975, immediately after the new year holiday, the big move from the old county jail into the new county jail commenced. With security on high alert, the tension thick in the air and the Lake County sheriff deputies itching for action, the exodus turned volatile. During this time, an attempted escape ended in a big shoot out in the middle of town. The deputies and Sheriff's Department were working with a zero-tolerance policy, cracking heads and suppressing even the slightest opposition. The violence between prisoners and our keepers raged out of control for the first few months. Both sides suffered significant injuries: broken jaws, broken bones, and blood flowed until order was restored.

The new county jail was a state-of-the-art facility in 1975. The Sheriff's Department intended to command complete control from Day One, and they certainly accomplished just that. Everyone from the sheriff on down acknowledged the old jail situation had become a lawless hell hole, badlands where the devil's wickedness ruled. Drugs and other contraband were in abundance. The violence was often unnatural and went unchecked. Extortion, rape, and physical abuse ran rampant. Once a person was placed in a jail section in the old county jail, it was every man for himself. There were no safe havens and no rescues or protection from the jailers. This was an environment where even the lion hearted could easily become prey or submit to extortion. A person's gang affiliation may or may not have saved them from some of the rough stuff, but assuredly, subservient functions included washing someone's underwear or giving up an occasional meal, and if a prisoner got a little money, hands would be in his pockets.

The jail officials knew how bad things were in the old county jail and they also knowingly accepted the fact that they had lost control. Our Jailers had a saying coming into the new county jail: "You guys ran the old county, now we gonna run the new county." And right away, they proceeded to clean house using brute riot force to accomplish their goal. Where the overall conditions surrounding the old jail made it virtually impossible to control prisoner behavior, the conditions at the new jail were absolutely perfect. The jailers seemingly had only one attitude: zero resistance! They were running this show.

The Lake County Government Center was the hub for all county business, including the court system and the county jail. The County Government Center project was a massive undertaking that started from the ground up. The court system and the jail were the main two components. The Government Center complex grounds easily covered more than 100 acres; the jail alone was a huge five-story building that covered at least 30 of those acres. The new jail provided the cells, the units, and lockdown sections to completely control prisoner movement and better isolate predators and troublemakers, as well as those who needed protection.

Where the old jail had no rules, the new jail had rules that reflected being under a dogmatic, oppressive, totalitarian regime. Yet one rule alone caused a spontaneous revolt throughout the jail, leading to several weeks of fighting and rioting: The Dayroom Rule. This rule perpetrated and encountered the most resistance from prisoners in the move to the new jail. The entire situation came down to a matter of an intense power struggle between prisoners and their keepers: one side having not even a sling shot to fight with and the other side having a fully equipped arsenal and was combat ready.

I had been incarcerated approximately eight months and the jail was filled with prisoners who were locked up as long or longer. When moving into the new county jail, all personal property was confiscated except personal and legal mail. Reluctantly, prisoners surrendered or abandoned their contraband and the other items they had collected during their stay in the old jail. None of those things once allowed in the old county jail were allowed in the new county jail. Books, magazines, board games, clothes, toiletries purchased from the jail commissary, and all other items were confiscated. In exchange, prisoners were given a grayish prison jumpsuit made of a coarse jean material with Lake County Jail stenciled on the back. We were provided a new mat and pillow, new bedding, towels, and a toiletry kit.

Next, prisoners were assigned to a cell block or section. Juveniles started out on the fifth floor in a 16-man cell block. By the time we moved, the numbers in the juvenile section had increased to 8 and continued to grow during 1975. The juvenile section was a unit with two 8-man cells and a dayroom. The cells were constructed of steel and reinforced concrete was designed into bunkbed style with four beds welded to each wall that ran the length of the cell and a stainless-steel toilet with a built-in sink along the back wall. Everything was a tight fit and with a full house, you had a crowded and congested situation.

The dayroom area was also constructed of the same reinforced concrete and steel and had two stainless-steel picnic tables, two toilets, two sinks, and two shower stalls, everything being made of stainless steel. Upon entering the dayroom, to the left and right were tables, directly in front were the two shower stalls, to the left of the showers were the two stainless-steel sinks with stainless-steel mirrors hanging above them, and to the right of the showers, in plain view, were two stainless-steel toilets. The dayroom rule meant when prisoners came out for breakfast in the morning at roughly 6 am, they had to stay locked up in the dayroom all day until after dinner, at roughly 6 pm. That was The Dayroom Rule.

Now, from my personal experience, the first full day in the new county jail began with being woken up for breakfast and given about 5 minutes to get up, get dressed, and get into the dayroom to eat. Once in the dayroom, we ate from new real cafeteria trays, served a real breakfast meal like scrambled eggs, sausage, toast, milk, and coffee. Everything was completely new. We were the first to use or touch literally everything. The newness of things had me feeling optimistic about my situation in general and the meal was a huge and very welcome improvement. But my optimism began to fade fast once it dawned on me that we would be locked in the dayroom all day until after dinner. What do eight teenagers do, locked up under these conditions for 12 straight hours with absolutely nothing to do? You can only do so much sitting down or trying to lay down or pace the floor. The adult sections at full capacity would have 16 adults per dayroom, facing the very same conditions. We had 12 hours in this cage with nothing to do but with idle time. We were compelled to smell and see another man taking a dump, which actually constituted cruel and unusual punishment and required a lawsuit by the American Civil Liberties Union (ACLU) to bring the practice to an end.

Although we juveniles submitted and offered only hostile complaints, the adult sections started rioting almost immediately. Day One got violent and bloody before sunrise with every section revolting to one degree or another, some being more confrontational and rebellious than others. For the first couple of weeks, something went down somewhere in the building every single day. I recall the riot team dressed in full riot gear, staying in the control room around the clock. The jailhouse grapevine kept us informed about which side got the better of the fighting.

The zero-tolerance policy was best demonstrated in the juvenile section on Day Two or Day Three. Out of curiosity and a matter of just wanting to know the rules of the game, I asked what would happen if we did not come out for breakfast and was told those who did not come out would not eat all day: either misinformation or bad information. Never being a morning person and not a big eater, I decided to stay in my cell and forego eating one day. I believe this was on Day Two. Those of us in the juvenile section had no intention of being defiant. We did discuss our options and concluded we could either stay in our cell and not eat or suffer the dayroom. That damn dayroom was so brutal and purposeless until the lesser of two evils was like jumping out of the frying pan straight into the fire.

Three of us made the decision to stay in our cells and not come out for breakfast. I went right back to sleep, not worrying about food or anything else, for that matter. I had seniority, I had influence, respect, and the power to call the shots. I would eat regardless, even if it meant someone else going hungry. My sleep was interrupted by someone snatching me out of bed by my ankle followed by a blow to the head. I kicked as hard as I could at the person gripping my ankle, knocking them off balance and getting loose. I ended up on the floor where all I could see was boots and the lower part of legs that were all dressed the same, and I was surrounded by them. Blocking and dodging wild frantic blows from my jailers' riot sticks, I rolled under the nearest bed, where I found temporary refuge.

My keepers came prepared, dressed in full riot gear, complete with shields and four-foot-long oak riot sticks. Rolling beneath the bunk bed proved to be an excellent move because it neutralized the damage they could inflict. Dug in deep beneath my bed protection, I kicked and lashed out at the many hands reaching in to grab at me. Finally, one of them got a good grip on a leg and pulled me out. I remember getting to my feet and somebody hitting me on the head from behind. Confused, pissed off, and angry as hell, I turned to confront my attacker only to find myself being bounced around like a ping-pong ball as my keepers pushed and shoved me straight out of the section and into the solitary-confinement block. Things happened so fast that it seemed as if one minute I was in bed asleep and the next minute I was in an isolation cell, naked except for my boxers. As it turned out, all three of us were placed in a one-man isolation cell together, wearing only our boxers.

For the first few moments, as the dust of confusion settled, silence was the only sound heard. We were totally dumbfounded and without a clue as to what just happened and why. The isolation cell had enough room for a single bed, a toilet–sink combination, and a little walking space. With no bedding or mattress and wearing only our boxers, the three of us stood around questioning what had taken place.

Since I had been incarcerated for a while by this time, I knew most of the officers who worked the lock-up units and they knew me. The first chance I got, I started politicking for our release, relating what was told to us about staying in our cell and not coming out for breakfast. The rank and file officers sympathized but conceded there was very little they could do. Then, I got a chance to speak with a sergeant. I knew we had a good association and explained the situation to him. The sergeant assured me he would take the necessary action to straighten things out but advised me to remain patient because it would not happen that day. Before breakfast the next morning, we were back in our section. The dayroom rule would eventually phase out and the doors to the dayroom and cells would be left open until the nightly lockdown head count, but not without a fight.

Reese, facing life in prison for a robbery and shooting, became my new right-hand man and would tease me about the incident for years to come. Reese, at age 17, arrived right before the jail move and our friendship flourished until he was the closest thing I had to a brother. Once again, our jailers moved the juvenile section back to the original block after I picked the lock to the dayroom and opened the doors to the adult cells. Someone informed and that led to the juveniles being moved and the rest of the section placed on total lockdown. Reese would come almost immediately after this move. At that time, the juvenile section included Clifford, Eric, Reese, and me, all four of us facing a life prison sentence, all being treated as adults and to be tried as adults.

Through my friendship with Reese, I discovered a real strength in my character and in my commitment to a friend. From hanging out with Big Al Cross, I learned that true and genuine friendship embraces a person and the person embraces it back. Reese was my guy, so when the Fifth Avenue Insanes (a well-known Gary street gang) showed up six deep on a murder case and wanted to jump Reese, I felt a need to step in. To better understand the significance of what I was stepping into, I was going up against guys from my hood area that I knew and they were a stronger force in numbers, all in defense of a friendship I made in jail.

The Fifth Avenue Insanes were arrested for murder resulting from a shoot-out between two rival gangs where a little girl was killed when caught in the crossfire. In these days, no gang in Gary, Indiana, was even close to being as heavily armed as those Fifth Avenue Insane boys. The Insanes were robbing gun stores in the little surrounding towns like crazy, never realizing with every robbery they pulled would cause the store owners to circle their wagons tighter in self-defense. Those Insane boys continued robbing gun stores until those gun-store owners started shooting back. Eventually, both the police and the coroner needed to be called to the robbery crime scene.

Six members of the Fifth Avenue Insanes were arrested in connection with the shoot out and the killing of the little girl, who was 10 or 11 years old, and I knew two of them personally. Eugene and Frog were friends with both my brother David and my step-brother Kenny. Both were former members of the 18th Avenue Gangsters. On many occasions, I ran the streets with Kenny, David, and other members of the 18th Avenue Gangsters including Frog and Eugene. I often hung out with David and Kenny at the ages of 12 and 13, David sometimes running me off as big brothers do when little brothers want to hang with the big boys. I participated in the delinquency behavior and some of the same gang activities with Eugene and Frog along with the 18th Avenue Gangster when hanging out with them. From drinking wine and smoking, to shoplifting and stealing, to fighting and shoot outs, I was right there in the thick of things, getting my initiation into the ways of gang street life.

Eugene and Frog were both tough streetwise youths who would form and become the leaders of the Fifth Avenue Insanes. Eugene was much like France as an agitator and troublemaker, only Eugene possessed more courage and had a fighting spirit. Eugene had what I call a true gang members' mentality and character. The more back up he had, the tougher he was; the bigger the audience, the louder he got and the more he would act like a fool. It was Eugene who instigated the confrontation with Reese simply because Reese wasn't from Gary; Reese was from Hammond, Indiana. In a gang-territorial sense, this made Reese a rival and therefore an open target in enclosed quarters and in a very volatile situation. Reese would have to defend against the six Insanes alone, the kind of odds gang members mostly prefer.

When Eugene, Frog, and the other Insanes made a move on Reese, I found myself suddenly having to make personal-value decisions on the spot. The questions were, do I go up against my brother's friends, do I go up against guys I know and ran with on the streets, and do I take sides against guys from my hometown? Reese was someone I met in jail and knew for perhaps a month or so, yet Reese was my friend and that mattered to me. I found myself at the birth stage of making decisions that I was willing and ready to defend in armed struggle, if necessary.

My decision to take a stand along with my newfound friend was greatly influenced by Reese himself and his bravado actions. Although I recognized the signs of the storm brewing, once in motion things happened rather quickly. One minute I noticed Reese having words with Eugene and the next thing I know, Reese was standing on a table with his back to the bars and loudly shouting, "You mother fuckers ain't doing shit to me." Reese was the laughter type who enjoyed clean fun. Now all business, I found his fighting spirit to be admirable. Without hesitation, I got between Reese standing on the table and Eugene with his boys standing in front of me. I said, addressing only Frog and Eugene, "If you fuck with him, you gotta fuck with me." Once Clifford saw the direction I was going, he followed suit, taking up position at my side. I do not take credit for saving Reese's bacon that day; Reese had saved his own bacon. I was just being a friend.

The hierarchy in the county jail began with the cell boss and his enforcers. I would cleverly change the system later by making Reese my cell boss and Clifford my enforcer. I gave them the titles, but I kept the power. The Fifth Avenue Insanes would get out of jail, yet 1975 proved to be a violent year for juvenile crimes and the jail would be full of long-term juvenile prisoners awaiting trial. For me, control of the section and maintaining that control equated to self-preservation. I used logic and intimidation most of the time to get my way; when necessary, I applied outright brute force. Even if intimidated into listening to reason, it was better than suffering the alternative and the consequences that followed.

My biggest struggle for survival while incarcerated emerged through my emotional battles. As tough as I thought I was and needed to be under the circumstances, still underneath I was an emotionally sensitive kid. Throughout my incarceration, when mail was being passed out and I did not receive any, my feelings would be hurt. When others ordered from the jail commissary and I did not have money from home to make a purchase, I felt left out. But in those early days, when I first arrived at the county jail and did not get visits from home, those were devastating emotional blows that led me to gradually grow emotionally bankrupt and emotionally dead. Then again, I realized that I could not afford to have feelings under the circumstances; I had to stand on my own.

Visiting day was once a week. The first couple of weeks I did not get a visit from my family. I felt disappointed but remained optimistic. By the third week, after visiting hours and I still received no visit, I was completely crushed. I remember crying like a baby for the second and final time. Not getting a visit from family or loved ones did much more than make me feel alone; it made me realize I was alone in an unforgiving and morbid situation. I quickly acknowledged there was no room in my life for such emotions, and therefore, I systematically began closing down. With each disappointment I faced, I circled my wagons around my emotions until they had no room to breathe. I grew more and more nonchalant and emotionally dead until I had practically no feelings at all; that way, I could not be hurt or disappointed.

The occasional letters from my mother and the five or ten dollars she managed to squeeze from her welfare check to send me commissary money was enough to remind me someone cared, but not enough to sustain me. I did not get my first visit until after moving to the new county jail almost a year later. My mother was at a total disadvantage with seven more kids at home and literally on her own in raising them. She had no knowledge of the judiciary process and a limited education. My mother was in over her head, as was I. I was mature enough to understand all of this, yet there was no consolation accompanying my young understanding.

In the new county jail, I met the second real convict who greatly influenced my fertile mind. Philip J. was a gangster with proven street credibility, a big-boy reputation in and out of prison, and very militant in attitude. I met Philip J. while in a holding cell on the first floor and we started talking, mostly just me answering questions as he probed and sized me up. I made a statement about being in the juvenile section using the word Colored to describe the race of my cellmates. When I said "Colored," Philip J. politely asked what color. I felt instantly stupid because I was a James Brown "I'm Black and I'm proud" kid. At an early age, I had a budding sense of Black consciousness and Philip J.'s comment seemingly exposed a weakness with which I felt uncomfortable. Thus, this conversation may have been the beginning of my journey in search of my personal identity.

Philip J. also introduced me to the world of civil litigation by getting me on the class-action lawsuits filed against the Lake County Jail from the rioting. In and out of jail most of his life, Philip J. knew the law better than some college-educated lawyers. Being what the penal system called a jailhouse lawyer, he had already filed and won several lawsuits against the State of Indiana. I can't say we developed a friendship of any substance. There were traits I admired and respected about him, but I never trusted him for some reason. Yet, meeting this brother left an impression on me in more ways than one.

Philp J. got me involved in lawsuits against the county jail that led to visits from the ACLU and their legal team. Members of the ACLU legal defense team would be the first to demonstrate compassion toward me of any sort regarding my criminal case. With anger and blood in their eyes, they listened to me relate my narrative of being beaten and placed in solitary confinement for violating the dayroom rule. The one thing I remember most of all is receiving legal mail from ACLU. I read my copies of the lawsuits over and over and over until the pages were like limp noodles. I wrote down words, repeated them over and over, and used them in sentences when talking, further developing my fascination for words.

The ACLU's mere presence caused the Lake County Sheriff's Department to loosen its stranglehold on the jail and the ACLU's immediate involvement and legal actions caused the rioting to stop. Soon, we had books and magazines coming from home. The jail provided a little book cart of used books, old *Reader's Digests,* and *National Geographics.* My reading habit, although in its infant stage, would continue to increase. Then one day, I found a jewel on the book cart: a *Webster's Dictionary.* My reading became a self-education assignment where every day when reading I had a paper, pen, and dictionary readily available. I wrote down words to look up later, some words I looked up while reading, and this would become my regular routine. Words were intriguing and finding the dictionary was like a torch that revealed their hidden meanings. If I had to describe my first impression of the dictionary in one word, the word would be beautiful.

When we eventually got playing cards in the sections, guys spent all day playing cards. When TVs were allowed, guys watched TV and played cards all day. I played cards and watched TV too, but being a true introvert, I spent most of my time alone, reading. For some reason, improving my intellect was quite important to me, once again exposing a weakness I wanted to correct. Personal shame in areas I perceived to fall short would be my biggest motivations for making changes and adjustments in my life. I was not dumb by a long shot; I was uneducated and that made me feel ashamed.

When reading, I would write down sayings or quotations and occasionally wrote paragraphs or inscriptions in addition to writing down words. My initial philosophy-building process began with saying, "If you can conceive it, you can achieve it" and "The difficulty in dying for a friend is not as great as finding a friend worth dying for." I wrote these things down, committed them to memory, and quoted them whenever possible. I kept countless scraps of paper beneath my mattress. I had words written on pieces of brown paper bags, blank pages from books I had read, and on the back of my legal mail. I had words written everywhere. With a dictionary as my closest reading companion, I looked up the definitions of my words. I would also spend a great deal of time just studying the dictionary, speed reading through the words, and stopping to examine and get a better comprehension of those words I recognized.

Reader's Digest in particular played a pivotal role in my reading and writing development. I found the short stories easy to read and follow. I found good advice and suggestions in *Reader's Digest*. I would also find myself inspired to write short stories and poems as a direct result of reading the *Reader's Digest*. Those short stories and poems accumulated under my mattress too. I read articles on how to improve one's vocabulary only to discover I was already using many of the techniques described. The most significant thing *Reader's Digest* did for me was give me confidence in my reading abilities and encourage me to read even more.

Action, espionage, and westerns became my favorite pass-time read-ing material. When my options were limited, I read whatever was avail-able, making science fiction and horror my very last choices. Of course, reading was my temporary escape from my predicament: my primary escape into another world. Through my reading, I traveled and explored the world like an adventurer of sorts. How some authors depicted and described certain scenes so vividly not only created a picture in my mind, but also demonstrated the power of the written word. Suddenly, I saw writing as a science and an art form, like painting. I wanted to be artist, painting pictures with words on paper. During my practice writ-ing, I would make a list of words and use them all until I drew a mas-terpiece to my satisfaction.

My attorney, Jay Given, was a good man who was highly respected in the Lake County Criminal Court system. Well connected and consid-ered one of the top lawyers in the county, Mr. Given was a court-ap-pointed attorney, and although I did not see or hear from him often, he proved to have my best interest at heart. Attorney Jay Given petitioned the court for a psychiatric evaluation on my behalf, citing temporary insanity as my legal defense. The court appointed two state psychiatrists to interview and examine my mental stability. I played the crazy role well enough to convince the doctors to send me to the state mental hos-pital for a 90-day observation. This move turned out to be one of those times I would overplay my hand.

Transferred to the state mental institution for the 90-day observation put me in a whole new and different environment, worse than the county jail. I remember being escorted down a hallway at the hospital the first day I arrived and seeing patients walking around like zombies. Through-out the place, I heard the hollering and screaming of madness, and for once I became scared, not of those around me but afraid of becoming one of them. The Indiana State Mental Hospital was located in Westville, Indiana, and had a unit for juveniles suffering from mental issues; I was housed with them.

At dinner, I sat at a table with one kid who obviously had serious behavioral problems because they had him strapped to a chair. He was bound with leather straps at the wrists and attached to the arms of the chair; everywhere he went, the chair dragged behind him. At dinner, he seemed to eat in slow motion and his food kept falling from his mouth after hardly chewing it. All I could say to myself was "how in hell did I get myself in this mess?" I was not prepared for this kind of madness and felt I was in over my head. I thought the temporary insanity move was a great idea, thinking six months or so at the mental hospital and I would be free again. But six months in that place, I would have been as loony and as all-out crazy as my fellow residents.

The next day, I met with three members of the hospital psychiatry team for my intake examination. After a series of seemingly harmless questions, one doctor asked if I was stoned when the crime occurred. Back then, my hood did not use the "stoned" terminology and the only time I recall the word being used is my grandfather saying he was stone sober. I sat stunned and rather perplexed for several moments, unsure how I should answer the good doctor. Finally, I replied with yes, thinking like my grandfather, "yes, I was stone sober." Thank God I did not express or convey my thoughts in full because doing so may have gotten me committed as a patient. I knew in advance that being intoxicated would negate a temporary insanity defense and it was my error saying I was stoned during the criminal act. No, I wasn't stoned during the commission of the robbery murder, but incorrectly or ignorantly saying I was probably saved me from becoming a nut case for real.

The temporary-insanity defense would not be a get-out-of-jail-free card, as I thought it would be. Although my county jail experience was hard time, I remained confident I could handle and survive that element, whereas I had absolutely no confidence I could handle or survive the state mental hospital environment. The doctors concluded and reported to the court from their interviews and examination that I was illiterate, mentally retarded, and incapable of learning, but not temporarily insane during my criminal offense. After only two days, I would be transported back to the Lake County Jail to await trial and was grateful the temporary-insanity move failed.

Perhaps a month or so after moving into the new county jail, Clifford started getting called out for court alone. I immediately knew what was going on. Clifford and his lawyer were negotiating a plea agreement to turn state's evidence and cooperate with the prosecutor: his testimony in exchange for probation. This was a typical prosecutor's move in a multidefendant case: negotiate a deal with the less culpable defendant first. I did not hesitate to confront Clifford with my suspicions and he admitted a plea deal was in process. His lawyer and his family wanted him to cooperate with the prosecution and testify against me. I was not surprised and subconsciously expected this move to eventually come to pass.

Clifford looked up to me. He held me in high regard and had real brotherly love for me, but Clifford did not have the grit or the fortitude I possessed. Clifford tried to give the impression that he was indecisive about making the deal, yet I knew he had already caved under the pressure. When discussing the matter with him, I went into damage-control mode. The die had been cast and there would be no dissuading him, and I knew this. Being more understanding rather than getting angry, I would coach Clifford, suggesting he minimize my involvement as much as possible. Then one day, Clifford was called out for court and never returned to our section. They moved him to the adjacent section. I knew right away what the move meant. My only question was how much damage he would do in the long run.

In June 1975, the wheels were in motion for my case to proceed with a jury trial and a tentative date was set. The prosecution offered me a chance to plead guilty to a 15-year prison sentence, but before I could accept, the plea offer was withdrawn. The prosecution obviously thought it would be an all uphill battle to convict a 15-year-old juvenile, considering I was the youngest on a case with three adult codefendants. Once all four of my codefendants turned state's evidence and took plea agreements, which included testifying against me, the prosecuting attorney had a better shot at a conviction. A second deal was offered for a 15- to 25-year prison sentence, which my attorney suggested I decline, saying he felt we would do much better taking a jury trial.

I remember stressing and contemplating the decision and, although I trusted my lawyer, I could not see a favorable outcome proceeding with a trial by jury. If convicted, I faced life in prison and chances were very good a guilty verdict would be rendered. After all, I would have four codefendants getting on the witness stand to testify against me. I believe my attorney, Jay Given, proposed a strategy revolving around convincing a jury that my codefendants were placing the blame on me because I was the youngest, using me as the fall guy. No matter which way I viewed my dilemma, I reached the same conclusion. Either accept the 15- to 25-year plea deal or take my case to trial with a life prison sentence lingering overhead. Neither proposition appealed to me and I laid up nights worrying and thinking about my destiny and what the future held.

One night, I got out my writing tools and wrote a letter to my attorney asking that he try to negotiate a plea agreement on my behalf for a 2- to 21-year prison sentence. Jay Given was a power player in the Lake County Court System and had all the right connections. Working his magic, Mr. Given went to bat for me and came back with the 2- to 21-year plea deal I requested. Under this sentence, I would be required to serve no less than 2 years and no more than 21 years.

Mr. Jay Given was not only a mover and shaker in the Lake County Judicial System with a reputation as a fixer and an excellent trial lawyer, he was also a power player in the Lake County political circle. While incarcerated, I would later learn Mr. Given was murdered, his death believed to be the result of a contract killing. Rumors implied his death was politically motivated with a chief of police and a mayor involved. Lake County has a long history of corruption, bribery being an internal component. Justice was for sale if the price was right and obviously matters could turn politically street violent to protect the order of things.

I genuinely liked and respected Mr. Given because he demonstrated he had my best interest at heart. In the court system, from top to bottom, no one cared about what would eventually happen to me. My understanding is that I was to be made an example because juvenile violent crimes were on the rise. Mr. Given managed to get my neck out of the noose from a life sentence in prison, but those who followed would not be so lucky.

5. The Journey

My journey into the Indiana Prison System began with my arrest and subsequent conviction as the youngest person incarcerated as an adult in the Indiana Department of Corrections. From the county jail, I would be transported to the Reception Diagnostic Center where the determination of prisoner placement is made. Once per month, all convicted and sentenced prisoners are loaded onto a bus and taken to the RDC. My codefendants, Span, Gamble, and Jessie, were among the prisoners who made the trip with me to the diagnostic center. Clifford received the promised probation and the other three received 10 years each, according to their plea agreement. For once, I noticed neither Spann nor Gamble had a blackened eye or bruises that were common when I saw them during court hearings when the five of us were brought together.

The Indiana Reception Diagnostic Center is supposed to evaluate prisoners to determine to which correctional facility they will be sent. At the time, only one of the three correctional institutions was available for consideration: the Indiana Youth Center, the Indiana reformatory, and the Indiana State Prison. The Indiana Youth Center housed younger prisoners with a minimal criminal record and short prison sentence, and being White also seemed to be a prerequisite. The youth center, according to prison standards, was a soft laid-back joint with extra perks; Blacks rarely got sent there. The Indiana Reformatory, better known as gladiator school, housed prisoners with a more extensive criminal record, more hardened and dangerous, but with less than a life prison sentence. The Indiana State Prison, the Big House, and better known as The

63

City, housed lifers and diehard criminals and those incarcerated more than 25 years and those doing significant prison time, the Bad Boys of all Bad Boys in the state of Indiana.

Because of my age, those in authority at the RDC only allowed me out of my cell for meals until I began protesting and started acting a fool. They threatened to put me in isolation if I did not calm down and, as a punishment for my behavior, my keepers kept me locked in my cell for three days and brought my meals to me. While everyone else was out moving around throughout the day, taking IQ tests, and having physical and psychological examinations, I saw a psychiatrist just once. On average, a prisoner's stay at the RDC lasted approximately three weeks taking these so called placement tests. I would spend all my time there reading and sleeping, not allowed out of my cell for any of the extracurricular activities afforded the adult prisoners, yet on my way to an adult prison to serve my sentence.

State-appointed psychiatrists had already concluded and advised the court that I was illiterate, mentally retarded, and incapable of learning. A record of their findings and conclusions would follow me throughout my incarceration and be made part of my permanent institutional record. I often wonder what my keepers were thinking when they made the decision that the Indiana Reformatory should be my destination. At age 16 and classified as a retarded person, they sent me to the gladiator school for punishment and rehabilitation. This could have never been a move for my benefit or my welfare, nor a sincere effort to rehabilitate me or help me. I would grow up among hardened convicts and, for the sake of survival, became a formidable gladiator at the Indiana Reformatory myself.

On July 3, 1975, a bus loaded with approximately 20 or 30 fresh prisoners left the diagnostic center heading for the Indiana Reformatory. My three codefendants were also designated to serve their sentences at the Reformatory and the four of us rode out together. I may have dealt with Gamble and Spann in a cordial manner, but beneath the surface, I couldn't stand either one. Really, I did not know them and in prison I had no inclination to get further acquainted. Jessie, on the other hand, was my frequent running buddy on the streets. We had a history between us and our families knew each other well. During the bus ride, I met Jomo through Jessie and we eventually became good friends over the years. The nucleus of my prison circle of friends would begin with this bus ride.

The mere sight of the Indiana Reformatory was rather intimidating and caused me to experience a brief moment of anxiety. The 30-foot walls that wrapped around the prison, mounted with gun towers, was a clear indication that I was about to step into a totally different world. The dirty, lifeless, and grey concrete walls spoke loudly of the morbid and empty existence of those confined behind them. I went numb as the prison bus pulled up to the massive iron gate at the prison rear entrance where life as I once knew it would change forever. I had never seen a gate quite so huge and menacing in appearance, and movies on TV do little to convey this sight compared to the up-close experience. I remember thinking to myself "ready or not, this is it!" There was no way out of whatever lay ahead and my only option was no option at all, other than to hold my own ground at all costs.

The gate opened and the bus pulled into the rear entrance port, an area large enough for the bus with a prisoners' holding tank and a guard shack. The building had a second large gate immediately in front of the bus which led into the prison compound and a guard tower station above the port area, with armed guards posted. A cut-out walkway was constructed directly beneath where the bus was parked so officers could walk to inspect the undercarriage. All supply or delivery vehicles in and out of the prison came through the rear entrance port for a thorough inspection, coming and going. The back gates, as we called them, were where one entered the prison upon arrival and where one left upon departure, once the sentence was completed. The Indiana Reformatory was built in the early 1920s on more than 30 acres of land enclosed by the giant prison walls that separated convicts from the rest of the free world.

The transport officers in charge of the new commitments exited the bus first to store their weapons in the guard shack for safe keeping. At this point, only the officers in the tower were allowed weapons. After several moments of waiting patiently while the transport officers checked in their weapons and turned over the necessary paperwork on the new commitments, we were finally escorted off the bus, hands and feet in shackles. We were ordered off the bus and made to stand in a single line in the rear gate port area. One by one, the shackles were removed as a tough-talking officer gave his speech about what was expected of us during our stay there. Then into the holding tank we went. Seeing the transport officers collect their weapons, get back on the bus, and back out as the big gate opened only served notice that my life in prison had actually begun.

A short time later, an officer from behind the walls appeared. It was his job to escort us through the initial prisoner intake process. In single file, we were marched through the prison compound. Onlookers aware of the scheduled new arrival observed us from a distance. Some shouted, "New fish in the house." Others looked for familiar faces. Still others simply indulged their curiosity. Several called out Jomo's name in greeting and one or two called out to Jessie. Jomo was a gang leader, I would later learn, but the kind of gang member who could stand on his own like my brother David and my step-brother Kenny. Jomo was a very likeable guy and I immediately discerned he was also highly respected and had a solid reputation from the streets.

Our first stop was the clothing and receiving department, where each man had to strip naked and be searched, again. This included bending over, spreading one's butt cheeks, and coughing. Next, we were sprayed with bug juice, lice spray, and sent to shower. I found the whole procedure humiliating and rather demoralizing. But now in Rome, we had to submit to Roman law or suffer the consequences. I never got used to the invasion of spreading my butt cheeks and coughing. My jaws get tight with contempt from the mere thought even now. The day would soon come when I openly rebelled against this particular practice. Before I left the reformatory, my keepers understood some Roman laws just did not apply to me, yet along the way I would pay the cost to live with what dignity I had left. When deprived of all else in prison, a man had only two things worth hanging onto: his manhood and self-respect.

After showering, each individual was called one at a time. The personal belongings that arrived with us were searched and inventoried.

Those things we could keep were given to us. The rest could be sent home at our expense or trashed. If trashed, depending on what the item was, it would eventually find it was way into the prison population and become the property of someone else. If one was man enough, they could take it back or demand it back on sight. Next, we were given three sets of prison blues: pants and shirts. The shirts all had our prison number freshly stamped over the right pocket. We also got three pairs of socks, t-shirts, and boxers; a bed roll with blankets, sheets, and pillow; and finally, a pair of state boots that I refused to wear during my entire incarceration.

The group of prisoners were then escorted through the main prison compound to J-cellhouse where new arrivals are held for orientation and classification. The walk took us through the heart of the prison grounds, past the major's office and lock-up unit, the prison mess hall, and the hospital. The main compound opened to reveal a maze of sidewalks leading in multiple directions and all areas of the prison. What stood out most to me during the walk to J-cellhouse was how well kept and perfectly manicured the lawns were. The heart of the prison compound was easily the size of a football field with only a flagpole in the middle, surrounded by the well-kept lawn and intersecting sidewalks. From first appearance, one could mistake the Reformatory for a military academy of sorts, and I could feel a sense of order and discipline in the air.

J-cellhouse was a large building like most structures scattered about the institution. The concrete stairs leading up to the front entrance matched the building's overall dimensions. Once inside J-cellhouse, all we had was an officer's station immediately to the left and nothing but cells for human warehousing: three tiers on the front side and three on the back side that ran the length of the building, approximately 50 cells to each tier. New commitments were assigned the first 25 cells on the bottom tier until classified and permanent housing assigned.

The prison had three cellhouses similar to J and an honor dormitory. When I arrived, the prison was already overcrowded and prisoners were being doubled up. My first cellmate would be an older stick-up man from Gary who was down for his second robbery conviction. William was a small-time criminal with a history of petty crimes and mom-and-pop store robberies under his belt. All his crimes related to supporting an out-of-control drug addiction. William would be an easy cellmate to live with, which was very important when two men are forced to live in such close quarters together for any length of time. The wrong two personalities locked in a cage together tend to turn ugly very quickly, and prisoner placement was a delicate balancing act for prison officials.

My education began from my first night at the Indiana Reformatory; every day was class day, every day was a test, and every day bared a lesson. Learning to mind my own business in prison was finally driven home and forever carved into my mind when my curiosity got the best of me one day. No more than two or three weeks into serving my prison sentence, I had been in front of the classification board and assigned to H-cellhouse and enrolled in school. While returning to the cellhouse from lunch, I heard a commotion and saw a crowd of guys gathering and guys looking over the tier at the action on the far side of the cell block. Being so inquisitive, I ran up to the crowd, trying to peep through the gathering mob of onlookers and action seekers. Being a little fellow, I couldn't see over or around the crowd until suddenly the mass of bodies parted, like Moses parting the Red Sea, and standing before me was a wide-eyed panic-stricken prisoner leaking blood, a prison-made knife in one hand, a frantic look on his face, looking around as if he did not know who was or was not the enemy. I completely froze in place as he came directly at me, half expecting to feel the puncture of the blade hit me. I heard a voice saying calmly from within, "do not move." The words were clear and conveyed reassurance. The wounded prisoner, obviously fighting for his life, ran past me and disappeared around a corner. I stood right there for a moment, feeling stupid and very vulnerable. Never again would I be one of those who raced to the scene to observe or witness a personal fight between prisoners; I would start minding my own damn business.

Most everyone from Gary, Indiana, knew of me due to the nature of my case. The prison grapevine was just as vibrant as that in the county jail, perhaps even better informed and more reliable. Guys at the Reformatory knew I was coming there before I even knew where I would serve my prison sentence. I became acquainted with the entire Gary crew, but being a loner by nature, I would mostly travel alone in prison and, to a large extent, always felt like an outsider. For some reason, I had very little in common with them or with other prisoners in general, and I seemingly marched to the beat of a completely different drum. Although I was much younger, my thinking was on a more mature level and I saw in most of them strength that only derived from numbers. Few had what it took to stand alone and everyone had gang affiliations. I saw false pretenses in their characters as they pretended to be more than they were, and I had little interest in the things with which they identified. But more importantly, I resented the subtle attitude of those who thought they held a higher status because they got regular visits from home and made commissary weekly.

H-cellhouse, predominantly Black, was the roughest and most ruthless cellhouse at the reformatory. Some prisoners were assigned to H but others preferred protective custody or solitary confinement over H-cellhouse. I had no problem living among these rowdy elements, as my own rebellious side emerged. From Day One, I had difficulty following the rules and stayed in trouble all the time. At first, it was simple infractions like being out of place or not attending school classes. As punishment, I was put on cell restriction, allowed out of my cell only for meals and school. I continued to break the rules until the level of punishment increased. My behavior and rebellions would also increase. Eventually, I violated every rule except rape and murder. With a serious little man's complex, a hair-trigger temper, and a bad disposition for following the rules or taking orders, I would do my time as I wished, defying officers and fellow prisoners along the way.

My little-Caesar complex kept me in combat mode and made me a walking powder keg, always feeling a necessary need to prove myself. Being a proud and very sensitive young man with a chip on my shoulder, no one could raise their voice at me, talk disparagingly to me, or show the slightest disrespect. For some reason, my young mind translated all acts of hostility into an issue of size, thinking if I was bigger, these things would not happen. This was no exaggeration on my part because I saw how bigger men in prison received more room for respect, regardless of deserving it. I also saw bigger prisoners who I knew to be big and soft use their size to intimidate and bluff their way around the joint. My little-man complex would lead to countless physical and verbal confrontations with my keepers and fellow prisoners. I had to prove I could not only slay any Goliath, but I, too, was a giant who others had to respect and reckon with. Subconsciously, I believed it necessary to be more demanding and more aggressive in commanding respect due to my size, and those who tried me instantly felt my wrath, bar none.

Rainbow, a big tough youngster from Gary in his early 20s who stood well over six feet and weighed well over 200 pounds, would be made my first example. Rainbow had a reputation for being a bully and ran with a bullish crew of pushy brothers. Approximately six months into my sentence and still in the early stages of my outright rebellion against the system and submitting to life in prison according to my principles, I felt compelled to shut him down. Violence in prison is a universal language and no one misunderstood the message when you spoke it. I would learn to master this language and speak it fluently. With Rainbow, I saw an opportunity to make a power statement that I was nothing to play with and a true force to be reckoned with, if provoked.

The incident occurred during the lunch break when all prisoners returned to their designated cellhouses. I was living in G-cellblock at the time. This unit was identical to H-cellhouse by design and on the opposite side of the prison compound. Where H was predominantly Black and rather rowdy, G was predominantly White and laid back. I had been transferred to G-cellhouse after getting out of solitary confinement for one rule infraction or another. I was still at the stage where I believed rules were made to be broken. Breaking the rules as usual, I hid out one day so I would not have to lock down in my cell and wait for my tier to get the chow-line call. Chow call was on a rotating schedule with six tiers per cellhouse and 25 cells per tier and my tier was scheduled near last. I had all sorts of tricks for getting out of my cell and running around the cellhouse, hiding from the officers on duty until the coast was clear, and then blend in with the normal prison flow. I was up to my old tricks of playing hide and seek when I found myself in front of Rainbow's cell. I don't remember why I stopped there or what was actually said, but I do recall some verbal sparring between us, but I thought lightly of the exchange and moved on.

The prison chow hall during lunch time is full of buzz and activity, with a seating capacity for perhaps two hundred prisoners and two lines that stretch out the door at mealtime. The chow hall was also racially divided right down the middle with Whites on one side and Blacks on the other. You could take either line, but everything had its order and mode of operation. I took whichever line was the shortest. Officers were posted throughout the chow hall for all meals, but a heavier presence is on location during lunch, along with all the high-ranking brass. Even the warden made his appearance at this time on occasion. Jessie, Jomo, a brother named Whopper, and I were eating lunch when Rainbow came and stood towering over me and threatened to kick my ass if I ever talk to him like that again. I guess he meant our verbal sparring match from earlier. I didn't care what he meant. I heard only the threat and instantly went into full-combat mode.

Rainbow proceeded to sit at a nearby table with his boys, thinking it was over. I, on the other hand, felt it was the opportune moment to make a power statement to all those present: "Observe and witness my work." Without saying a word, I got up and headed straight for Rainbow. Before he could sit down, I was on top of him with a chow hall chair that I grabbed along the way as my weapon of choice for the occasion. The stainless-steel trays we ate from or the durable steel chow-hall chairs were the best two readily available weapons in the chow hall and I've used both. My attack on Rainbow drew all attention, but not before I got a couple of good solid blows in on him, drawing blood and sending him ducking for cover. Officers on security responded almost immediately, pouncing on me and wrapping me up in a submission hold until they had me handcuffed and thoroughly subdued. I had been itching for a fight. My little-man complex had been simmering for months and I was subconsciously looking for an opportunity to express myself as a true big boy, worthy of the utmost respect. I would make an example of Rainbow so others would quickly get the message that I was not a man you could threaten and walk away from. To not move on him so aggressively would have been my downfall, opening the door for others to talk down to me or treat me like a punk, and I was having no part of that in my life.

The attack on Rainbow got me put in solitary confinement for six months and boosted my reputation for being a young up and coming gladiator who took no prisoners. Solitary confinement was the dreadful lock-up unit where individuals spent 23 hours a day locked in their cells. Most feared the lock-up unit, but I did not. My entire stay at the Reformatory was spent in and out of lock-up. Solitary was my rite of passage into becoming a hardened convict and for being acknowledged as a stand-up guy. The lock-up unit is also where I concentrated on my serious studies to obtain my penitentiary master's degree. I would stop reading fiction and begin reading books on self-improvement and developing the inner self. I studied meditation, subliminal suggestion, metaphysics, and the science of the mind. I read anything regarding improving oneself from how to get a better night sleep to how to control one's personal world and pursue one's goals in life. I read *Think and Grow Rich, I'm OK—You're OK,* and so many others that I can't remember.

I studied African American history too, only to grow bitter and enraged as I learned of the atrocities perpetrated against the African American people. Although I grew up in the South under Jim Crow and was part of the first school-desegregation experiment following the *Brown v. Board of Education* decision, I still had no real concept of racism. But my keepers at the Indiana Reformatory would change that and clear up my ignorance on this matter, causing me to grow even more callous at heart. My keepers taught me to hate with a passion. They were racist to the core and made no effort to conceal it. Indiana being the birthplace of the Ku Klux Klan, the Indiana Reformatory was located in the heart of Klan territory. One Black officer was on staff and two Blacks worked in the education department. The rest of the prison employees were all White.

My militant side would emerge as a result of my studies and my intellectual side matured as I nurtured my hunger for knowledge and an insatiable desire to better myself. On lock down for 23 hours a day, all I did was read from the time I got up until I went to sleep. The one book that left the biggest impression on me during those days was *The Rise of the Fourth Reich.* Conspiracy theories didn't faze me. I could already see those in power controlling and manipulating the world in which we lived. I was more intrigued by the power of such men and how to amass such power myself. Always the idealist and a true humanitarian in spirit, I wanted the power to change the world. Those in authority held a selfish objective, their agenda motivated by greed. They viewed the common people as mere pawns in the game being played on the world's stage; this was my militant opinion.

The struggle and championing the cause against oppression everywhere became a major interest for me. From South Africa to the backcountry roads of Mississippi, I learned as much as I could about the struggle and those involved. I stayed abreast of current events around the world that pertained to the political movement for social change and spoke out against oppressive government policies. I absorbed everything from the Kent State tragedy to the Attica conflict, from the Watts riots to the Vietnam War. Malcolm X and Muhammad Ali would become the only two men I felt worthy of looking up to as my personal heroes and were men I greatly respected. Malcolm took a stand according to his truths and gave his life. Muhammad Ali stood his ground in accordance with his principles and sacrificed material wealth and worldly prestige for his cause. I found in them the kind of resolve and commitment of purpose that was truly admirable, and I too wanted to possess such qualities in my character.

The radical philosophy I was developing was preventing me from appreciating the works and contributions of brothers like Rev. Martin Luther King Jr. and Booker T. Washington. I felt Dr. King was much too soft with his nonviolent approach and Mr. Booker T. Washington was an Uncle Tom and much too servile. After reading Rev. Martin Luther King's popular *Letter from the Birmingham Jail,* my opinion changed dramatically and a closer examination of his life led to a greater appreciation of his work. I still held the same views regarding Mr. Washington, but the end results of his accomplishments overshadowed my personal perceptions of the man. I would evolve as my understanding matured, and as a young man, establish my own identity. All the personalities I studied and their works had some influence on my growth and development, some more than others. The books I read were littered with precious jewels and I pocketed as many as I could.

As a very young man growing up in a hostile environment in search of himself as an individual while also dealing with the identity crisis of being a Black man in the United States, I incorporated the things into my life that best served my survival needs at the time. My militant attitude allowed me to flourish as I adjusted my forever present little-man complex. I redirected my anger toward what I considered to be the struggle and any prison revolutionary cause we could manufacture. Sometimes the causes were legitimate, but more often than not, they were a matter of looking for an excuse to vent. Information and logic helped solve my identity crisis as a Black man in the United States and a descendant of former slaves, and a people the entire world seemed to hate and despise. Coming into a higher level of consciousness, I reasoned that I could never be labeled Colored, Black, or Negro to reflect my nationality. If Colored, what color was I before being colored. Was I green and then colored or was I red? My pigmentation was too brown for me to identity myself as just Black, and Negro came across sounding like a Caucasian stigma. Neither seemed to establish my nationality, yet I would continue to grow and evolve.

The guys I met on lock-up were rebellious rule breakers like me: guys who fought against the system or refused to tolerate being treated less than a man by our keepers. I selected a small circle of friends from among these prisoners, guys I could trust and respect. Giz and Priest were two such brothers. On lock-up for attempted escape along with several other guys from Indianapolis, these two were shot callers for the Indianapolis mob. Gary and Indianapolis coexisted in prison like Russia and the United States during the Cold War. Both were equally strong and heavily represented behind the walls and considered the two superpowers that ran and controlled almost all illegal activities in the joint. Gary and Indianapolis shared a delicate relationship that could erupt at any moment or come together in unity, if necessary. As always, I befriended individuals based on content of character; race or where they were from had no value for me. Giz and Priest embraced me as a comrade in the struggle and I embraced them back.

The lock-up unit had only four tiers, two on each side of the building with 25 cells per tier. When not reading, I occasionally played chess long distance with either Giz or Priest. Guys would hold conversations with one another from a long distance: idle talk or reminiscing about the streets. Being the quiet one, I didn't engage much in tier talk. Mostly, I was not heard on the tier unless I was calling out a chess move. I found a great deal of unnecessary tier talk caused some to unknowingly expose themselves in many ways. Simply listening, I became what I would call a trainer observer. When people talk a great deal, I found that inadvertently they tell others who they really are beneath the surface. They indirectly divulge their inner thoughts and feelings, revealing subtle hints of their true character. I would study those around me as if studying for a final exam in human nature. I concluded that the majority of those incarcerated at the Reformatory were shallow, superficial, and failed to represent the individual they verbally claimed to be, and I totally disliked a fake.

Giz and Priest had a no-nonsense, take-no-prisoners mentality similar to my own and we shared a great deal in common with our prison and political philosophies. On the lock-up unit, we led hunger strikes, pushed others to sign petitions, and spearheaded riots. Many of the positive changes in the Indiana penal system derived from the work that guys like us put in. Working for prisoners' rights was still very unpopular at this time and few had the courage to fight for change. We believed the choices were to stand up for something or fall for anything. Perhaps more radical in our approach due to the circumstances and the frustration of being under the yoke of incarceration, we were self-proclaimed vanguards of prison reform and members of the struggle from behind prison walls. We willingly accepted the consequences of our actions, allowing the chips to land as they may. Giz and Priest would eventually end up on death row and suffer execution by electric chair, and I would spend more than 25 years in prisons and jails.

My loyalty was unconditional once given, but in my youth I had a tendency to extend this loyalty without question to those I embraced as friends. Following my six-month stint in solitary confinement for the assault on Rainbow, I returned to the general prison population to learn a very valuable lesson about where and with whom to place my loyalty. This lesson would come by way of my boy Reese, a friend from the Lake County Jail days, who arrived at the Reformatory shortly after I did. Reese already had a brother incarcerated there named Willie. In fact, Reese had two brothers who were in and out of the joint for most of their lives and Reese would follow suit. Willie was a seasoned convict when I met him: muscular and very athletic like Reese, a boxer with excellent hands, and a shot caller for those from Hammond, Indiana. In my opinion, either brother possessed the raw skills and athleticism to be world-class boxers. I learned to box from them during my early days at the Reformatory. I personally had no desire to become a boxer in a professional sense. I used boxing to stay in shape and to develop my defensive skills.

Reese came to my cell one day after lunch and asked if I had a knife he could use because his brother and he had a beef with other prisoners from their hometown, Hammond. Without questioning the nature of the conflict, I offered my support: a mistake I would never make again after the dust settled and I learned what the altercation was about. On the weekends after lunch, prisoners were shown a movie in the chapel, mostly low-budget movies with no significant plot. Two full-scale riots with shooting, tear gas, and bodily injuries resulted from the showing of these pointless kiddy movies while I was there. On this particular occasion, I went to the movie with Reese, his brother, and a couple of other guys. As we left the chapel after the movie, Reese and Willie exchanged heated words with another prisoner. Once we reached the cellhouse, they caught up with this guy standing in front of another prisoner's cell, talking with his codefendant and partner in crime from the streets. The codefendant's name was Mousy, a tall lanky brother from Hammond who respected Reese and Willie, yet refused to bow down to any man. Mousy was locked in his cell, having not come out for the movie call, when Reese and Willie approached from the back side of the cellblock and commenced to pound on the guy from the chapel. The guy broke and ran, but they caught him and pounded on him some more. Mousy, locked in his cell, saw all this, yet was unable to assist his codefendant. Mousy went ballistic, raging and issuing threats. I never touched the brother, but I was there. I call myself being there for a friend, if needed. From what I was seeing, they didn't need my help. Yet still, I was there and that counted me in as far as Mousy was concerned.

Most of the cellhouse were out on the tiers waiting for the lock-down call, which comes once everyone returned from the movie. Onlookers gathered here and there to peep at the action, curious about what was going on. They spoke among themselves, trying to piece together what little they knew of the event. From there, things seemingly unfolded all at once, yet in slow motion. I recall hearing the lockdown announcement and the cell doors bang open simultaneously. I looked to my left and saw Mousy storming out of his now-open cell. I looked to my right to see Reese and his brother disappear around a far corner. Suddenly, I heard someone yell, "run." I looked to my left again to see Mousy approaching fast, and this damn fool had a baseball bat in hand. Well, Mousy bowed down to no man and I ran from no man. I took my eyes off Mousy for a brief moment, turning back to face him a second too late. I saw the baseball bat coming straight at my head, having only enough time to roll with the blow just enough not to absorb the full impact. I saw stars in brilliant colors and heard bells ring, but remained coherent and now thoroughly pissed off. Mousy drew back to strike again, only this time I was ready. I ducked under the second swing and charged him. In a sudden rush, I had him pinned against a cell using my shoulder in his chest and gripping the cell bar with my left hand. I hit him several times with right hooks until I saw the bat trapped between us. With all my might, I reached and wrestled the bat away in one quick motion. Just as I got control of the bat, Captain Walker appeared and some ass kisser trying to score points grabbed me, pretending to be a peacekeeper, and within minutes, officers were everywhere, shouting orders and securing the cellblock.

I didn't feel a thing when Mousy hit me with that baseball bat, but the next day, the damage was clear and convincing. My head was pounding as if a crew with jack hammers were doing construction work on my brain. The entire left side of my face was swollen, my left eye swollen completely closed, and I had about 10 jagged prison stitches along the side of my left cheek bone, less than an inch from my temple.

The slight roll I made upon the bat's impact probably prevented a direct blow to the temple and perhaps saved my life. I would remain in the prison infirmary for several days, replaying the events over and over in my mind as they had unfolded. I remember being hurt and very disappointed because I felt a sense of betrayal from Reese and Willie. Once I learned what the confrontation was all about, I felt like the biggest fool on planet Earth. Mousy and his codefendant had a sissy boy and Willie wanted him. In prison, fighting over another man didn't go down very well with me and how the brothers vanished when the battle kicked off disturbed me even more. The brothers had raced to their cells for the lock-down call, not wanting to deal with Mousy at that time, not while he was on the war path wielding a damned baseball bat.

They left me in the middle of some mess they had created, knowing Mousy was no pushover. I lost total respect for Willie and never broke bread with him again. The bond between Reese and I would remain to some degree, yet things would never be the same between us and never again would I even so much as consider helping him in matters of personal conflict. My concept of friendship and loyalty came under question to the extent that I had to rethink who was and who wasn't worthy. The saying, "the difficulty to die for a friend is not so great as it is to find a friend worth dying for" would follow me the rest of my life. I found the ultimate test of friendship is manifest under adversity and tribulation when only the sincere at heart showed consistency. But most importantly, the veil of illusion regarding convict ethics and the street code of ethics was lifting, revealing that very few practiced what they preached and many talked the talk but didn't walk the walk.

During my short stay in the prison infirmary, I met the notorious Cold Soup Campbell, a former enforcer for the equally notorious and vicious street gang called The Family that controlled the illegal drug-trafficking on the streets of Gary, Indiana, in the early '70s. Cold Soup Campbell was one of the last true original gangsters from Gary. Very few honored and lived by the street code as he did. Soup was in the infirmary for a bad asthma condition and we quickly became very good friends. Soup was well informed, by way of the prison grapevine, of all that happened throughout the prison and it was he who told me what the beef between Willie and Mousy was about. I wanted to catch Mousy and permanently put his ass to sleep. Soup would be the one who negotiated the peace between us later.

Soup was feared and commanded the utmost respect. At age 25, his name was already legendary. Street rumors had Cold Soup Campbell being one of the deadliest young members of the organized crime crew known as The Family. Many throughout the Midwest heard of The Family street crew because they made Gary the murder capital for two or three consecutive years. They demanded total control of the drug market. One bought and sold only The Family product or suffered the consequences. These brothers came on hard and strong, suppressing all opposition with unchecked violence. The Gary Police Department put together a taskforce to deal with The Family and those boys proved to be just as deadly and violent as The Family; police gangsters with a badge and gun were commissioned by law to stop the takeover of the Gary streets by The Family crew. Some in the know claimed many of the unsolved murders during those times could rightfully be attributed to the drug taskforce. The police and The Family had gun battles in the middle of the streets, in front of the police station, and even at one funeral, with local police and the FBI. We're talking wild west, shoot-on-sight running gun battles between outlaws and those wearing badges.

Political and police corruption ran rampant in Gary, Indiana, and in my opinion, this corruption gave birth to Black organized crime like The Family. Everyone was in our neighborhood making money on illegal operations—gambling, bootlegging, prostitution, the numbers—and it was all approved and endorsed by those in power. The Family would put the squeeze on all illegal operations with the saying, "cut us in or cut it out." Eventually running the Irish, the Jewish, and Italian mob operators completely out, they tried to hold onto power by putting a Black figurehead out front, but The Family made the cost of doing business a matter of live or die under their rule. One group of drug dealers would band together, refusing to submit to threats and intimidation from The Family. They called themselves The Organization. Although this second gang had some real gangsters in its leadership, they were no match for The Family, the undisputed kings of the Gary underworld.

Once discharged from the prison infirmary, I hit the general population one last time before being put in solitary confinement for the duration of my stay at the Indiana Reformatory. Many thought my rebellious behavior was reckless and foolish, but there was a method to my madness. I had already concluded that my release would not come any time in the immediate future, so why play by the rules? Also, I was in pursuit of a reputation for being acknowledged as a force to be reckoned with by my keepers and fellow prisoners. Many of the things I did were calculated moves to enhance my developing bad-boy image. Most guys came to prison and instantly became model prisoners, going months, years, or even their entire prison sentence without breaking a single rule. I would accumulate more than 50 conduct reports and write ups in the two and a half years I spent at the reformatory. The majority of my offenses revolved around disobeying a direct order and refusing to lock down. My defiance derived mostly out of spite and a total lack of respect for my openly racist keepers.

I did not respect the warden or his assistant. I held no respect for the captains, lieutenants, or sergeants and I definitely had no respect for the open foot soldiers who masqueraded as tough boys, abusing their position and authority. During my studies, seeing the photos of young Black men being hung and Whites gathering around to watch in a festive spirit greatly disturbed me. Seeing my keepers perpetuate the same mentality and support similar conduct only caused bitterness to grow in my heart. The assistant warden in particular had an extreme stance against prisoners' rights in general and possessed a Nazi approach to the policies he implemented. My studies revealed that the world power structure was still lily White; African American life was still expendable, oppression was very much alive and well, and men like the assistant warden were still in control of our world.

In my last days at the reformatory, I became more militant and engaged in more revolutionary activities from behind prison walls. Cous, Giz, and Priest were perhaps the three strategists among us always coming up with a plan of action and protest. Cous was 17 when arrested and subsequently convicted of home-invasion murder, along with Giz and Priest. Cous was talented, with a brilliant intellectual mind. Giz was a jailhouse legal genius, and Priest was a smart quiet individual with the heart of a gunfighter. Cold Soup Campbell and a brother named Dirty Red were also participants in what is better known as the prison struggle and the movement behind the walls. We were all frontline soldiers who identified with and supported the armed struggle against a racist system and oppression against people of color. I grew to love and respect these brothers because there was no falsehood in them. They said what they meant and meant what they said. Individually, each of us posed a threat and was considered a force to be reckoned with, but collectively we could and did make the administration lock down the entire prison often.

The prison system continuously recycled prisoners with guys coming and going, some going home and some being transferred to other institutions. By the time I was 18, the joint had changed over tremendously and so had I. On January 2, 1978, I would be transferred to the Indiana State Prison located in Michigan City, Indiana; Indiana State Prison was also called the Big House and known as "The City." Dirty Red and I monopolized control of the lock-up unit by this time and pretty much had things our way. Our natural talents seemed to complement each other perfectly. Dirty was a born leader like no one else I ever met and I possessed the uncanny ability to see a benefit even in times of adversity. Dirty and I would get so out of control that they made special cells for us. The front bars of our cells were covered with mesh wire, leaving only a slot for the food tray. We didn't have a problem throwing something in an officer's face or reaching through the bars and grabbing someone. We extorted and intimidated the prisoners who worked on the lock-up unit. These job were usually reserved for snitches, and although we were always getting informed on, we never got caught directly.

Then one day, a White lock-up unit worker and I had some words and I promised we would get a chance to discuss the matter further when the bars were not between us. I was locked in my cell at the time and he was on the tier working. Fate was not in his favor because a couple of days later, my cell door popped open for my one hour of recreation time: 23 hours locked down and one hour out. It was lunch time and the unit worker with whom I had words was moving from cell to cell, pouring Kool-Aid for the guys on lock-up. He was four or five cells away when my cell door suddenly opened and I was out in a flash and went straight at him. I hit him with a solid right hand, knocking him backwards, and he came back at me with the metal pitcher he was using to pour Kool-Aid, catching me on the forehead. I got in real close to neutralize the pitcher and kept hitting him until he fell to the floor. I heard the officers on duty sound the alert and I knew they would be coming in full force real soon, but not before I finished my work. I continued to beat him until officers got there to pull me off. I beat him into a coma and they had to take him to an outside hospital. This incident led to my transfer to The City. I graduated from gladiator school confident I could survive anywhere.

At age 18, 19 days before my 19th birthday, I was transferred to the state prison where one had to be 25 and older or have a life sentence. Under the best interest of the institutional clause or for security reasons, my keepers could practically make any move they wanted or excuse the mistreatment of prisoners according to their whims. Shipping me to The City at age 18 with only a 2- to 21-year prison sentence really amounted to a devious and felonious attempt to throw me to the wolves. Although I would be the youngest kid on the block at the Indiana State Prison, I was no longer the youngest person incarcerated in the adult department of corrections. Dirty Red's codefendant now held that distinction, being 14 when arrested, tried, and convicted, and inevitably sentenced to life in prison. The story of this kid read like a Greek tragedy: in words similar to Brother Malcolm X, society has been hoodwinked, bamboozled, and outright fooled to believe incarceration alone is how best to deal with society's young rejects.

Sending me to The City was like sending me to study for my master's degree as a career criminal.

6. I.S.P.

I believe it's very important to say here that I made the decision early in life to pursue a divergent path that included a life of crime and breaking the law. Of course, I drew from the influences of my environments and experiences; yet ultimately, the choice was mine. Under this pretext, I'm compelled to accept full responsibility for my actions and deeds. The choice on my part was too much of a conscious and premeditated move to blame anyone or anything else for how I lived my life or how I chose to have lived my life. I wanted to live the life of an outlaw in the sense that the law was obsolete and not applicable. Being infatuated with the street life was no more than a misdirection of positive energy: a positive energy potentially capable of anything humanly possible. I often wish someone was around to provide me with better guidance in those days, but that someone was not there so I would become the man I was destined to become.

From beginning to end, I believe I was largely under the influence of what I coined "the Robin Hood syndrome," a strong desire to steal from the rich and give to the poor. Living the street life was no more than a vehicle by which to carry out my lawlessness. There was a point in time when all I wanted to be was a gangster/hustler/player. My dreams revolved around being a highly respected figure in the underworld. I had absolutely no desire to be a lawyer or doctor or part of any other profession. Chasing tax-free dollars and living outside the law was my life ambition. The so-called glamorous and adventurous life of crime held an alluring appeal in my eyes: a brotherhood of honor and principles, an institution only a brave few had the courage to join. Survival depended on the individual's street savvy and ability to make things happen on their own. I did not aspire to be like any of the street personalities I saw in the neighborhood. I wanted to be bigger. I dreamed bigger and aspired to overshadow them all.

While at the Indiana Reformatory on lock-up, I would study to improve my intellect as well as my criminal knowledge. I read anything I could get my hands on about high-profile crimes or criminals. I loved reading about a good, well-planned criminal scheme, pulling off million-dollar capers and the cunning of a viable get-rich-quick plot. I read about all the infamous American Western outlaws and the American gangsters of modern times. I concluded my life would have been short-lived and violently ended had I lived in Western days. Of the notorious American gangsters, I felt the Meyer Lansky and Lucky Luciano combination would have been the only formidable challenge worthy of serious consideration. Chicago's Al Capone, whose signature move was the St. Valentine's Day Massacre, was all about brute and muscle followed by violence. I would have out muscled him at his own game, and with finesse.

Prisons are, in fact, fertile learning institutions for those with criminal ambitions. My transfer from the Reformatory to the Indiana State Prison was like leaving child's play and high school and going off to college, where every day was test day and the game is played for keeps. Everything about The City proved as different as night and day compared to the operations at the Reformatory, from the mentality of the prisoners incarcerated there to how officers ran the prison. Most everyone serving a prison sentence at the state prison was doing life. They were seasoned convicts, serious-minded men with little or nothing to lose and many resigned to the belief they would never be free again. These men were institutionalized to the point where prison life was all they knew and the only place they could function, and they were willing to protect what they had and the prison positions they held. The very worst of the worst of Indiana's criminals, rejects, and social outcasts were incarcerated at the Indiana State Prison. Those at the Reformatory were still taking baby steps as wanna-be criminals, whereas those serving time at The City were taking giant steps and still putting in work behind the walls.

When I arrived at Michigan City in January 1978, the prison was on total lock-down, meaning absolutely no prisoner movement at all. Guys confined to the maximum-security solitary-confinement unit had taken several officers hostage, broke off the lock-up unit, and seized control of a five-hundred-man cellblock. The prison would remain on lock-down for my first week or so there. Because I was in solitary at the Reformatory prior to my transfer, they kept me in solitary confinement upon my arrival at The City; thus, I did not go straight into the general prison population. It would be perhaps two months later that my keepers released me into the prison population among Indiana's finest.

One brother in particular, who I connected with on the lock-unit when I first got to The City, was a fellow named Jerome. He was also on the lock-up unit with me at the Reformatory. Jerome was doing a life sentence. He killed one guy while in prison and was on lock-up for attempted murder of another prisoner. Jerome had over 20 years in when I met him and had served most of his time at The City and therefore knew everyone. He was transferred back to Michigan City a couple of weeks before my transfer. Jerome got weed for me and schooled me on the lay of the land at The City in general, but I never trusted him; the first time I gave him money to buy me weed, I let it be known that I would not stand for a loss. Granted, Jerome was a killer, but I was not afraid to speak my mind and get an understanding about my business dealings with him. Also, I saw what I considered a very serious weakness in him. He liked young White boys and I saw a gayish manner in him I could never trust.

Once again, I discovered that prisoners from Gary, Indiana, knew of me and were aware of my case and why I was in prison. I would meet several guys on the lock-up unit who expressed being familiar with the circumstances surrounding my arrest and incarceration. I no longer had the distinction of being the youngest person incarcerated in an adult institution. A 14-year-old youngster named Tippet would take that title. Tippet received a life prison sentence for his involvement in a string of robbery murders. I would be the last juvenile the Indiana criminal justice system would show any type of leniency toward teenage violence in Lake County, as juvenile criminal behavior grew worse around the country. The Lake County courts started handing out life prison sentences to young teenagers during this period, as if handing out weekend vacations. I was in the county jail with a youngster who killed his mother and father and another who broke into the house of an 80-year-old woman and killed her by stabbing the old lady to death, striking her more than 30 times. No doubt teen violence and teen violent crimes had become a very serious issue around this time and sending these young men to prison for life to deter such behavior became the quick-fix solution to the problem.

One day prior to being released into the general prison population, a Sergeant Blake was making his rounds in the lock-up unit. I remember him walking past my cell only to do a double take and instantly come back to stop directly in front of my cell. I vividly recall him standing there looking at me with a bewildered expression playing across his face as if he could not believe his eyes. At age 19, I still looked very much like a kid and here I was in the toughest and roughest prison in the State of Indiana and Sergeant Blake knew this. Talking to me with genuine concern in his voice, he inquired as to why I was in prison, how much time I was serving, and the like. He concluded by promising to look into getting me off the lock-up unit and telling me that if I had any problems at all during my stay at Michigan City, I was to immediately get in touch with him. Sergeant Blake's last statement came across sounding as though I was fresh meat, and possibly doomed to the unnatural appetites of prison predators. Although Sergeant Blake had good intentions and perhaps wanted to save me, years later it would be I who saved him.

Finally released into the general prison population, my education in prison life would take yet another turn as I found myself surrounded by true hardened and tried convicts and criminals living life in prison with nothing to lose. Assigned to B-cellhouse, I remember feeling a sense of apprehension as to what to expect next from my new prison environment, but not once did I entertain the thought of fear. My attitude remained consistent with the decision I made when first incarcerated; I would rather die on my feet rather than live on my knees. I moved into my new assigned cell in B-cellhouse, two doors down from Superfly Terry Walker, an older brother from Gary, Indiana, who immediately embraced me as a little brother. Fly was doing a five-year prison sentence for a firearms violation and was at the end of his sentence when he was abruptly indicted for murder and subsequently hit with a life sentence. Superfly Terry Walker and I became good friends and shared a bond that still exists to this very day.

Although I continue to move around as a loner, Fly would introduce me to the major players from Gary and pull me into the crew with which he associated. Fly's acts of brotherly love made my transition into life at the Indiana State Prison go smoothly. I still had to earn my own respect, but the way I carried and conducted myself was to my advantage. I had a very subtle cockiness about me that was borne from a deep-rooted sense of self-pride and self-confidence. All the older convicts with whom Fly connected me were true old school and more or less embraced me as their knew little brother and helped me settle in. These guys could call shots or knew someone who knew someone. They would actually create a job for me and assign me to the gym. My job was to work out on the boxing team. These guys also ran or were involved in drug smuggling, gambling, and countless other illegal operations going on throughout the prison. The number one such operation in 1979 was converting a one-dollar U.S. money order into a three-hundred-dollar money order. This was a multimillion-dollar penitentiary racket, the brainchild of a Mississippi prisoner, yet perfected and totally exploited by convicts at Michigan City.

The Indiana State Prison—The City—was very much like a city within a city, along with its own commerce and currency. Unlike the Reformatory, The City had no petty rules and no strict suffocating policies to follow. The prisoners had a great deal of breathing space and the atmosphere was a great deal more relaxed and somewhat peaceful. More than 90 percent of the prison population was doing life or big numbers and the majority of those were career criminals, in and out of prison all their lives; the rest were institutionalized men, guys who had been incarcerated so long they would be completely lost out in the free world. Officers were dealing with true and proven killers and did not take for granted that they would be going home at the end of each day. Officers were there for security purposes only and the other staff members working in the prison served in only supervisory positions. The prisoners actually ran the prison and kept literally everything up and running. Everyone knew the score and, for the most part, everyone stayed in their own lane.

I had a rude awakening of sorts one Sunday while in the prison chapel talking to the chapel clerk, an old convict of 70 plus years. I don't recall why or what I was doing there. I do recall the nature of our conversation, which left a shocking impression on me. I had read about a guy named Grisby who held the world record for having served the most time in prison and he had served that time there at the Indiana State Prison. Out of curiosity, I asked the chapel clerk if he knew Grisby. He said "yes" and went on to tell me stories about the man. What sent me into a head spin was what he told me about how much time he and others still there had served. The chapel clerk had over 40 years in and another convict had 55 years in. The clerk reeled off a list of prisoners with 20 or more years in until it dawned on me just how real prison life was for those who were promised no way out. That exchange alone would haunt me for the duration of my criminal lifestyle, and the fear of growing old and eventually dying behind prison walls became very real to me.

Suddenly, my friends were mostly lifers, guys doing a life prison sentence, and most of them were in their early 20s. A brother name Razz would become one of my closest partners and someone I connected with on an intellectual level. Razz was doing life for murder and was probably 21 at the time we met. Ace was another prisoner with whom I connected on a mental level. He was from Detroit, Michigan, and serving a 10- to 25-year prison sentence for armed robbery. Both were on the boxing team, both were light heavyweights and, as a flyweight, I had to do battle with both of them in the boxing ring before being accepted into the club. In the ring, I had to spar with middleweights, light heavyweights, and heavyweights because no one else on the team was my size or in my weight class. Once I demonstrated my courage and heart in the ring, the whole team embraced me. I was one of them and nobody messed with members of the boxing team.

Razz and Ace were perhaps the two individuals who elevated my thinking to a completely new level. After working out in the evening, we walked the prison yard talking Greek philosophy—Socrates, Plato, Aristotle—until the sun went down and we had to go in for the nightly head count. Ace and Razz were intellectually sharp in their own right, Razz being superior book wise and Ace more superior streetwise. I was a new student to their discussions. In the early days, I just walked along and listened, absorbing their conversation like a sponge. Passing books on to me, the two of them would gradually engage me in their discussions, questioning me and challenging me at every turn, causing me to verbally defend my every comment, and I grew to love and look forward to our dialogs. You couldn't misquote a passage or mispronounce words with these guys or they would tear you to pieces, having no mercy.

In my first two or three weeks at The City, I matured a great deal. I was surrounded by serious-minded men who didn't play the childish games often present at the Indiana Reformatory, so I quickly learned to conduct myself accordingly. Although my reputation was solid and preceded me to a large extent, It would take a three-round bout with Pee-Wee Lamar to erase any doubts as to whether I was a man or a mouse. One of the guys who ran the gym instigated and promoted the fight between PeeWee and myself, constantly teasing PeeWee and saying I was there to take his title as the best pound-for-pound fighter in the joint. PeeWee Lamar was in my weight class, give or take a few pounds, and was a legend throughout the prison system for knocking out heavyweights with either hand, back in his prime. In and out of prison all his life, now at 40 and a seasoned convict, all he did was gamble and get high all day. But make no mistake, PeeWee was as dangerous as they come and to a large extent, reflected an older version of me as a little man casting the shadow of a true giant. We both carried reputations as little big men, his already proven and tested and mine looming large on the horizon as a young up and coming player.

When the date for our fight was set, it became the talk of the prison and the planned event took on a life of its own as the hype built. Like a real prize fight, bets were made and trash was talked; despite my youth, the odds were split down the middle as to who would win the contest.

Although I talked a good game leading up to the fight, I had real concern about the punching power of the old sly ring veteran. PeeWee was the real deal in the boxing ring and in his younger days, had the man boxed professionally, he would have won world titles. Pictures of PeeWee from 20 years prior still hung on the gym walls at the Reformatory, and although his speed and reflexes may have diminished over the years, a boxer's punching power lingered and I knew this. At age 40, the man was still knocking people out outside the ring, so I was under no illusion. I could be his next victim and get put on my back with my lights out.

Most of the guys on the boxing team usually did their road work in the mornings: ten laps around the recreation yard equaling a five-mile run. We did calisthenics, sit ups, push-ups, jumping rope, and shadow boxing all in the mornings. During the afternoon hours, we did our ring work. The day came when PeeWee and I laced up the gloves and climbed into the ring to do battle. I remember only a few gym workers and several prisoners who hung out in the gym being present when Pee-Wee and I got in the ring. I had Razz and Ace working my corner. Pee-Wee had his codefendant, named White Folks, working his corner. White Folks was actually Italian, I believe, but acted and sounded Blacker than most Blacks. PeeWee and White Folks had been codefendants on cases since the beginning of time, always in and out of prison together, and were considered inseparable. The referee was a convict named Kojo, a big man who towered over PeeWee and me as we came center ring to touch gloves and begin the fight.

When the bell sounded for Round One, only 10 or 15 guys were standing at ringside to watch the action. The number would double by the end of the first round. I would lose all track of time and my concentration focused solely on PeeWee as he pressured me and landed one solid punch after another. I remember seeing his feared overhand right coming my way and couldn't get out of the way or slip it. The punch landed and rung my bell. It was PeeWee's signature knock-out punch and I absorbed the blow and thought to myself that he couldn't hurt me. I found myself in the clinches with him and applied my own pressure. The old sly fox of a fighter spun me around like an amateur and skillfully evaded my assault. We stood toe to toe and exchanged blows, neither of us backing down an inch. I felt invincible and as the fight progressed, I grew increasingly more confident. By the third round, Pee-Wee was getting winded. I, on the other hand, was primed to go a full ten rounds. I remember landing my own overhand right, a punch I would use on Big Country, the powerhouse heavyweight on the team. Whenever I landed this sucker punch on Big Country, it made him so mad I had to run for my life until he settled down. PeeWee ate my overhand right and came back with everything he had.

To call the bout exhilarating would be an understatement. Both of us seemed to be in a zone of our own, our adrenalin and our will preventing either man from going down or from giving his all. The fight ended with both of us standing center ring, hugging each other with big smiles on our faces and showing the kind of respect for each other that derives from two combatants having thoroughly tested each other. What would surprise me most was the standing ovation we received after the fight. During the heat of battle, I didn't notice how thick the crowd had become since the opening bell. Now we had a complete full house of onlookers. They extended congratulations and cheers, handshakes and hugs, as we exited the ring and I had never before experienced a more natural high.

Neither man would be declared a winner or loser. PeeWee demonstrated he could still hold his own in a young man's game, and I proved to myself and others that I could hold my own against one of the very best in the business. What impressed me most about PeeWee was that he fought from his heart and not from physical conditioning. In preparing for his bout with me, he made a single frivolous attempt to work out, spending his day in the gym at one of the gambling tables playing cards instead, part of his known daily routine. The Police Athletic League, a boxing team from Gary sponsored by the police department, brought in a lightweight fighter who was knocking our guys out until he matched up with the old man. At age 40 and going three-minute hard and physically demanding rounds, PeeWee would do it having never worked out. Three-minute rounds are no cake walk. I greatly respected PeeWee Lamar because, as a fighter, I understood what it took to get in the boxing ring and grind out three hard rounds against a formidable opponent. Yet,

I would witness PeeWee pull this off several times with pure heart and sheer drive and determination at age 40, and without any preparation whatsoever. Truly, the boxing world missed something great and extraordinary with PeeWee Lamar not fighting professionally. Then again, I could say the same about other wasted talent I saw withering away behind prison walls.

Eleven months after my arrival at the Indiana State Prison, I was scheduled for a fourth parole-board appearance. My chances looked quite good because my rebellious behavior had taken a 360-degree turn. While at The City, I had no write ups for bad conduct, insolence toward staff, or rule infractions. On paper, my turn around had to look impressive, I imagined, and I really got myself together for my parole-board hearing. This was unlike my previous appearances when I knew I didn't stand a chance. This time I could really strike gold. Razz and Ace prepared me mentally and had me operating far above the rim. Other guys gave me sound advice and shared glimpses of convict wisdom. Still, no one understood my situation better than me and no one saw all the cards I held to manipulate the outcome of my parole-board hearing as I saw and understood them.

The parole board continued my case for further review pending a psychological report, which led to me meeting the prison psychologist, Doctor Daberry. The Doc was a big dark-skinned man with a wildish head of curly grayish hair that made him look very distinguished. He had a professor's scholarly look about him, and although he always dressed nicely, you could tell the man was not big on making a fashion statement. A button could be unfastened or his ever-present bowtie lopsided, and it didn't faze the good doctor. Once he came in dressed looking like a rainbow and when I commented on his attire, he simply stated he had dressed himself. On another occasion, he came in dressed really impressive, and I complimented him. Dr. Daberry said his wife had dressed him. It dawned on me in that instant that the Doc was not joking about who dressed him each day, and you could definitely tell when he picked out his own attire for the day or his wife laid out his clothing for him.

From our very first meeting, Dr. Daberry and I developed a rather unique bond that transcended the doctor–patient relationship or the prisoner–staff boundaries. We both genuinely liked each other as individuals and talked for hours on whatever subject came to mind. These conversations had nothing to do with the parole-board evaluation request. Whereas the board wanted to get a professional opinion of my mental stability, Dr. Daberry had already concluded that I was far more intelligent than my prison record implied and there was nothing wrong with me on that level. In fact, our discussions had nothing to do with whether I was mentally fit to be released back into the free world but were more or less a student–teacher exchange. Dr. Daberry had an office full of books, my kind of books—mind builders—and I never left his office without some new reading material. Long after the sessions required to satisfy parole-board needs, I continue to visit and talk with the Doc because I enjoyed our conversations. He seemed to understand and accept me in ways no one else did, was never judgmental, and was always thoughtful and objective. To some extent, he took on a surrogate father role of sorts, an unspoken condition to which we both consented without categorizing.

With Dr. Daberry's assistance and his psychologist report recommending my release, I would be granted parole after serving 4 years and 10 months on my 2- to 21-year prison sentence. His recommendation included a change in environment, citing that a return to my old surroundings would most likely hinder a successful reentry into society as a productive citizen, and therefore suggested I be given an out-of-state parole. Dr. Daberry's report was complete with information detailing where I would relocate and with whom I would be living. We made arrangement for me to transfer my parole to Norwich, Connecticut, where I would live with my Uncle Willie, my mother's oldest brother, a Vietnam War veteran who was on the front line during the height of the war.

7. Recidivism

I was released from prison in February 1979 after serving 4 years and 10 months on a 2- to 21-year prison sentence. Being paroled under the condition that I relocate to another state, I was released into the custody of my mother's brother who lived in Norwich, Connecticut, where our family lived when I was a kid. I left prison with many high-minded ideas about living large, enjoying life, and having the very best of everything. While in prison, I daydreamed and fantasized about how I would one day make it big once back on the streets. Other prisoners who had been in and out of the prison system drew vivid pictures of the good life anticipated following release. For almost 5 years, I heard the glamorous stories, including the conquest of beautiful women and having pockets full of money. Few of these stories carried any real weight or validity; most were exaggerations and the rest were flat-out lies. Still, I could see myself getting out of prison and living a player's lifestyle, foolishly thinking a world of pleasure and delight would be a served to me on a silver platter.

The rude awakening of reality would quickly slap me in the face and dispel my grandiose fantasies and player dreams. No one rolled out the red carpet. The women did not pursue me like a rock star and there was no influx of cash to fill my empty pockets, as I had imagined. Rather, I was sort of at a loss because the world I lived in before going to prison had changed a great deal during the short period of my incarceration. I had learned to live and survive in prison, yet found myself struggling to make the proper adjustment once back in the free world. I was so far behind the times that one day, when taking the city bus, a little boy had to show me how to get off. I remember rejecting the notion that I had become institutionalized. Still, there were occasions when I seemed to feel more at home and comfortable in prison than I felt on the streets. Nothing went according to plan and less than six months later, I was on my way back to the joint, once again for robbery.

My second tour of incarceration in the Lake County Jail found me in a very familiar environment where I had already been tried, tested, and proven myself worthy as a future force to be reckoned with. I was only 20 years old and considered an experienced convict, well on my way to becoming convict-wise and literally a career criminal for the next 35 years. When the dust finally settled, I would spend a total of 26 years incarcerated in jails and prisons throughout the United States. My thuggish ambitions came with consequences that required payment in full upon demand, and I paid. The price for the lawless lifestyle I embraced extracted a heavy toll to which I reluctantly submitted, yet this was a lifestyle of my choosing: I would learn to become a man who accepted the good, the bad, and the ugly consequence of my actions.

My codefendant on my second armed robbery case was known as Whopper. He was only a couple of years older than me and already had street credibility for being a stand-up individual who could hold his own. Whopper grew up on the mean streets of Gary, Indiana, and had an extensive juvenile criminal record, including several trips to boy's school. I met Whopper in the Lake County Jail my first time around and we ended up serving time together at the Indiana Reformatory during the early days of my incarceration. Whopper was street hardened and as tough as they come. We both had the heart and soul of gladiators, which made it easy for me to join forces with him to commit this robbery. Whopper came from a decent hard working-class family. He was just a bad seed caught up in the street life like me. He would get out of jail on bond for the robbery charge and was never to be seen or heard from again, leaving me to fight the robbery charge alone while rendering no assistance from the outside. I was on my own once again and as a direct result of being disappointed by yet another codefendant, I vowed to never have partners in crime again. I was learning firsthand, through personal experience, that the street codes of conduct were principles to which very few actually lived by.

Back in the Lake County Jail facing a 20-year prison sentence plus a violation of parole charge, I saw my years of incarceration extending way into the future. I remember the anger and humiliation I felt being prison bound again after such a short time on the streets. It was perhaps during those hours that my failures would produce my greatest strength and determination to succeed. My ego was shaken right down to its very foundation, yet my confidence remained strong that I would overcome my adversities. I was my own biggest critic and from deep inside, I demanded more from myself than anyone on the outside looking in. Dealing with the trials and tribulations I faced was like the pressure that turned coal into diamonds. True enough, I found that the hardships and struggles that didn't break me ultimately made me stronger.

One day, after being in the Lake County Jail for approximately 2 or 3 months, I stood looking at myself in the mirror and was absolutely shocked at the image staring back at me. I didn't recognize the reflection of the stranger looking me squarely in the eyes. The man in the mirror was definitely not me and I had no desire to be him. The image I saw looking back at me was cold, nonchalant, and emotionally dead. In every aspect of his features was a story to be read that no one could see or comprehend but me. All I had been through and was going through appeared to be written all over my face. My youthful innocence was long gone, replaced by a very scary-looking individual who I created for the sole sake of survival. When saying I was shocked at what I saw is truly an understatement because it ran far deeper than that. This proved to be such a profound experience and moment of introspection that it cause me to break down and cry. I cried because I did not approve of what I saw myself becoming and I prayed a tearful prayer, asking God to help me find my way. I did not pray for my release from jail. I did not pray for mercy from my transgressions, nor did I pray for relief from the burdens I carried. I sought and prayed for only one thing: to find my way back from what I saw myself becoming. I had seen a potential beast in the making and a borderline psychopath in the mirror, and it really frightened me.

I spent about nine months in the county jail, awaiting trial. When my court-appointed attorney came to me with a plea agreement offer and suggested that I take a ten-year deal, but I rejected it. Defiant and stubborn, I demanded my day in court and a jury trial, knowing the odds were against me. I was poorly equipped to put up any real courtroom fight in my own defense, and my public pretender—excuse me, I meant public defender—was only going through the motions in representing my case. Tried by an all-White jury of my peers who never lived in my world and detested my very existence, I was found guilty of robbery and subsequently sentenced to 16 years in prison, plus a mandatory parole violation. My fate would be dictated by me and my own actions and deeds. I could have taken the ten-year plea agreement that, in retrospect, was the intelligent thing to do. Yet there was absolutely no way to convince me to willingly sign off on giving up ten years of my life and freedom without at least putting up some sort of fight. I had the heart to fight but not the tools or skills. This would change in the years to come, as I learned to master the law and the judiciary system far better than most lawyers. I learned how to fight and became hard to handle in a courtroom; never again would I be taken advantage of.

Following my trial and conviction, I was sent back to the Indiana State Prison to serve out my sentence. I felt knee high to a grasshopper as the prison bus arrived at the rear gate of the prison and dropped off the new commitments. I had to face brothers who thought very highly of me, brothers who considered me a rising star, brothers who would bet their last dime on me, and I had let them all down. There was a miserable feeling in the pit of my stomach regarding my quick return to prison that took me a long time to overcome. Having let others down was only one side of the equation. The personal shame and humiliation I felt within ran much deeper.

I returned to the Indiana State Prison around June of 1980. Reagan was running for the Republican Party. Reagan's campaign platform included a promise to get tough on crime, among other issues that would directly affect prison conditions across the country. I remember thinking to myself and predicting life in prison under a Reagan administration would be a living hell. I don't recall all the campaign rhetoric he was pushing, but he said enough for me to conclude a prison break was the only avenue of escape if he became president. I would make the decision that if Reagan became president, I would make my own jail break. He did, in fact, win, and I made my escape attempt by trying to climb through the ceiling of the prison administration building, but to no avail. For the next ten years, I continued to contemplate a prison break while still fighting to have my conviction overturned. At the end of the day, there would be no escaping and the appeals court provided no relief, leaving me no choice but to serve out my sentence.

Prisons were already overcrowded before Reagan came into office. Suddenly mass incarceration became a big business and the concept of rehabilitation was obsolete. I lived through these years with first-hand experience, seeing the prison system change into merely warehousing men indefinitely. More and more prisons were built and eventually the private sector got involved to exploit the slave labor prisoners provided. Reagan delivered on his campaign promises and prisons evolved into a profitable industry. Later, President Clinton enacted policies to stop the bleeding revolving around America's imploding crime-and-punishment problem. Yet the one who put the country on the fast track to mass incarceration would be no other than President Bush through the war on drugs: a war disguised to attack young Black men. All these laws and policies, passed over four decades, would lead to the indiscriminate incarceration of Black youths all over the country. There were those on the outside looking in who opposed these laws and recognized them for what they were, but their stance against passing such laws fell on deaf ears.

My life would change significantly upon my return to the Indiana State Prison. Shortly after my return, a brother I met in the county jail as a juvenile invited me to a Muslim service. His name was Stone and he received a life prison sentence at the age of 17. Bobo was one of his codefendants and he also received a life sentence at age 17. Bobo was the same brother who introduced me to the paper-route business. My grade school friend Ant would also end up at the state prison, serving a 15- to 25-year prison sentence, arrested and convicted of murder at age

16. The cards of crime and punishment had dealt all of us a pretty ugly hand and we had no choice but to live them out.

When Stone invited me to the Muslim service, I had absolutely no interest in Islam or in becoming a Muslim. I believe both of our objectives were purely selfish at the time because it was the Muslim open house we wanted to attend. All the clubs and organized religious groups were allowed one open house per year where approved visitors come in to spend a couple of hours with their loved ones. The Lifer's Club was, by far, the biggest open house affair of them all because most everyone in the joint was serving a life sentence. Yet it was the extravagant Muslim Eid Al-Fitr that everyone in the prison sought to attend, even prison officials. The Eid Al-Fitr is celebrated following the holy month of Ramadan, the month of fasting for Muslims all over the world. You had to be a Muslim and observe the month of fasting to attend the Eid Al-Fitr festivities, so I agreed to fast with the Muslims for the sole purpose of going to this open house. Little did I know that trying to be slick and clever for the sake of attending the Eid turned out to be like the hunter getting captured by the game.

What started out as a selfish aim would evolve to become the single best move I made in life because I actually began to study the religion of Islam and found myself becoming a Muslim. Embracing the religion of Islam was far more than a light bulb moment for me: it was the awakening of a sleeping giant. Everything seemed to become crystal clear and questions I had not even considered before were answered. I found myself on a journey that provided structure in my life in every aspect. My eyes were opening and my spiritual thinking became more universal. Islam would define my purpose as a human being and as a man in general, with God being the only supreme authority over me. I yielded and submitted to nothing in my life as I would willingly yield and submit to the religion of Islam. I always processed everything mentally—love, life, or religion—and my analytical mind found real substance in the Quran and the teachings of Islam, which completely captivated me and appealed to me intellectually. Further, the Quran revealed my own potential for greatness because in all creation, only the human being possesses the nature of free will and is anointed the sole vicegerent on earth. Literally everything in creation is intended to serve or be subservient to mankind and I found this knowledge to be so overwhelming.

The wisdom and teachings I would discover in the Holy Quran were so profound that my senses became acutely fine-tuned. I embarked on a quest for knowledge and understanding using a verse from the Bible as my foundation. Proverbs 4:7 "Wisdom is the principal thing; therefore get wisdom; and with all thy getting get understanding." I never relied on someone else to define God for me or identify what my relationship with God should or should not be. I learned through my own personal studies, reaching my own conclusions and understanding. Islam opened the doors for my spiritual journal and the Quran provided the necessary guidance needed to emerge from the darkness into the light. I often reflect back on the experience I had in the county jail and seeing the man in the mirror, praying to God to help me find my way. Today, I strongly believe it to be only a matter of destiny that I travel the path that led to where I stand as a man at this hour in life.

Born James Edward Faison, I changed my name to Abdul-Jameel Mugtasid Taajwar upon becoming a conscious-minded African American Muslim. My reason for the name change served two personal objectives: a matter of freeing myself from the slave master's name that identified us as property, and establishing my own identity according to how I wanted to be recognized by man and God. My first name, Abdul-Jameel, is attributed to God and means servant of the beautiful and God is the most beautiful. Mugtasid means wise-intelligent and Taajwar means prince, king, the one who wears the crown. Metaphorically speaking, I would kill James Edward Faison so I could live. James E. Faison would become an expendable liability who I was certain would undermine and destroy me if I allowed him to continue existing.

I got a job working in the Muslim office, which was just a small room sectioned off at the end of a trailer large enough for a desk and three or four chairs. Put in charge of the Muslim newspaper, I was given a runner's pass that gave me extra leeway to move about the prison with ease. I used my runner's pass like it was a get-out-of-jail-free card and pretty much went anywhere in the joint I wanted to go. I pressed on once seeing how my runner's pass opened doors closed to the general prison population, pushing past one security gate after another, all except the security gates leading to freedom. Most prisoners with a runner's pass walked lightly. In contrast, I moved freely in and out of restricted areas until someone refused to let me pass. I frequently visited death row, where I had three friends awaiting execution. Only a handful of guys in the entire prison could make this move. I got away with making certain moves in the joint by simply carrying myself with a sense of purpose, as if I belonged wherever I was going. Also, to a large extent, I moved as I did in defiance of the limitations my keepers held over me, still being a rebel at heart.

Approximately six months after becoming Muslim, I was appointed to the position of Assistant Imam (Muslim minister). The brother in charge was grooming me to take his place, but before I got settled into my newly appointed position, I ended up in solitary confinement for assaulting an officer. One evening, while on my way to the recreation yard, a sergeant stopped me at the Main Street checkpoint and went out of his way to directly harass me for no apparent reason. The sergeant claimed he stopped me for not wearing my prison ID tag, which was ludicrous because no one followed or enforced this petty rule. The sergeant had me locked in a holding cell until his shift was over, but on our way to the holding cell, I told him everyone we passed without an ID tag better get stopped or there was going to be trouble. My words fell on deaf ears as we passed one prisoner after another not wearing their ID tag. The whole incident had me furious beyond any sense of reason and before the night was over, thing got a great deal worse. Held in the holding cell until well after midnight, I was then handcuffed and escorted to my cell where two officers searched and tore apart my living space and stepped on my personal property with total disregard. I stood watching, not saying a single word, my anger and contempt toward my keepers growing. I didn't clean up the mess when they were finished and laid down with my cell looking like a tornado hit.

The next morning, I asked the guy in the cell next to mine to look after my things and left the cellhouse, looking for Mr. Sergeant. All night long I thought about what I was going to do and the ensuing consequences of my actions. With a fresh sentence in front of me, I felt the need to make an example of the sergeant and set the record straight that I would not tolerate being disrespected by anyone. Finding the sergeant at his regular job in the prison laundry, I went at him with an oak stick and a knife with the intention of giving him an old-fashioned whipping with the oak stick. The knife was actually intended for intimidation purposes only; I only planned to use it if things got out of control. The sergeant never saw me coming as I approached and struck him on the head several times before he broke and ran, with me in hot pursuit. I caught up with him again as he attempted to wedge a laundry cart between us. I rewarded his efforts by delivering a blow to his knuckles. I continued to chase the sergeant around the laundry in attack mode until back-up arrived. Along with his reinforcements, about ten Muslim brothers arrived simultaneously, surrounding me and making it clear I was not to be manhandled, an action for which they were notorious. I have no idea how they learned about what I was up to, but they mysteriously appeared, seemingly from out of nowhere.

Prison is a dangerous and often a very violent environment and I learned early that some messages are best communicated through violence. I understood the mentality of violence and the behavior of violent men. After all, I did grow up with them and lived among them most of my adult life. Hundreds of far more dangerous and deadly men were incarcerated at the Indiana State Prison, and having nothing to lose, I wanted my message to reach them too. My intentions were to let it be known that I would strike out at anyone who provoked me, staff or prisoner. I didn't want to seriously hurt the sergeant. I merely wanted to shake him up thoroughly from head to toe. I knew exactly what I was doing, the price I would pay, and the possible rewards that would follow. I also knew my actions would be the talk of the prison for days to come on both sides, which is also what I wanted. For the most part, my move was like engaging in the art of psychological warfare, penitentiary style, with violence as a medium.

I was given 18 months in solitary confinement by the conduct adjustment board (the prison court of law) for assault on a staff member. To my surprise, the sergeant in charge of the lock-up unit befriended me from Day One, telling me I should have whacked his coworker a few times for him. Simply put, the man was contemptible and everybody knew it. This officer never would have considered pulling over countless other prisoners for such a petty reason as he gave me for calling me out that evening. He had a bully attitude, a big guy who threw his weight around when and where he could. I was a little man with a little man's complex who loved to prove himself by bringing down a giant whenever the opportunity presented itself. The incident had the makings of an explosive situation because all I had was my pride and dignity and would not compromise for anyone or anything.

I spent a year in solitary confinement, locked down 23 hours a day, which was a small price to pay to live on my feet rather than on my knees. I spent the majority of my time reading; I read from the time I got up until I went to sleep. Like my beloved brother Malik El-Shabazz, "affectionately and better known as Malcolm X," when the light in my cell was turned off at night, I sat on the floor next to the bars using the dim lighting from the catwalk to continue reading. I recall my thirst for knowledge was unquenchable as I focused on improving myself intellectually. My friend Razz, who was a teacher in the education department and serving a life sentence, got me interested in getting my G.E.D. (high school equivalency) soon after my return to prison. After taking the G.E.D. test and passing it, he encouraged me to take college courses by way of correspondence through Indiana University. Razz was a mathematical genius and a highly intelligent brother and received his master's degree while incarcerated. Razz would no doubt be the biggest influence in my striving to educate myself throughout my stay in prison.

Aligned with Department of Corrections policy, prisoners only served half of their lock-up timing, providing the prisoner did not cause any more trouble. In my case, the warden ordered I serve out my entire sentence. A true convict named Rich, who not only knew how to manipulate the prison system but also had tremendous clout and power in the joint, would assist me in circumventing the warden's order. Rick stood about six four and weighed over three hundred pounds, a White guy doing a life sentence for killing a state trooper. Neither his size nor his crime was the reason Rick commanded so much respect from prison officials. The man possessed a brilliant legal mind; he had his own paralegal class equipped with hundreds of law books and legal journals, all bought and paid for by him. Rick had contracts with judges and lawyers for whom he did legal work and got paid royally for his services. Rick had also filed and won several lawsuits against the Indiana Department of Corrections and prison officials were intimidated by him. Also, Rick would seriously hurt an officer if they pissed him off. I personally witnessed him go off on them.

We waited until the warden went on vacation and Rick convinced the assistant warden in charge to release me back into the prison general population. Using my connections through the Lifer's Club, the president of the Lifers got me a job in the prison library as the library clerk. The Lifer's Club was the strongest organization in the joint and the president had enormous power and influence. My networking abilities were evident in my younger days and continued to improve over the following years. I also signed up for Rick's paralegal classes and discovered a newfound love for researching the law. I took to legal research and law books like a fish to water. It seemed to come second nature to me and I found it quite intriguing. Rick also ran a business class and I took that too.

While on lock-up, I heard that prison officials got rid of the boxing ring and there was no more boxing team. I made plans before getting off the lock-up unit to establish a new boxing team called the Wrecking Crew. With the support of the Lifer's Club and using the same sergeant I assaulted as my sponsor, we got the ring back and the boxing team was up and running almost immediately. After my assault on the sergeant, he was promoted to lieutenant and I was given a green light to move freely about the prison with no trouble. Things went according to plan once again, but only I truly understood the method of my own madness or unconventional approach to doing things. I remember one prisoner asking how I managed to get the boxing ring back because they had tried to no avail.

A second unplanned assault on another officer about six months later landed me back in solitary confinement with a two-year sentence. This time the warden served notice that once I finished my time, I would be transferred to the maximum-security lock-up for an indefinite period up to five years. The maximum-security lock-up unit housed those prisoners who could not be controlled or coerced into conforming to the prison rules: the bad boys of all bad boys. The second assault on an officer came when I straight armed this officer to the face, knocked him down, and took his radio to prevent him from calling for back up. Again, I had to manipulate the situation and the prison system to avoid being locked up in solitary confinement indefinitely. When my time was almost up, I wrote a letter to the same assistant warden who had previously bailed me out, asking that I be transferred to the Indiana Reformatory. In my letter, I gave him my word that I would cause no trouble at the Reformatory and further stated that I wished to be transferred back to the state prison when appropriate. My request was honored and a few days later, I was on my way back to the Reformatory where it all began.

8. Return to Gladiator School

I was in my mid-twenties when I returned to the Indiana Reformatory, now a hardened convict and no longer a 16-year-old kid trapped behind a 30-foot prison wall learning how to survive in prison on his own. I had evolved in every sense of the word to become a true reflection of my prison environment. I no longer possessed the youthful innocence of my early years of incarceration. I was a young man molded and shaped by the prison experience I faced each day over the years: a hardcore convict in the making and well on my way to becoming a man who lived the life of a prisoner, according to the hand he was dealt.

Although prison life and the prison experience did have a dynamic and very crucial impact on how I saw and dealt with life in those hours during my incarceration, I found myself evolving on yet another level of even greater importance and significance than my personal determination to stand up as a man at all times and at all costs while in prison. Islam was opening new doors to a higher knowledge, broader ideas, and a more profound understanding of life in general. I was, perhaps, advancing into my third year of being a Muslim when I returned to gladiator school. Islam had me more disciplined, more thoughtful, and considerate of my actions. Islam was reshaping and fine tuning my entire philosophy of life and had me carrying and conducting myself on a higher and more disciplined level. The quick-tempered and rebellious kid with the little-man complex returned to the Indiana Reformatory a totally different man: full grown, con wise, and coming into my own.

In Islam, we are taught to seek knowledge from the cradle to the grave, even unto China. I found myself on a path that took me anywhere and everywhere my quest for knowledge led. I soon discovered that knowledge also possessed its share of power and influence among men during these days. My intellectual and spiritual evolution would emerge, framed by the religion of Islam. I sought knowledge and fully understood its power; Islam taught me to respect my teachings because I will be held accountable for what I know. As a Muslim, I studied the Bible in greater detail, along with the Dead Sea Scrolls, Masonry, and a little of all the several liberal arts and sciences. I traveled the world through books and my studies, uncovering countless gems that I incorporated into my life. Books were my most intimate companion while under the yoke of incarceration.

When I arrived at the Indiana Reformatory in 1975 at age 16, I was practically an empty vessel, lacking real substance and personal identity. No one taught me the essence, the values, or the true principles of being a man. Here again, I had to teach myself and learn on my own, and piece by piece cultivation of the man I would eventually become. Like many other African Americans struggling with our lost and suppressed history, I felt a burning desire to discover my place in the world as a people. We were labeled Colored, Nigger, Negro, and Black to identify the African race born in America under the oppression of slavery, all of which I rejected.

Now upon my return to gladiator school ten years later, a totally different man was on location. Although the sleeping giant had awakened and was fully conscious, I remained a promising piece of work still in the making. My reputation as a stand-up guy with convict credibility had grown tremendously over the years and word of my return to the Indiana Reformatory was resounding on the prison grapevine. Old friends welcomed my return and provided whatever assistance I needed in getting settled. In contrast, the prison administration and the ground officers seemed to monitor and maintain a watchful eye on my every move. My prison record clearly indicated that I was far from being a model prisoner or on the straight path to reform. My behavior and individual conduct reflected a propensity to solve any differences with a violent response, which was exactly the image I wished to depict.

In my first week upon my transfer back to the Reformatory, I would inquire into and get up to speed regarding the status of the Muslim community there. I immediately learned that although a number of individuals demonstrated an interest in the religion of Islam, the organization had no real structure and the brothers present had limited knowledge and understanding. I reached out to members of the Muslim brotherhood to learn who was supposed to be in charge, only to discover discord in the ranks and hypocrisy in leadership. Prisoners who were not Muslims but who respected the religion of Islam came to me with stories regarding un-Islamic behavior and activities in the Muslim community and I vowed to put an end to it all and clean house.

At this time, I did not realize how far my shadow of influence extended, but the word got around concerning my personal disenchantment and the tension would grow. The talk was all over the prison that I would not allow the present leadership of Islam to stay in place. This penitentiary rumor would prove absolutely correct, as I clearly expressed my uncompromising position from Day One. Since embracing the religion of Islam, which came naturally for me, I committed myself to a way of life in a way I had never committed myself before to anybody or anything. I love and respect Islam to such an extent that I would willingly give my life to defend the tenets and dignity of my religion.

Granted, I was nowhere in the vicinity of sainthood and possessed my fair share of faults and shortcomings. I still nurtured my gangster mentality and had my thuggish ways. Yet, I had my boundaries and moral parameters and left no room to compromise or surrender them under any circumstances. I learned the brother who was supposed to be in charge and his so-called assistant were lovers, an abomination that went totally against the grain of Islam. I wasn't homophobic. I could care less about what one engaged in or who they did it with. I simply saw no place for homosexuality representing the leadership and nobility of the teachings and religion of Islam.

That first Friday when attending the Jum-ah Friday Muslim prayer service, I arrived early and prepared to set the record straight and lay down the law. I was focused and determined to impose my will and exert my influence to demand change, and ready to pull the trigger on any opposition I might confront. The other brothers trickled in gradually, each man quietly waiting for the service to begin and anticipating what might happen next. These brothers supported me and the stand I was taking. Each of them expressed their grievances and disapproval of how the Muslim community was being run and looked to me for direction. Young and new to the religion, these brothers were striving to find themselves, and although they were uncertain and lacked the fortitude to initiate change, I had no such problem.

Muslims all over the world are instructed to drop all business ventures and any other such preoccupations and join the Friday assembly, the Jum-ah prayer. Neither of the two brothers in question would show up for service and came around only once or twice during my entire stay at the Indiana Reformatory. My planning did not take into account this sudden unexpected move and I found myself pressed with the responsibility of having to conduct the prayer service myself. Unprepared and having never engaged in public speaking, and being a man of few words, I was suddenly front and center with all eyes on me.

Collecting my composure, I proceeded to nervously perform all the essential duties of conducting the Friday prayer services. I had absolutely no idea what I was going to say as I approached the podium to address the brothers waiting patiently to hear my first public speech. As soon as I began to speak, I recalled the advice given to the brothers in a previous speech given by the Imam who I came up under during my early days of embracing the religion of Islam. He said a brother should always be prepared to give a talk expounding on our religion by addressing the five pillars of faith. All nerves and jitters on the inside, I projected a confident front and went on to deliver a lecture on the five pillars: faith, prayer, charity, fasting, and the pilgrimage to Mecca at least once in a lifetime, if one can afford it. Once again, it was my studies, reading those self-help books and published articles on public speaking, and being a better conversationalist that enabled me to convey my first public address.

I was made the leader, or Imam, after being unanimously selected by the members to represent the Muslim brotherhood. My involvement in prior civil litigations and class-action lawsuits against the State of Indiana demanding equal protection of the law and the rights for Muslim prisoners to exercise their religion would prove helpful. I was well aware of the consent decree handed down by the U.S. District Court outlining provisions the prison administration was compelled by law to make available to the Muslim community. We were receiving mere tokens of what the consent decree ordered. I took charge and started pushing and pushing until we got everything we had coming.

Assigned to the education department, I enrolled in the architectural drafting class, which I enjoyed. The drafting class was very therapeutic for me because I was still a headstrong young man who had trouble following rules, and gladiator school was an institution of rules. The drafting classes gave me something constructive and meaningful to do with my time and kept me out of the line of fire from clashing with correctional officers, as the relationship between my keepers and me would remain adversarial throughout my incarceration. In the concrete jungle of prison walls, officers and prisoners were seemingly predatory enemies. The clear and present face of racism at the Indiana Reformatory would also keep me in combat mode with my keepers. I didn't like them or their fake and superficial superiority attitude and they didn't like me or my defiant disposition.

Unlike at Michigan City, my keepers at the Indiana Reformatory believed in vigilante retaliation. By this time, I had learned there was no way prisoners could ever win in a physical confrontation with the prison administration, a tried and proven failure repeatedly demonstrated over the years. Officers at the Reformatory had an unhealthy reputation for making a prisoner disappear if they were assaulted or touched. Fully understanding what I was up against, I had to modify my approach in how I dealt with my keepers for the sake of self-preservation. As rebellious and defiant as I might have been, I had enough common sense to know my limits and did not want to disappear into the middle of a one white-hooded night. Minding my own business, I said and had as little contact with my keepers as humanly possible, and quietly did my time at the Reformatory the second time around.

I had given the assistant warden at the Indiana State Prison my word I would cause no trouble at gladiator school, if transferred there following two assault charge against staff. Focused on staying beneath the radar and walking the fine line drawn in the sand between me and my keepers, I learned how to consciously make the best of any given situation. Regardless of how challenging or suffocating things got, I found a way to produce positive results by seeing the glass half full and adding up my gains instead of perceived losses. It was perhaps during this period in my life that everything seemed to converge; mentally, physically, and spiritually, I found myself in a great place.

I met an older brother at the Reformatory who knew the Bible like a scholar and learned from him ideas I never heard in church or heard mentioned by a pastor. Muslims believe in the biblical knowledge revealed in the Bible and in the prophets who came with the divine message. The New Testament was the first book I ever read from cover to cover, but reading the Old Testament years later during my studies, I immediately discovered that the entire world was not destroyed by the flood of Noah's time as I was once led to believe. The Bible tells of a people who lived on the other side of the great flood. The history of Masonry can also be found in the Old Testament in the building of King Solomon's temple, which provided me a clearer understanding of that fraternal order. It would be the timeless wisdom depicted in the books of proverbs and psalms that I found most intriguing and spiritually rewarding.

Gladiator school was an institution of violent young men who were not yet fully grown enough to grasp or embrace the essence of manhood. Imagine fifteen hundred young, rowdy, and high-strung men prone to mischievous and unpredictable behavior warehoused in a confined environment. These guys could snap spontaneously and send the prison into a full-scale riot at the drop of a hat. Being late with the prisoner's mail, the joint would explode like a powder keg sitting on a red-hot fire. On the weekends, prisoners were allowed to watch movies in the institution chapel. On several occasions, boring or childish movies led to inherent chaos, causing the entire prison to be placed on total lock down for days. Fist fights were a common practice to settle any and all personal disputes and were frequent occurrences. Stabbings and cold-blooded murder were the answer to some personal conflicts and the death toll would increase during my stay at the Reformatory.

Two homicides in particular caused me to grit my teeth in anger, providing a clear reminder of how death could suddenly appear, unannounced and unexpected. One was the murder of a young African American prisoner who was about 20 years old and only days from being released. Penitentiary rumor had it that he sodomized a young White prisoner who would eventually extract retribution. The offender was housed in solitary confinement, doing a disciplinary sentence for his loathsome and deviant conduct when being escorted to the prison infirmary, at which time he was stabbed to death. According to prison rumor, the event was part of a grand conspiracy between Klan-affiliated prison officers and the White prisoner's father, also Klan affiliated. Tremendous circumstantial evidence implied these rumors were true.

The prisoner was being escorted to the infirmary for a routine pre-release physical examination. He was going home within days and getting his medical clearance. With his hands cuffed behind his back, the White prisoner came seemingly from of nowhere and proceeded to stab his totally helpless victim to death while two White officers looked on. Gladiator school was a strictly controlled facility and all the stars had to be aligned in your favor with a rabbit's foot in your pocket plus a whole lot of inside help to execute such a move. Standing around waiting for someone to kill by chance, even with the best of planning, was as improbable as walking out the front gate. Under the circumstances, we couldn't move five feet around the prison compound without being stopped, questioned, and searched. Movement was totally and completely controlled, with no exceptions, and we were not allowed to even approach a prisoner being escorted to or from the lock-up unit. The sidewalks are cleared of all foot traffic during these moves.

The second murder was of Fat Cat, a shot caller and drug dealer from Gary, Indiana, with a big-boy reputation and serving a double life sentence for two drug-related homicides. Fat Cat was a cold-blooded, self-serving individual with a strong following in the joint and thought he couldn't be touched. Another White prisoner would join forces with a Black prisoner from Indianapolis, and together they would throw gas into Fat Cat's cell and burn him alive. Fat Cat had slapped the White prisoner over an unpaid drug debt, and one just doesn't slap another killer in prison and expect it to be the end of things, nor can one assume they're the only killer in town or think they're too big to be reached by the violent hands of death behind prison walls.

The murder of Far Cat wasn't just a prison killing; it was an agreed upon execution and a quietly kept conspiracy to hit a Gary leader by other convicts. Considering Fat Cat's status in the joint, prisoners couldn't move against him and miss, nor could they move against him from a position of weakness or without a green light from other shot callers in the joint. Burning Fat Cat in his cell meant absolute and certain death, regardless of whether the fire department was right on the spot with hoses at the ready. Once enough gas is thrown in a cell followed by fire, the prisoner can count himself among the dead. There is no help, no way out, and no counter move for this convict-style assault, an old school move among those playing for keeps by any means necessary.

I would experience mixed emotions about each of these killings because I fully understood how helpless both of them were in each situation. I was once locked in my cell during an accidental electrical fire in the cellhouse and I stood helpless as the smoke grew suffocatingly thick. I knew the feeling of helplessness from having one's hands secure behind their back because I lived like that myself. One side of my thinking called the killers cowards in both situations for not giving their victims a prayer of a chance. Then, the other side of my thinking said sometimes you just have to get your man any way you can; it comes with the territory. Being helpless and unable to defend myself was one of my biggest fears behind the walls. I also had a major fear of being killed in prison and did not want to see my life end there. I would selfishly deem my life to be more precious and significant than any other life in the joint and was willing to get as down and dirty with the next man as necessary to defend my stand.

I came into prison from Day One standing on my own and I lived in prison from Day One standing on my own, learning life-saving lessons early to mind my own business. Being a solo act in prison and a loner by nature, minding my own business would come easy for me and be one of the main keys to surviving the prison experience in general. But in facing all my fears, I would fear even more what I saw within myself if provoked and how far I was willing to go to live standing on my own accord in all aspects behind those prison walls. Being under the yoke of incarceration has a tendency to debase even the best of us and bring out the pure diabolical nature that exists in mankind, and I had become a true reflection of my prison environment by this time.

I learned to gracefully traverse throughout the Indiana Prison System, avoiding the minefields and many pitfalls that led to life or death confrontations. To a large extent, I was well liked and respected by most and possessed an uncanny ability to network across all lines of separation. Being a shrewd networker enabled me to build allegiances with other power players in the joint, which I used to my advantage when proven necessary. I would also discover that I commanded substantial organizational skills and I put those talents to work at the Reformatory in establishing the Muslim community and putting our house in order. The prison system housed three different Muslim sects: the Nation of Islam, The Moorish Science Temple, and the Sunni, which I practiced. Sunni beliefs of the universal teachings of Islam was the only religion lawfully recognized and accepted in the Indiana Department of Corrections. I would subsequently organize all Muslims, provide a platform for the Nation and my Moorish brothers so they could exercise their beliefs, opening the way for a united Muslim brotherhood. The prison administration would thus label me a manipulator and perhaps I was manipulative in order to serve my purpose and obtain my goals and objectives, all of which revolved around establishing the brotherhood.

Being the recognized leader of the Muslim community caused me to give a great deal of thought to leadership in general and the responsibilities that come with the status. In reading biographies, especially autobiographies of men considered great or renowned leaders, I looked first at the integrity of a person and their cause, then at individual fortitude when facing adversity. From the Bible to the streets of Gary, I saw leadership in many different facets and wondered where I fit in. My experience upon returning to gladiator school clearly demonstrated that circumstances can easily thrust a person into a sudden position of responsibility. Once again, I was a loner by nature, yet realized I must be capable of becoming a leader when life circumstances required that of me. The one book that helped me identify and define the leadership philosophy I would eventually embrace was *The Prince,* by Machiavelli. I wanted to be fair and just: a man who stood on his word and had the fortitude to firmly defend his personal convictions. Just don't cross me or provoke my dark side to manifest itself, because there was a very thin line between my willingness to be peaceful and humble and the quiet storms of my aggression.

After spending eighteen months at the Indiana Reformation, I was more than ready to transfer back to the state prison. I had grown a great deal during my eighteen-month stay at gladiator school by way of commanding more self-discipline and becoming more of a thinker. I walked through my stay at the Reformatory without getting a single conduct report for rules infractions. The power of the pen became my weapon of choice when it came to doing battle with my keepers. Spiritually, I found myself operating on a totally different level, still evolving and building the man I would eventually become.

I would complete the architectural drafting class and immediately request a transfer back to Michigan City following graduation.

9. Back to the City

It was probably later in the summer of 1985 or '86 when I was finally transferred back to the Indiana State Prison. The prison conditions at Michigan City had changed a great deal during the time I had been gone. Freedom of movement was now more limited, the new breed of convicts were emerging and overshadowing the old timers, and prison life in general behind the walls of the Indiana State Prison was taking on a new look. On average, the prison population was much younger and produced a new breed of convicts. The culture was perhaps more deadly and violent during this period of my incarceration than at any other time. The different mobs and cliques that ran the joint were playing for keeps on all fronts, leaving bodies behind close to death or with fatal stab wounds to prove the point. What could you tell a posse of young brothers fresh in their twenties with a life sentence hanging over their heads, blinded by rage because of the daily situation they faced and seeing no light at the end of the tunnel, no matter how hard they looked? These guys travelled in packs five or six deep and all they had left were their manhood, self-pride, and dignity, none of which you could violate without inviting the winds of death to blow your way. This was the stormy environment and hostile conditions under which I returned to the Indiana State Prison.

Back at Michigan City, I received a warm embrace by those I sincerely counted as friends or close associates, and received an embrace of true brotherly love from my fellow Muslim brothers. My transfer back to The City was like returning to an old neighborhood and I wasn't fazed in the least by the lay of the land on the prison compound. I was glad to be back at the state prison, although some might consider my thinking a bit crazy. I felt truly relieved and as though freed from a tremendous task: a task that improved me as an individual and challenged me for the sake of determining if I had a breaking point. My stay at the Reformatory became a significant trial and test in the practice of self-control and operating under discipline. To a large extent, my problem revolved around my ego, my contempt for my keepers, and my rebellious nature. I needed to learn humility and my experience at the Indiana Reformatory was merely the beginning of a long journey toward achieving this objective.

With the religion of Islam as the essential focus in my life, I immediately got involved with the Muslim brotherhood upon my return to the Indiana State Prison. Within a couple of weeks, I had secured a job assignment working for the Muslim office again, which allowed me considerable freedom of movement and no direct supervision by prison staff, both being much appreciated after being under the totally controlled environment at the Reformatory. I was given a runner's pass ID to move around the prison to conduct Muslim business and went anywhere I wanted to go in the joint by conducting myself as if I had a green light to move as I was moving, and for the most part, I was not questioned. My approach to moving throughout the prison was simply a matter of attitude, acting like I had legitimate reason to go wherever I was going and pushing forward with confidence in my stride until someone ordered me to stop.

In my absence, the Muslim brotherhood had won another long-fought legal battle demanding a place of our own for religious services. Court litigation and perseverance eventually caused the prison administration to accommodate the Muslim quest for their own place of worship. In the past, we were like a caravan of gypsies traveling from one place to the next for our daily prayers, never knowing where we would meet until the last minute on most occasions. The Catholics and Protestants had their own place of worship, we reasoned, and therefore the Muslim community should be afforded the same.

So after several years of persistence and remaining steadfast, Muslims won the prize of an old condemned building located in the recreation yard area. The building was old, like the majority of the buildings congesting the prison compound, and had seen better days. I was not present during the cleanup and renovation phase of this project, but I saw the before and after photographs and the brothers had done some amazing work, bringing life back to our new place of worship. This building had not been occupied in several years, during which time prisoners would sneak into it for countless forbidden reasons. At the top of the list was engaging in homosexual activities or to use illegal drugs or other contraband substances. Convicts walking around the walls of the prison recreation yard frequently used the building as a public restroom, urinating and defecating on the floors. The roof had several leaks that contributed to the general deterioration of the building overall infrastructure and the place was littered with assorted rubbish and garbage. The photographs clearly depicted the repugnant conditions of the building prior to the Muslim community acquiring it.

I would hear numerous stories about the many laborious hours brothers put in to clean up the building, painting and fixing up the inside and scraping the peeling paint from the exterior brick walls and resurfacing them with a fresh new coat. I was told of the major effort the brothers put forth in repairing and retarring the faulty roof, and how the best prisoner electrician in the joint came in to rewire the entire building. Absolutely every aspect of this undertaking was carried out by prisoners, leaving the officials at the administration level baffled as to how quickly the task was accomplished and even more stunned by how little assistance the Muslims requested. It was like the prison administration gave the brothers a building borderline beyond repair thinking the project would prove a complete failure, an erroneous assumption on their part.

Returning to the Indiana State Prison to discover the Muslim community finally had their own place of worship impressed me a great deal. But of the many fascinating achievements in my absence, the acquisition of a thorough and complete library covering every aspect governing the Islamic religion impressed me tremendously. The library offered a wide collection of literature from the basic principles on which Islam was founded to books exploring the profound ideologies of the religion, expounded by well-respected scholars from every corner of the Islamic world. Not like the brothers at the Indiana Reformatory, the brothers at Michigan City were more mature religiously and far more studious. These brothers could be found studying and researching issues that represented the heartland of the Islamic religion, and could direct a fellow prisoner to the source of their information if challenged. The Muslim library would also provide a tremendous wealth of knowledge and information to anyone seeking to better understand the Muslim way of life.

I had been back at The City following my transfer from gladiator school for perhaps two or three weeks when I came to my Muslim brothers with a business proposition. We had a small room that more or less served as our kitchen area and I proposed a plan, asking that I be allowed to use it to start a small restaurant business on the recreation yard. We were perfectly located for my business venture because the yard had constant free-flowing traffic all day long, and everything happened on the recreation yard, and I do mean everything.

Being that the little kitchenette room was conveniently removed from the main player area, I argued that my business operation would not run interference in any way with our normal daily activities, and by adhering to such a strict religious diet, I contended the brothers would no longer have to worry about the conditions under which their food was being prepared. I further offered to provide all Muslims with a fifty-percent discount across the board on all food items sold. I delivered my proposal concisely, while touching on all the pertinent points I knew would be of utmost concern to my Muslim brothers as a whole. In the Muslim community at Michigan City, I was well respected and the brothers honored my request without question. My proposal was put to a vote and passed unanimously!

What suddenly encouraged me to become a penitentiary entrepreneur is still a question to be answered; perhaps it was just the hustler in me just doing what I do. Although I had no initial capital to get my business off the ground, I entertained absolutely no doubts regarding my ability to accomplish my intended business goal. It was not a matter of faith that motivated or drove me; it was a matter of self-confidence. I could see my way through my business plan with clarity from beginning to end, and once I had this type of focus, even the impossible was possible. Making an idea materialize was only a matter of taking action and breathing life into it. I discovered this talent in myself a few years earlier and came to hold dearly the saying that anything conceived can be achieved.

Once I got the green light from my Muslim brothers, I spent the night considering my next move, which of course was how best to raise the funds necessary to get my little business up and running. I pondered several options before finally deciding to approach the Old Man, a seasoned convict who was not only extremely business minded but also played for keeps when it came to collecting a debt. According to prison rumor, the Old Man was serving a life sentence for a contract murder and was a prison loan shark. Although he carried himself as a mild-mannered individual, the brother was as lethal as a loaded .45 with the safety off. At the time he was perhaps in his later forties, yet those with whom he shared a close relationship referred to him as the Old Man, perhaps because most of us incarcerated at Michigan City were so young. Over the years, the Old Man had quietly acquired a great deal of power and influence throughout the prison system, being highly respected by convicts and prison staff members wherever he went. He had a hand in almost everything that went down in the joint that concerned getting money and he definitely ran the biggest loan shark operation in the prison, running it with an unforgiving business attitude. He was a major force in the joint and no one to play with and I knew going in that I would have to honor any business commitments I made with him in full.

Many convicts were reluctant to do business with the Old Man because of the high interest rates when loaning money and how the Old Man ruthlessly applied the rules of the game. If one borrowed five dollars from him, they paid him back ten. If they missed their timely payment, it doubled to twenty and continued to double each time they failed to pay off. Everyone charged these same sort of compound interest rates in one form or another, only the Old Man was more ruthless and truly unforgiving when it came to collecting on what was owed him. During my incarceration, I had patronized the prison stores and loan sharks very few times because I saw how borrowing a single pack of cigarettes could easily turn into owing a whole carton. Plus, that was one of the two things Big Al taught me as a kid when learning the ropes. He often said, "little man you remember to mind your own businessman, and whatever you do, don't you go borrowing shit from them damn stores."

I had no viable source of income to repay a loan should I forfeit on it, yet I was rather confident in my ability to succeed in my business venture. I would approach the Old Man with my business plan, knowing in advance that failure was not an option and could inevitably turn into a life or death situation. The Old Man was an individual who was deadly serious about collecting any debt owed to him, and I was well aware of his reputation and that he was inclined to settle money disputes with violence. I also knew he was better than myself at playing that game.

I sought the Old Man out. He was a cellhouse worker in D-block, one of the older and larger cell blocks on the prison compound housing with more than five hundred men. I remember it being soon after the morning work line was called out and the cellhouse was rather empty, except for those who worked in the unit and a few stragglers. Although prisoners were not allowed to visit cellblocks they did not live in, I managed to get around the prison compound fairly well. But for one reason or another, I could not finesse my way past the officer on duty in D-block on this particular day. Therefore, I sent another prisoner who lived in D-block to get the Old Man for me. I waited at the huge steel gates that led to the unit for about five minutes before the Old Man appeared with a big pleasant smile playing across his face. He greeted me with a firm handshake, extending a hand through the steel bars of the gate to take mine into his. I remember the Old Man had a look in his eyes that said he truly welcomed my visit and what took me so long to gravitate his way. Over the years, the Old Man and I had done no more than exchange greetings when passing each other on the prison compound, having never engaged in any dialog of substance.

After a brief exchange of small talk, I explained to him that I wanted to discuss some business with him and we both agreed to meet on the recreation yard later. We shook hands again and I stepped off, promising to meet up with the Old Man later as planned. The conversation didn't take more than two of three minutes. Not a word was wasted, yet it seemed like a great deal was covered in the short span of time we talked. I walked away thinking that now was the time for me to shine but at what expense, and I questioned whether I was about to make a deal with the devil.

I ran a few errands to check my personal traps around the joint before going to the recreation yard and the Muslim office. It was not long before the Old Man showed up with Blind Billy in tow. Together, they headed for the gym where they usually engaged in their daily chess wars. Blind Bill was a truly remarkable brother who I greatly admired for his courage and fortitude to not succumb to adversity. After spending approximately ten years in prison on a life sentence for murder, Blind Billy began to gradually lose his eyesight. Many thought Billy was perpetrating a fraud in an attempt to gain his freedom, whereas he was truly losing his vision until eventually he was totally blind. The Old Man and Blind Billy were always close friends, but it seemed that as Billy lost his vision more with each passing day, the Old Man increasingly assumed the responsibility to look out for his blind friend and comrade. The two were inseparable in every sense of the word and it was a rarity to see one without the other.

Moments after observing the Old Man and Blind Billy enter the gym, I too headed in that direction. I immediately found them in the weight pit, preparing for their daily workout. The Old Man greeted me with the customary politeness that was typical of him as I approached. Blind Billy's keen sense of awareness, enhanced by the loss of his sight, also quickly acknowledged my presence with a warm friendly smile. Both men extended their hands and I received each in a strong brotherly grip, shaking the hands of both brothers in turn. We would first indulge in the general penitentiary small talk surrounding prison life, my brief tour of duty at the Indiana Reformatory, and other such passing conversation regarding life behind the walls.

Then suddenly, the dialog turned to serious business as the purpose for my meeting with the Old Man came to the surface. I recall briefly detailing my business plan and explaining to the Old Man how I had already received the blessings of my fellow Muslim brothers to activate my plans. I concluded by stating that I came to see him seeking the necessary finances to get my little operation off the ground. The Old Man listened attentively as I outlined my business proposal. Blind Billy, who appeared preoccupied with other thoughts, was in fact mentally processing my every word and smiled approvingly when I finished my sales pitch. Without hesitation, the Old Man asked how much I needed. I replied that two hundred dollars should be sufficient to successfully get my little prison restaurant up and running. The Old Man was a shrewd and very serious-minded penitentiary businessman, and no doubt the biggest loan shark in the entire joint, the latter being the reason I approached him with my problem in the first place.

After hearing the amount I needed and wanted for my initial investment, the Old Man asked a second question: How long did I need this loan? I told him to give me thirty days and I would have his money back. The Old Man quickly calculated his response, his sharp business mind rapidly digesting the pluses and minuses in dollars and cents balanced by the time factor I quoted. Then he flatly stated, "No!" I thought this was his final answer, but after a brief moment, he continued on as if giving his next words careful thought. "You take sixty days, little brother," he said, "because you're going to need time to get established first, before you start seeing a real profit." It was in that instant that it dawned on me that the Old Man truly wanted me to succeed for some unexplained reason and was willing to extend a full hand toward assisting me.

Once the fundamentals were discussed, a single question remained. How much interest did the Old Man want in return for the two-hundred-dollar loan? Once again his answer stunned me, because when I asked how much he wanted, he replied, "Nothing," and went on to say, "Concentrate on getting your business going, little bro, and occasionally I might stop in for a sandwich or something, that's all." Again, the Old Man was notoriously known throughout the joint for being on the paper chase in hot pursuit of the all-might dollar, and when most convicts described him, it was usually connected to how serious his attitude was regarding money; his money in particular. To not demand interest on a loan from the Old Man was unheard of, and he only allowed thirty days to repay him. He charged dollar for dollar interest on all loans, meaning under normal circumstances, I would have to repay him four hundred dollars at the very less.

Granted, I only asked for two hundred dollars, but we are talking about a great deal of money considering the nature of the situation behind prison walls. First, cash is illegal contraband behind the walls. Second, only a select few had ready access to large amounts, let alone enough to extend a two-hundred-dollar loan without hesitation. The old convicts who hustled in the joint kept an illegal bankroll by one means or another. They were the true movers and shakers in the joint. Many prisoners spend their entire period of incarceration and rarely see more than a ten or twenty pass through their hands, whereas those who knew the ropes and understood how to manipulate them saw hundreds and thousands. The Old Man was definitely in the thick of things behind the walls. He had probably seen thousands passed through his hands and probably had a few thousand stashed away when he agreed to give me the prison loan I requested.

Although the Old Man did not want any interest on this loan, it was nevertheless silently understood that we were dealing in blood money. My paramount concern was repaying the money according to the established agreement between us. Yet, I found myself embarking on new waters once again. I had confidence in my business plan, but I had no real experience in running a business. Still, I was a natural hustler and could see clearly throughout my plan from Point A to Point Z. I knew deep down in my heart that I would succeed and embraced the challenge.

From Day One, my little restaurant business took off at a promising pace, the demand being so great that I needed help from one of my Muslim brothers. That first day, from start to finish, I remained busy cooking and making sandwiches until the recreation yard closed. The word spread quickly around the yard that my business was open, and before long, I had a list of orders with more pouring in. My business was an instant success, but I soon learned that I was driven more by the challenge of my business venture than by the desire to run and operate a successful business. The restaurant got off to a fantastic start and immediately produced a profit. Everything went perfectly according to plan. Still, it did not take me long to lose interest in the restaurant business and move on to other prison hustles behind the walls.

During this period, I was assigned to A-cellhouse, an old structure resembling a large warehouse with cages for approximately four hundred prisoners. Upon my return from the Indiana Reformatory and being assigned to this particular cellblock, the day-shift sergeant in charge of the unit gave me free rein to come and go and practically do as I pleased. The sergeant and I got along great on a personal level; he was well aware of my bad-boy reputation around the joint and gave me my space. The cellhouse clerk was also my right-hand man and this guy pretty much ran the day-to-day operation of the cellhouse, more than the officers on duty. With the sergeant and the cellhouse clerk on my team, I received preferential treatment across the board in A-block.

Big Zake, the cellhouse clerk, stood about 5' 10" and was built like a German tank. He had a strong reputation on the prison compound by the time I met him. With Big Zake in my prison-people network, I would create a power base in A-cellhouse that allowed me to spread my wings in new directions. Of all people, the cellhouse clerk knew more about the operations, what was going on in the unit, where every single prisoner in the block lived, and their prison number. The convict assigned to this job had complete and total freedom of movement throughout the cellblock. He was the first one out of his cell in the morning and the last to be locked down at night. The cellhouse clerk was also the prisoner with clout in the cellblock and was privileged to valuable information as a result of officers talking freely around them. Pulling Big Zake into my social and business network opened an additional door of opportunity for me as I took my prison hustle to another level.

With a stronghold in A-cellhouse, I had everything going my way considering the circumstances. As long as I did not cause any trouble or problems in the joint, I was left alone to pretty much do as I pleased.

Every prison has a class of convicts who the prison administration either kept locked in segregation or left alone due to their reputation. I wanted to be left alone, and during my incarceration, I repeatedly sent this message to my keepers through my actions and deeds until they eventually heard me. I understood the image I projected by my reputation because I created the character others saw: a character with an attitude built for survival behind prison walls by whatever means proven necessary.

I had a cellhouse store where I loaned out cigarettes and other commissary items two for one. I still had the little recreation yard kitchen going, but allowed another Muslim brother to run it, for the most part. My attention suddenly turned to another lucrative penitentiary hustle: gambling. One day, I decided to house a dice game in my cell and things went so well the first day that it became a regular game. Housing a dice game was much like refereeing a championship prize fight and if you lost control of the game, things could get ugly quite fast. I had already been a witness to the deadly violence associated with these dice games in the joint and knew exactly what to expect, and I knew how to expand my alter ego to match that of the next man. Housing these dice games was definitely not for the weak or the timid because one bad call would cause blood to spill and you had no friends during the game.

We started the game betting packs of cigarettes and as the game progressed, the cash started to gradually emerge from its many hidden places. First, the ten- and twenty-dollar bills came out, followed by the fifties and hundreds. I always knew there was money on the prison compound. Now I was seeing it and was surprised at how much I was beginning to see. More importantly, by housing the game, I cut out my share as the house and began to build my own penitentiary bankroll. My time to shine had arrived and the convict side of me seized on the opportunity.

With a stash of cash and a cell full of commissary, I stopped eating in the prison chow hall altogether. I did not wear prison-issued clothes with my number stamped on them and removed myself as much as possible from being dependent on my keepers in any way. I only spoke to officials when absolutely necessary and continued to stay in my own lane and mind my own business. My objective was the same since Day

One of my incarceration: to survive my prison experience living on my feet rather than on my knees and to retain as much of my personal identity and sense of freedom as possible. My keepers only held my physical being in captivity while my soul and spirit and the essence of the man I had become fought tirelessly to remain free.

One day, Big Zake came rushing into my cell filled with excitement and propositioned me with a Godfather deal; a deal I could not refuse. Zake already had an officer working the cellhouse who would bring us a joint or two of marijuana on occasion. Then a high school friend of his started working at the prison as a cook supervisor in the prison chow hall. Big Zake had finally convinced the cook supervisor to smuggle marijuana into the prison for him. The only problem was, Zake did not have the capital to finance the move and came to me with a partnership offer. In prison, behind the walls, I had accumulated more cash than I ever had at one time before. According to penitentiary standards I was penitentiary wealthy and when Big Zake said we needed five hundred dollars to initiate the marijuana operation, I would agree to the arrangement without hesitation.

Together, Zake and I met with his high school buddy to work out the details of our marijuana smuggling plan. My first impression of the cook supervisor was not good. He was young and very naïve. Every convict on the prison compound laid in the shadows waiting for someone like the cook supervisor: someone easily manipulated into crossing over to the dark side of life behind prison walls. For his own safety and longevity, I would explain and stress to the cook supervisor that it would be wise to limit his dealings to just Big Zake and me, advice I eventually learned fell on deaf ears.

Our first marijuana shipment came through smoothly, but that was the beginning and the end. By the time we made arrangements for a second shipment, the cook supervisor had already taken money from several other convicts and had failed to deliver. The tension grew thick between prisoners laying claim to the next package coming in, and the cook supervisor faced pressure from the type of convicts who would seriously hurt him. Things were spiraling out of control fast and there was nothing I could do to salvage the operation because the damage was already done. If we were discussing the problem on the prison compound among ourselves, it was definitely only a matter of time before informants told prison officials.

Still fighting my conviction for the robbery sentence, my keepers received a court order for my appearance at the Lake County Superior Court. Before the issue with the cook supervisor was resolved, I would be transferred back to the Lake County Jail to await my hearing. Never giving in to my robbery conviction, I fought the charge until the day I was released from the yoke of incarceration. I filed my own "post-conviction relief motion" because my understanding of the law had evolved over the years. Also, I was genuinely interested in the law and sometimes feel I missed my true calling in life and should have practiced law.

In challenging my robbery convictions, I cited violations of my right to due process of the law, use of an unlawful line-up or photo display, unlawful search and seizure, as well as ineffective assistance from counsel as reasons the court should reverse my conviction and grant me a new trial. Although I was guilty of the crime and everyone else was convinced I was guilty, they had to cheat and violate my constitutional rights to convict me. I fought to the bitter end against my conviction, all to no avail, and discovered people on my level in life did not have the same protection of their rights as those more privileged. I knew and understood going in that my chances of getting my robbery conviction overturned were as good as a snowball's chance in hell. For me, to a large extent, it was mostly about fighting for a cause and a willingness to fight against the odds to defend myself.

I spent perhaps two months in the county jail and got extremely lucky right from the start by being housed on the fifth floor of the jail where several officers already knew me. One Black officer in particular had watched me grow up in jail, always expressed concern for my well-being, and always showed me brotherly love. Within reason, this officer would honor any favor I asked of him, such as give me extra food at mealtime, allow me to use the jail phone to call home, and move my packages around the jail. I could get the brother to pretty much bend or perhaps even break any rule, but nothing close to anything illegal. I met this officer as a kid in jail facing a life sentence and he knew I was about to encounter a very hard life ahead. He acknowledged me as a full-grown man now with real credibility, and I could see he was happy and impressed by how well I had survived against all odds.

It was quite astonishing how quickly the landscape of the prison environment can change in a matter of weeks. By the time I was transported back to the Indiana State Prison after a mere two months at the county jail, things had changed unfavorably for me. I can remember arriving on a Friday and hitting the prison compound only to feel a very strong sense of apprehension in the air. Long before the prison grapevine began to speak, I knew something was wrong. My survival instincts recognized the signs of pending trouble and my guard was up; I was on full alert.

Immediately upon entering A-cellhouse, someone informed me that Big Zake was on lockdown in segregation. Once settled in my cell, different prisoners came by with bits of information that drew a vivid picture of what had happened in my absence, and it was not good at all. The more I learned, the more disturbed I became and the more my anxiety increased. It appeared that, while I was gone, Big Zake's homebody and another cook supervisor were apprehended for smuggling contraband into the prison. This second cook supervisor was a White employee who had been secretly involved in a homosexual relationship with a prisoner for years. The supervisor would only bring cash for his convict lover into the joint until Zake's friend and the employee's lover convinced him to smuggle drugs. After getting caught bringing one-dollar U.S. postal money orders and marijuana into the prison, both cook supervisors told everything they knew. The two men were escorted from the institution in handcuffs and taken to the local jail. The White cook supervisor immediately made bond and was released, only to go home and commit suicide.

Since I returned to the Indiana State Prison on a Friday, the prison administration did not move against me until the following Monday. I spent the entire weekend half thinking I had dodged a bullet and would not get caught up in the prison drug-conspiracy dragnet. Big Zake and several other brothers were already locked down in solitary confinement for their involvement in the conspiracy. I would inevitably meet the same fate.

The prison administration investigator would call me to his office early that Monday morning for questioning and I left his office in cuffs, segregation bound. The investigator was a big fellow, standing well over six feet and weighing over three hundred pounds, and used his size and an aggressive attitude to intimidate his subjects. I always had a no-nonsense approach to dealing with my keepers; I never compromised and met the prison investigator in the middle when questioned. The rat chasing the cat game between us continued until the investigator realized his efforts were fruitless and the interview was suddenly terminated.

My keepers charged me with drug trafficking, conspiracy to violate institutional rules, and being a habitual offender. The prison investigator, in writing his final report, asserted that I was the shot caller in the drug-smuggling conspiracy and continued to orchestrate the operation even from the Lake County Jail, which was absolutely ludicrous. I had no contact with my fellow convicts while at the county jail and had no idea or knowledge as to what was happening at the state prison while I was away. Once again, my keepers would label me a clever manipulator capable of calling shots from afar. Granted, I had grown strong behind the prison walls over the years and had my sphere of influence on the prison yard, but by no means did my keepers have the equation right.

Sentenced to one year on lockdown in solitary confinement and housed in my cell for 23 hours a day once again, I settled in to make the best of a bad situation, rearranging my daily schedule to make the necessary mental adjustments to do lockdown time. Being in solitary confinement was not new to me and I took my unfortunate predicament in stride. I would sleep mostly during the day and read or write all night when it was a nice and quiet and seemingly peaceful. Within reason and under the circumstances, I served my lockdown time my way, using my acute convict tactics to govern my situation and keep things in my favor as much as possible. Days and nights in solitary confinement were like living in a world alone, with just my private thoughts to contend with. A man gets to know himself very well under these conditions, as he faces his own human nature: the good, the bad, and the ugly that lives in all humankind.

I never saw Big Zake again. Penitentiary rumors suggested he was transferred after turning informant. I found these rumors to be true later, as I read court documents from a lawsuit I filed against the prison regarding the entire incident. Big Zake, in a malicious and underhanded move, pitched a story to the prison investigator that drew a picture making it appear he was a mere pawn in the game. My lawsuit charging the prison with violations of my constitutional rights also included claims of cruel and unusual punishment. A federal judge would issue a court order demanding prison officers turn over documents they once denied me, and I learned about Big Zake, as well as other prison informants connected to the case.

Due to good behavior and causing no problems in the lockup unit, my keepers released me back into the general prison population after serving nine months of my one-year segregation sentence. Once back on the prison yard among my fellow convicts, I returned to doing my time and minding my own business. I did a great deal of soul searching while in the lockup unit. I was still evolving as a young man and the spiritual side of me emerged stronger following my nine months on lockdown. Resisting the temptation and the devilish whispers to pursue the illegal penitentiary hustles, I made my image on the yard obscure. The light of Islam was clearly showing me a more promising way to live my life and I embraced it. While in segregation, I studied diligently to cultivate my inner and spiritual self and, upon leaving the lock-up unit, found myself traveling on a totally different level altogether.

Back in the general prison population, I kept my hands clean and my conduct mischief free, not because I was intimidated or feared the wrath of my keepers, but because I wanted to govern my actions and deeds according to the dictates of Islam. I gave my undivided time and attention to Muslim functions and Islamic activities on the prison compounds, keeping myself sucker free from the many pitfalls and snares of prison life.

On the surface, I appeared to be a model prisoner who was just serving out their sentence, and thought I was no longer on the prison administration radar. Then one day, straight out of the blue, my keepers sent for me along with a message that I was to pack my personal belongings because I was being transferred to another correctional facility. The Muslim brotherhood was in the middle of Friday services when the message reached me. The news made me furious and I exploded in protest of the transfer. My Muslim brothers had to calm me down and convince me to listen to reason because I had completely lost my composure and was on the war path. We all felt the transfer was unfair and maliciously motivated, and in my support, they all accompanied me to the prison administration building to challenge the move. The sight of twenty or thirty angry Muslims converging on the administration building was an alarming sight to prison officials, but our protest and challenge to the transfer was to no avail, and I would be shipped off to the Indiana State Farm.

10. The State Farm

Due to the overcrowded prison conditions in the Indiana Department of Corrections, the Indiana State Farm was converted from a misdemeanor facility to a low-level felony institution. Mostly short timers, first-time offenders, and young kids were sent to The State Farm. With my prison sentence coming to an end, my keepers decided to send me to The Farm to serve out the remainder of my time. Prison officials alleged that rival gangs were about to start a drug war as the reason for my transfer to The State Farm. So for my own protection and in the best interests of prison security, about 20 other convicts and I were transferred to different joints throughout the state. I seriously doubt whether my keepers' reason for the transfer had real substance. Perhaps they were playing it safe rather than being sorry later because the convicts incarcerated at the Indiana State Prison could be extremely dangerous when provoked.

The Indiana State Farm was just that: a farm sitting on well over four thousand acres of land. The prison compound was surrounded by a mere 12-foot high fence and you could practically walk away from the joint, but I would not advise it because The State Farm was very much like a family-owned business ran from the top down by mostly all family members. Brothers, along with their wives and children, maintained the security aspect of the operation. They all lived on the property around the prison and the majority of the other employees also lived around the prison grounds. The Indiana State Farm was in the heart of Klan territory, a lily White town where everybody knew one another. This was especially true for those who lived close to the prison grounds. Those who were not prison employees living around The Farm were always on the lookout for escapees because there was a standing bounty on our heads. White prisoners would face difficulty walking away from the joint. A Black prisoner, in contrast, attempting such a move would be playing Russian roulette with a loaded gun.

Upon my arrival at The Farm, I was placed in a lock-up unit apart from the other prisoners, my anger still simmering over the transfer. Spending the weekend in the lock-up unit did not help matters and by the following Monday, I was cruisin' for a bruisin'. Things would escalate when I went to the property room to retrieve my personal belongings. They took everything from me that prisoners were not allowed to have at The Farm: my street clothes in particular, and other possessions I had for years and valued. A very heated exchange between the property-room officer and me took place and subsequently, I found myself being escorted to the captain's office, supposedly for an attitude-adjustment talk.

Once in the captain's office, the man sitting behind the desk looked up at me, taking his eyes off a folder in front of him to size me up. The captain was a small man like me, but I could feel his energy and see strength in his character. Looking me straight in the eyes, the first words the captain uttered were, "We do things a little different around here." The captain knew who I was and the folder he had been reading was actually my institutional record, a concise report of my history behind the walls. The manner in which the captain delivered his assertion made it perfectly clear who was in charge, and my bad-boy reputation did not mean a thing to them. He would also make it crystal clear that his complete loyalty was to his subordinates and fellow correctional officers. Telling me directly, right or wrong, he would take his officers' word over mine. This revelation came to the surface as a result of me expressing a complaint about the property-room officers' conduct and behavior toward me.

My rebelliousness naturally wanted to get aggressive, but reasoning and common sense told me an aggressive confrontation would end badly for me. I literally hated my transfer to The State Farm with a passion.

Granted, The Farm was an easy, laid-back joint, but I was a seasoned convict raised among hardened prisoners; I had a convict mentality and a convict approach to dealing with my keepers and those incarcerated with me. I found the vast majority of the prisoners on The Farm to be young, immature, and somewhat irresponsible. I felt a great deal like a lion captured from the wildland and tossed into a pit of trained and toothless circus cats pretending to be lions.

My first couple of weeks at The State Farm proved to be a test of my self-restraint and commanding discipline under adversity. Once again, my seeing-the-cup-half-full attitude came into play. Over the years of my incarceration, no matter how turbulent things became, I learned how to extract something positive from the experience. Making the best of a bad situation, as always, and turning tasteless negative circumstances to my advantage, I could clearly see that the captain was right in saying they did things a little differently at The Farm and I did not want any part of the joint.

With my options being limited, I decided on a peaceful-agitator approach to force my keepers to transfer me back to The City, the state prison. Understanding the power of the pen and having adequate knowledge of the law, I started a grievance campaign and filed a grievance regarding everything I found wrong around the institution, laying the groundwork for future lawsuits. Prison officials at the administrative level literally hated the prisoner's grievance process and the paper trail it left behind. My keepers were thoroughly trained to address physical confrontations, but the power of the pen was a force they could not contain. Using my pen as the only weapon at my disposal, I sought an avenue to become a headache that my keepers did not want.

My grievance campaign immediately began with me filing grievances two or three times a week. These were rather petty complaints on my part. I knew in advance, my intentions were to become a nuisance and nothing more. At my first grievance hearing, the lieutenant in charge of the process sat me down for a long one-on-one talk, telling me directly that he knew what I was attempting to do and informing me that my scheme would fail. He also mentioned the manipulator concept with which my keepers had labeled me over the years, giving me the impression that this conclusion about me was recorded in my prison files somewhere. If they meant I manipulated things in my orbit to survive my prison experience to my advantage, they were absolutely correct, and I was proficient in doing so. The lieutenant went on to suggest that I settle down and give my stay at The Farm a chance. He would also advise that I come straight to him if I encountered any problems in the joint before going off on a tangent of rage.

The talk between the lieutenant and me lasted about one hour and I remember it being a man-to-man exchange. The lieutenant encouraged me to accept my situation as one of those things I could not change, and he had a valid point. Nonetheless, I pressed on with my grievance campaign until it dawned on me that my efforts would continue to no avail. After filing a grievance about the unsanitary conditions of the food trays in the prison chow hall, they put me in charge of the dish tank to inspect the trays as they came out. They outsmarted me with that move, making it clear they could be as creative with a response to my grievances as I was in coming up with them.

All things considered, I must admit The State Farm did have its advantages and was a stress-free environment where stabbings and killings were nonexistent. An occasional fist fight was the extent of the worst drama to be found on The Farm, and these were like kids on a playground hoping someone would quickly break them up. My biggest issues revolved around the mentality and attitudes of those with whom I was suddenly incarcerated with, prisoners and officials alike. Having practically grown up behind prison walls the hardcore way, I learned to live hardcore and by the hardcore rules of prison life. The passive prison yard and environment at The Farm was totally new to me.

Acknowledging my situation for what it was, I eventually faced the reality that I was at The State Farm to stay, and on the farm I would serve out the remainder of my prison sentence. Gradually, I adjusted to my new surroundings and settled down to do my time, and with each passing day I grew stronger. I was perhaps 28 years old when my prison journey led me to the Indiana State Farm. With 13 years of prison time under my belt, I was considered an old convict. No one at The Farm had more time on the yard than I had and my reputation proceeded me once again.

The brothers from my hometown, Gary, Indiana, all fell in line behind me, and the Black prisoners at The Farm in general turned to me for guidance and leadership. The White prisoners rallying around their Nazi flag and Klanish dogma were not so Klanish once I confronted them after hearing racist rhetoric coming from that crowd. I had a strong voice in the joint and people heard me when I spoke and recognized me as a legitimate force to be reckoned with. I would use my status and influence to promote peaceful relationships between the Black and White prisoners, and also to resolve personal conflicts between my Gary homeboys. I often felt like a babysitter, overseeing grown men who did not have a clue as to what prison life was all about.

Upon my arrival at The State Farm, I found the Muslim community there to be just four or five brothers expressing an interest in the religion. They knew very little about the fundamental teachings of Islam or the proper way to conduct the Friday services. All they had was good intentions. The brother in charge immediately stepped down when I arrived because I was far more qualified in every aspect to govern the Muslim brotherhood. To a large extent, these young brothers reminded me of myself in my early days behind the walls, lost and striving to find the best of myself spiritually. They were attracted to the radiant light of Islam and hungered for the knowledge and understanding incorporated in its teachings. I felt the strong obligation to do my part to share all I knew and provide the best guidance within the limits of my capabilities.

After a couple of weeks on The Farm, the murky waters engulfing my disdain over the transfer began to clear, but the vestiges of my contempt would remain and I openly wore my feelings on my sleeves. The space around me was still like a mine field and anyone entering "my space" did so at their own risk. The bad disposition that possessed me would linger for a while, but not to the point of becoming self-destructive or picking losing battles. Seeing my glass half full on The Farm, the best in me manifested itself. At the end of the day, my experience at the Indiana State Farm proved to be another moment of personal growth and development.

Still in confrontation mode, I befriended a White prisoner named Jim Bo who had his right leg amputated at the knee. In my early days at The Farm, Jim Bo was the only one I allowed to get close to me and I went off on a tangent when I learned he was being extorted by another prisoner. I had known the weak and spineless brother extorting Jim Bo from my first trip to gladiator school, the Indiana Reformatory. I also knew he had turned informant and testified against two brothers I highly respected, Giz and Priest, landing them both on death row. He would not last a hot second at The State Prison or the Reformatory. But in the passive environment of The Farm, he fronted like a tough guy and ran in a group of young blind followers who did not know any better.

Using my convict approach, I confronted the guy extorting Jim Bo while surrounded by some of his followers on the yard, walking straight up to him and saying, "Man, I know you. You testified against Giz and Priest and got those brothers a death sentence." Although my assertion came out sounding calm and composed, the look in my eyes told a completely different story. All the oxygen was seemingly sucked out of the air and things fell silent. My word power punched holes through the weak image the guy was attempting to portray and exposed him as a rat. Getting no response to my matter-of-fact statement, I went on to say Jim Bo was a personal friend of mine and I would appreciate him being left alone. Calling another man a rat openly and to his face in the joint is instant fighting words if you could not stand on what you claimed. I could, and I never saw that guy again on the prison yard.

Living behind the walls, I taught myself to be a trained observer, being fully aware of everything going on around me. On The Farm, we were housed in dormitories holding approximately three-hundred men, and as a common practice, I watched and observed those around me closely. We had phones in the dorms used to make collect calls home, which could get rather expensive over time. Guys ran up family and friend phone bills to the point where phone services were terminated or had collect call blocks placed on their phones. I noticed one White kid who stayed on the phone and I suspected, from my position of observation, he was using some sort of gimmick. One day, pulling the White youngster to the side, I inquired about how he managed to use the phone so frequently. I addressed him in a manner that implied I knew a lot more than I actually did, and the kid, who was probably 18 or 19 years old, gladly shared his secret.

The process was quite simple. He kept hanging up the phone rapidly until an operator came online. The system would lose the number he was calling from and when the operator came online, he told them he was making a third-party collect call and gave them a bogus number when asked where he was calling from. Once I learned how to manipulate the phone system, I was off and running. My new friend had asked that I not reveal his secret to anyone and I honored his request. This is the first time since then that I have mentioned tricking The Farm phones. I knew and understood that the quickest way to mess up a good thing in prison was to tell too many people or tell the wrong person.

At the Indiana Reformatory and the Indiana State Prison, we were allowed to make one 15-minute collect call per month. Ready access to The Farm phones, along with a little trickery, and I was suddenly able to call my girl, Katherine, whenever I wanted to. I met Kathy through one of my correspondence campaigns about two years earlier while I was in solitary confinement. I wrote a letter to a small-town newspaper asking for pen pals and Katherine responded. From the very first letter exchange, I perceived something special and lasting in the makings between Katherine and me. She became a great deal more than a mere pen pal and friend. Kathy would establish a significant place in my life and become the one person I loved and also respected unconditionally.

Katherine came along at a very crucial moment in my life when I was striving to grasp and manage my empty emotions. Systematically, I had locked my emotions down over the years because I could not afford to have feelings behind the prison walls. I applied due diligence in improving myself mentally, spiritually, and physically during my incarceration. But emotionally, I was bankrupt, dead, and lacked the essential tools necessary to properly compartmentalize my feelings and deal with them. My nonchalant attitude toward anything that did not concern me personally was deeply ingrained and my emotions grew dormant over the years.

Katherine awakened and resurrected my innate human nature to know and to feel love on a mature level between two people. We wrote and exchanged long love letters getting to know each other in ways few people will understand. Kathy was very intelligent, thoughtful, and sincere, which manifested in her letters. I found our intellectual exchange on paper to be very rewarding as we explored the depths of one another. We discussed every subject imaginable openly and honestly, discovering all we may or may not have in common. I completely lowered my guard around my emotional defenses and allowed Kathy to enter the inner sanctuary of my heart. She accepted me as I was and with no false pretenses when the rest of the world seemed to look down on me disparagingly, as if my existence was insignificant.

I first met Kathy while she was going to an all-girls Catholic college. From Day One, none of the superficial mirrors reflecting the quality and character of an individual came into play between Katherine and me. We both saw past skin color, social status, or stereotypical opinions. I never saw Kathy as a White girl; I only saw a loving, caring, and very understanding person with whom I connected in a profound way. I did not obsess or cloud my thinking with her physical attraction, and she was, in fact, a beautiful young lady. But it would be the spirit of the woman, her inner beauty, and the totality of all that I saw in her that intrigued me most and won my heart and utmost respect.

Tricking The Farm phones became my lifeline to Katherine and our relationship flourished with the regular and direct communication between us. We eventually arranged for a special three-day visit that turned out to be the most memorable experience of my incarceration. On average, a prisoner is allowed one two-hour visit per week, but since Katherine lived in Minnesota and was traveling from out of state, we were granted the privilege of a special visit. For three days, Katherine and I met in the prison visiting room like two happily married newlyweds. We took to each other as easily as we gravitated toward one another through correspondence, and it was a simply beautiful union. I did not get visits from friends, family, or loved ones and Kathy's visits was like much needed food for the soul. After spending more than 13 years behind the walls, I probably had received two visits from home altogether, I really did my time alone and on my own. My visit from Katherine was more than a welcome treat; it was a reminder that someone cared enough to embrace me for who I was, faults and all. It was also a reminder that someone deemed me to be significant and worthy of love and affection. I would credit Kathy for nurturing my dead emotions back to health, for teaching me how to love, and for being an extraordinary friend under extraordinary circumstances.

At the Indiana State Farm, I hit the gym and became a beast in the weight room as a power lifter, bench pressing 325lbs with no spotter and dead lifting 500lbs with a legal 405lb squat. I started working out with a brother named Young Blood from Detroit, Michigan almost immediately upon my arrival at The Farm. Young Blood had served time in Michigan and possessed the kind of convict mentality I could identify with. We became quick friends one day after he watched one of my work-out performances on the heavy bag. I often beat on the heavy bag to work off my frustrations and built-up tension. In my early days on The Farm, I also used to work out on the heavy bag to send a message and to intentionally display my skills. I had very decent hand speed and the lethal punching power of a heavyweight. My timing and strikes were so precise they produced a rhythmic sound that often drew the attention of onlookers. Purposely, I showed off my hand work to openly demonstrate what others had to contend with when coming up against me.

Young Blood and I started talking after one of my intense heavy-bag workouts and discovered we were likeminded in many ways and had a great deal in common. Young Blood was a few years older than me, a very dark-complexioned brother who stood about 6'2" and weighed a solid 250 pounds, which was all muscle. He was a soft-spoken brother and the only man on the prison compound who I considered strong enough to meet me in the middle as a potential adversary. Still very much a loner who traveled about the prison yard as a solo act, I could regularly be found hanging out with either Young Blood or Jim Bo, a strong man on one side and an amputee on the other.

About six months into my stay at The Farm, the administration officials received a court order for me to appear before the judge in Lake County. This court order revolved around a motion for a sentence modification I filed following the affirmation of my original conviction by the appeals court. Still fighting for my freedom and knocking on every legal door in my reach, I filed a motion for a sentence reduction. My motion was inevitably denied, which came as no surprise because winning relief on a sentence-reduction petition required exceptional circumstances. But my return to the Lake County Jail would reveal to me just how much I had grown and matured in many pertinent aspects of my personal life.

A courtroom can be intimidating, subtly hostile, and a rather unfriendly environment for a defendant facing a court judgment. The accused often sits submissively and quietly at the defense table and allows the attorney to do all the talking. Over the years of my courtroom experiences, I came to understand that the worst thing a defendant can do is not address the court on their own behalf. In the past, I sat at the defense table quietly allowing my life to be dictated by others without even mumbling a word. No longer ignorant or naïve, confident and knowing no fear, I was absolutely prepared on all fronts for my courtroom appearance.

Back at the Lake County Jail once again, I was housed on the third floor in a single-man cell unit. I did not know the officers working the third floor and they did not know me, so there was no preferential treatment or special favors this time around. The cellblock to which I was assigned had about ten one-man cells, but only two or three were actually occupied. I would spend my time mentally replaying the expected courtroom scenario in my mind, considering the many variables and contemplating how best to position myself for victory against the odds I faced. I spent days and nights preparing a written statement I intended to deliver before the court. I would take about a week to carefully compose and write this statement, methodically placing every word. I even used a list of what I called power words; these words were designed to convey my intended message and command attention.

The solitude of my jail cell and being alone with only my thoughts had me in an incredible zone, almost to the point I felt invincible and could achieve anything humanly possible. It was my journey on the path of Islam that gave me the strength and fortitude to persevere. It was my journey as a Muslim that laid the foundation for my growth and development as I continued to evolve. The religion of Islam had greatly influenced every aspect of my life, from defining my values, principles, and beliefs to pursuing knowledge, wisdom, and understanding. It was my maturing as a Muslim and conducting the Muslim services that directly prepared me for public speaking. Islam also prepared me with the keys to unlock my inner self when necessary and to rise to the occasion in any given situation.

I remember the energy I felt during the hearing on my motion for a sentence reduction. My mind seemed exceptionally sharp and keenly aware of how the courtroom proceedings were unfolding. I felt a small sense of being in control for once by injecting my own influence into the hearing outcome. Succeed or fail, being on the front line of battle for my freedom gave an even greater purpose and meaning to my courtroom appearance.

The proceedings went as I anticipated and when the judge asked if I had anything to say on my own behalf, I got up to seize the moment. Reading my statement before the court felt like someone else was doing the talking. Articulating myself eloquently, I breezed through reading my statement to the court without missing a beat. I knew I was shining. It was one of those moments when absolutely everything and every word fell right into place. The courtroom echoed with silence as I concluded, but applause of self-congratulations rang inside my entire being for a job well done. Just listening to myself speak, I knew I had knocked the ball completely out of the ballpark and into another place and time. The judge was so impressed that he requested a personal copy of my statement. My lawyer gripped my hand in a handshake as if congratulating a colleague who successfully delivered his first oral argument. I could tell by the vibe in the courtroom that my performance was well received, and I remember it being a beautiful and exhilarating feeling.

My stay at the County Jail only lasted about one week before my keepers had me transported back to The State Farm. By this time, I had maneuvered and positioned myself at The Farm so that I had things my way, considering the circumstances. The Farm was a very easy joint in which to serve time and I had finally relaxed and dug in. The officers

on the yard did not harass me with petty rules and showed a higher degree of respect for my presence than they did for the much younger prisoners. I was conscious of my image on the prison compound and fully
aware of my range of influence among my fellow prisoners. Yet, I never
allowed my ego to consume me, nor did I allow myself to grow arrogant,
and I did not use my status in the joint for mischievous endeavors or to
exploit others. I often downplayed my true self and concealed my true
potential from those around me; in the prison environment in which I
grew up, the element of surprise was my number one weapon of choice.

The court would deny my motion for a sentence modification, but
soon after my return to The Farm, my keepers called me in for my an-
nual classification review and reinstated some good time lost due to bad
behavior. Restoring my lost good time suddenly put my release date
within immediate reach. The classification officer recalculating the
numbers for my new out date determined I had less than six months left
to serve on my sentence. The news came as a pleasant and very welcome
surprise, and I recall leaving the classification hearing with all smiles.

As the month of Ramadan approached, "The month of fasting for
Muslims all over the world," I took the initiative to get the Muslim
brotherhood ready for the thirty-day fast. Muslims fast from sunup to
sundown as a duty we owe to Allah so that a believer may learn self-
restraint and humility. Most of the new brothers were unaware of the
Islamic fasting month and had never fasted before. The prison administration officials at The Farm did not honor the Muslim month of Ramadan because brothers in the past had not taken advantage of those religious rights. I knew the law governing prisoners' religious rights behind
the walls and was part of the class-action lawsuit that resulted in the
consent decree my keepers were compelled to follow. I would push the
power of my pen once again to petition the prison administration to accommodate the Muslim brotherhood and honor our religious rights to
fast.

A brother name Hamid arrived at The State Farm approximately two
weeks prior to the month of Ramadan. Hamid was transferred in from
the Indiana State Prison like me. He was an older Muslim brother, well
versed in Islamic teachings and a former member of the Nation of Islam.

Hamid was taking his transfer to The Farm extremely hard and I had to constantly counsel him to be cool and to maintain his composure. I fully understood what he was going through and kept him close to me out of fear he would go off like a loaded .45 and incur the stern wrath of our keepers. I really liked Hamid. He was a good brother with good intentions. He simply did not wish to stay at the Indiana State Farm and would rebel. I had the foresight to see that Hamid's rebellious behavior posed a threat to himself and to others. He was a real-live time bomb, not merely waiting to explode but aggressively looking for a reason to suddenly explode.

Following my written petition to prison officials requesting accommodations be made for Muslims wishing to fast, they reluctantly complied. Provisions were arranged for us to have exclusive use of the prison chow hall for our meals twice a day, once in the morning before sunrise and again after sunset. Prison officials left the details and organizing of the fast entirely up to me, mainly because this was virgin territory for them with serious legal consequences at stake if undermined. From a legal perspective, I knew how strong my hand was, and my keepers knew I could be a formidable legal adversary, and for the most part, my every request was approved.

Ramadan is by far the greatest month in Islam to engage in self-reflection, to cultivate one's spirituality and striving to get closer to God. I looked forward to fasting during the month of Ramadan because it was the perfect time to work on my inner self. I still had my fair share of faults and shortcomings, and being a conscious-minded Muslim, I took Ramadan very seriously and put forth my best efforts to improve on my weaknesses. During the blessed month of Ramadan, I would grow as an individual in ways I cannot express or fully explain. Everything seemed enhanced intellectually and spiritually, as if seeing the world around me through fresh eyes. The benefits of fasting could be seen immediately for those who had the eyes to see.

Ramadan at the Indiana State Farm would reveal the extent of my personal growth and development over the years. I had the responsibility to run the Muslim brotherhood and my every decision would reflect directly on our image and reputation. My actions represented Islam and the Muslim community at The Farm, and my actions could jeopardize the welfare of the brotherhood. With this thought constantly at the forefront of my thinking, I would manage Muslim affairs to the best of my abilities.

Approximately midway through Ramadan, one evening when breaking our fast in the prison chow hall, my attention was suddenly drawn to a commotion between Hamid and an officer. I rushed over to where they stood exchanging verbal jabs to separate the two. I do not recall what led up to the altercation, but things would escalate quickly from there and Hamid only added fuel to the fire in his anger. As the other brothers gathered around us, showing support and solidarity, Hamid got more vocal and aggressive. Two more officers would arrive, thinking they could squash the matter by ordering us around and demanding we disperse, sounding arrogant and antagonistic as usual, only to see their orders fall on deaf ears.

I vividly remember at one point the lead officer saying he was taking Hamid. He did not say where he was taking the brother or what was going to happen to him. Hamid would turn to me and simply say, "Don't let them take me, brother." The chow hall fell piercingly silent and all eyes were on me. The overconfidence of the three officers seemed to instantly evaporate, replaced by raw fear. I had about 15 or 20 young and easily excitable brothers behind me who were high strung and ready to act out. The tension in the air was so thick I could feel it crawling up my spine and the wrong move could lead to an ugly situation very fast. Once this mischief-making genie was out of the bottle, there was no putting him back.

A surge of power enveloped me as the realization dawned on me that, for one moment in time, I temporarily held all the aces and the odds were to my advantage. A devilish impression whispering in my ear suggested I revert to my old militant mentality and revolt. Processing the predicament instantaneously through the eyes of my mind, I saw a scenario unfolding where the life and freedom of my fellow Muslim brothers were at stake. Visions of us taking the three officers hostage and inciting a full-scale riot played around inside my head. The whisper of mischief put forth its best effort to draw me in and instigate bad behavior, but I felt a tremendous sense of duty and responsibility to the Muslim community and could not lead us into self-destruction under any circumstances.

Once my thoughts broke away from the devilish whispers, I began to see clearly. I did not consider my own welfare or freedom at all. I only saw my obligation to protect the religion of Islam and the younger brothers under me. I knew some very rude boys who would have taken this incident as an opportunity to lash out and vent, prisoners who were forever adversarial toward the prison administration. I used to be one of those angry and rowdy convicts running wild and out of control, looking for an excuse to act out. But in the situation with Hamid, I saw my responsibility was to safeguard the integrity of Islam as far greater than any personal resentment I had toward my keepers.

Something truly phenomenal seemed to happen spiritually in my being and in that very instant, my thinking and overall attitude matured. The wicked whisper of mischief yielded to the prevailing voice of reason and wisdom. A profound sense of spiritual inspiration emerged shining a brighter and more positive light on the situation. I felt the presence of God all around me and my clairvoyance was intoxicatingly intense. I had been shown a clear vision of the advantages and disadvantages of making a decision influenced by a whisper suggesting wickedness versus a decision influenced by the superior voice of wisdom. I was thinking in harmony with the divine mind and felt I had greater support behind me than the group of Muslim brothers.

I pulled Hamid to the side and spoke to him as if negotiating a peace deal, telling the brother to be cool and go with the officers and I would make things right. Hamid's response was one of concern about being manhandled and assaulted by the officers once they were alone somewhere. Upon hearing Hamid's concerns, I spoke loud enough for everyone in the chow hall to hear my admonishment, saying, "They better not put their hands on you, my brother." Capitalizing on the tension in the chow hall, and using a little flare of theatrics, I spoke to Hamid but looked the officers straight in the eyes as I spoke. My Black militant temperament momentarily surfaced to impact my every word. I was in full charge of the entire situation and had the fearful officers' undivided attention. We all understood I was the shot caller for the moment.

As Hamid was being escorted from the prison chow hall, I issued one final warning, letting it be known that the brother better not be harmed in the least. More than half the brothers fasting were not Muslims. I had invited them to the fast because I knew the religion of Islam built character and provided substance to one's life and I wanted to introduce them to all that I had discovered. These brothers would repeat my warning using the kind of vulgar language we often use when in a rage. Everyone continued to express their concern for Hamid's safety in loud and compelling voices until the officers exited the chow hall with him.

The next morning, the warden sent for me and I remember being surprised and a little apprehensive because this was highly unusual. During my incarceration, this would be the first time the warden ever called me into his office. I rarely saw him on the prison compound or had the occasion to address him one on one. He was the most invisible man in the joint. Being called out by the warden incited my curiosity. I imagined the interview would be about the incident with Hamid in the chow hall but had no idea as to how I factored into the warden's equation. I was not worried or overly concerned about retaliation, being an upright convict who could stand firmly behind his words, his actions, and his deeds.

The meeting with the warden was rather pleasant, considering the state of affairs between us. I immediately got the impression his true purpose for calling me out was the size me up and measure the extent of my temperament. Indirectly, I heard him saying thank you for not setting off a possible riot the night before in the prison chow hall. I could also see he was having difficulty reading my character—something I was good at hiding—and my extensive bad-boy prison record did not reflect the same man sitting before him. Reading my institutional record, the warden saw the history of a rowdy kid growing up in prison, but what he saw in front of him defied the contents of my prison record. My past and my present would never match up and the distance between the two would continue to increase as I continued to evolve.

When the conversation turned to the matter of Hamid, the warden made an unusual and perplexing statement. "I'm going to let you have your brother back," he bluntly stated. Hamid was placed on lockdown overnight and the warden was saying he would forgive and overlook the chow hall altercation. Forgiving and overlooking a confrontation between a staff member and a prisoner, a potentially explosive confrontation like what happened in the chow hall, was unheard of. I was not sure if the warden's intentions were meant to gratify me for the sake of maintaining the peace, or to pacify Hamid to calm him down. I left the warden's office thinking my keepers had finally seen the light and acknowledged I warranted due convict respect.

Hamid was promptly released from the lockup unit soon after my visit with the warden, only to land right back in segregation a couple of days later for another encounter with a prison official. The warden called me into his office for a second time to discuss Hamid and his defiant behavior. I thought the "I'm going to give you back your brother" statement was a mind shocker, but in our second meeting, the warden went to the extremes when asking me what he should do with Hamid under the current circumstances. Prison officials do not ask a prisoner how to discipline another prisoner. They simply lock the bad actor down in segregation and throw away the keys. The warden asking me what should be done with Hamid came as a very surprising inquiry, but it gave me an idea as to how I could assist Hamid.

The brother did not want to be at the Indiana State Farm and remained insistent on being transferred back to The State Prison. I would tell the warden, if he really wanted to solve his Hamid troubles, he needed to transfer Hamid back to where he came from or the brother was liable to burn down the whole joint. I delivered my assertion, making it clear that Hamid would continue to act out and there was absolutely no stopping him. Hamid got his transfer soon thereafter.

11. The Second Time Around

Soon after the incident in the chow hall with brother Hamid, I was transferred from The State Farm to the Westville Correctional Center in Westville, Indiana. With my prison sentence finally coming to an end after almost ten years of prison life, my keepers decided to transfer me to the pre-release center located in Westville. The pre-release program was supposed to help those being released make a smooth transition back into the free society. While the pre-release program was a good concept, it did not provide me with any useful information that would further my successful reentry into the free world. I had done my own homework in preparation for my release and probably could have taught the pre-release classes myself.

The Westville Correctional Center was once a state mental hospital for those with serious mental conditions and those deemed criminally insane. I had spent a couple of days at Westville back in 1975 when it was still a mental hospital. The court ordered that I undergo a psychiatric evaluation that was supposed to last ninety days but was abruptly shortened. This evaluation came as part of the temporary-insanity defense pursued by my attorney, Mr. Jay Given. With the exploding prison population reaching record highs, Westville was converted into a correctional facility housing low-level and mid-level offenders.

The pre-release unit was located in a building near the prison main entrance, completely unsecured and one step away from freedom. I could see and smell freedom all around me and it was truly a beautiful feeling. Prisoners housed in the pre-release unit did not come in contact with the other prisoners incarcerated at Westville who were confined behind the fences of the main prison compound. We had our own rooms, ate our meals in the staff dining room, and lived in a totally stress-free environment where we were treated like human beings, for once. Of course I particularly looked forward to mealtime, especially at lunch hour, because the female staff members would come through looking like eye candy to deprived eyes.

The pre-release director remembered me from my early days at the Indiana Reformatory, when I was just a youngster and he was a young prison counselor new to his job. The director and I got along great. He had seen enough of prison life to better understand my convict mentality and gave me free movement throughout the pre-release center. The director also made it possible for me to go into the main prison compound to attend the Friday Muslim services. No one before me was allowed to make such a move and I found myself a pioneer once again for the future benefit of Muslims. The brothers inside the institution were amazed that I accomplished this particular move, though I never gave the matter a second thought. I was a Muslim and wanted to participate in the obligatory Friday services. My desire and perseverance overcame any obstacles. These sorts of achievements over the years would make me realize I could succeed at anything I focused on, if it began with a strong desire and a workable plan.

As I ponder my life experience, never have I blamed anyone or anything for how my life has turned out, always taking full responsibility for my actions and living with the consequences. Yet, fertile situations were forever present to encourage a life of crime or returning to a criminal lifestyle. When I was fifteen, the possibility of me reforming before growing into a hardened and callous convict were feasible. Where I was a misled youth, our crime-and-punishment advocates would unconsciously push me further into a corrupt way of thinking and living by sending me to the school of higher criminal education behind prison walls. The vast majority of my criminal knowledge was acquired behind prison walls and while walking the prison yard. I can only wonder what would have happened had someone taken a more optimistic and concerned approach to dealing with me and the crime I committed, placing rehabilitation on an even level with my designated punishment.

The states and the federal government spent millions, throwing good money after bad, in an obsolete attempt to curtail the growing youth problems in the United States. Since I first went to prison at age fifteen, the juvenile delinquency problem has multiplied at an alarming rate, becoming more violent and rebellious along the way. In later years, the State of Florida would go as far as to sentence a nine-year-old Black kid to prison for life. I can imagine how that kid will eventually turn out. Does anyone really care? I can personally attest that sending a kid into an adult prison environment will never solve the youth problem that has allegedly become a national concern. The concept of incarcerating kids and losing the keys for a decade or two and expecting positive results is a ludicrous and asinine way of thinking. Lawmakers and those in judiciary positions of power fail to realize that these very same youths will one day emerge from behind prison walls to confront society, psychologically damaged and scarred for life in ways few will ever comprehend.

The same money spent on keeping me in an adult prison from age fifteen to age twenty probably would have been better spent by putting me in a correctional institution geared more toward improving my behavior and correcting my erroneous ideals about life in general. Consider my being exposed to a program for five years aimed at rehabilitation instead of being sent to an adult prison among hardened career-minded convicts where a life of crime is glorified by day and by night. We are often found to be a product of our environment and my prison experience would produce a hard-core convict. At the age of fifteen, the human mind is still very impressionable and one's character and behavior are easily influenced to the left or to the right. While I do not claim to have the answers to the U.S. youth problem, I can speak from personal experience. The one thing I can assert for certain is that putting punishment ahead of rehabilitating our troubled youth is a major mistake.

I emerged as damaged goods after serving my first five years in prison, a kid having grown up behind prison walls and knowing little more than convict life. Once again, I was on my home following a ten-year stretch under the yoke of incarceration; this time, I would emerge thoroughly indoctrinated with an outlaw's mentality. I would be released soon after my thirtieth birthday and with a total of fifteen years of prison time under my belt. Half of my life was already spent behind prison walls. I had open wounds and battle scars that were buried so deeply and suppressed to the point that I was unaware of the extent they would continue to affect my life for years to come.

In January of 1989, I was released from prison far from being reformed or rehabilitated, but having good intentions to do the right thing and live a clean and crime-free lifestyle. Still, I had subconsciously built a trap door in my psyche, and my aspirations to excel as an exceptional street hustler and player merely lay dormant, waiting for the moment to surface. The strength of my faith as a Muslim at that time would coexist with the street life mentality I willingly embraced. The trap door that I speak of was an avenue I had left open that led straight into the world of being a notorious career criminal.

I would violate and totally disregard the conditions of my parole the first day upon my release by leaving the state without permission. Katherine and I planned this move for weeks prior to my release, knowing all the time that the move could lead to a one-way ticket right back to prison for me, if discovered. Headstrong and still entertaining a contemptible opinion toward authority, I had no problem violating my parole to be with Kathy. I was released on a Friday and had to report to my parole officer the following Monday. Katherine lived in Minneapolis, Minnesota at the time, approximately 12 hours away by bus. The plan was for me to travel to Minneapolis by bus and the two of us would drive back together to make my parole-officer appointment that Monday.

The union between Kathy and I was like a much-needed remedy for an emotionally deprived soul. Something about the prison experience severely stunts emotional growth and development of those who spend years behind prison walls. Part of the heart seemingly grows dark, lifeless, and nonchalant. Katherine would awaken my dormant emotions, breathe life into my heart, and actually teach me how to love for the very first time in my life. I had always been something of a lady's man, having my first sexual experience at age twelve and being sexually active throughout my teenage years prior to incarceration. As a young horny teenager, I was having sex with grown women more than twice my age and indiscriminately engaged in joy sex with no string attached. Yet with Katherine, things were completely different. We did not just have sex; we made raw, passionate love on a profound level. In prison, I had read and studied everything I could get my hands on regarding pleasing a woman. Articles by women about the gratifications of a woman's sexual needs and desires were my preferring reading material. In fact, pleasing a woman was another one of those subjects I would study like a science and I would use all that I had learned to unlock the secrets to pleasing Kathy.

Being incarcerated all my adult life at this point in time had me so far behind in the ways of the free world that I was like a small child relearning how to walk. Kathy would take me by the hand like a loving and overprotective mother and show me how to navigate in the new world to which I returned home. I remember her taking me around Minneapolis, shopping at the malls, and how strange and out of place I felt, no longer confined by prison walls or security fences topped with bonecutting razor wire. Katherine had an incredible way of making me feel at ease, as if she fully understood the transition I was experiencing. With grace and gentleness, she would help me pick up the pieces of a broken life a young kid had left behind, assisting me in every step along the way, making the necessary adjustments to reacclimate myself back into a free society that seemingly left me way behind in every aspect. The manner in which she treated me was a constant reminder that I had something good within myself worthy of saving as a human being.

Kathy and I spent a beautiful and loving weekend together, enjoying ourselves like two newlyweds. The following Monday morning, we got up before the crack of dawn to make the eight-hour journey from Minneapolis to Gary, Indiana, for the scheduled meeting with my parole officer. I remember being a bit concerned and kind of worried about making it in time, but with a big reassuring smile, Katherine would calmly dissipate my unwarranted anxieties and I found solace in putting my trust in her. The ride was a pleasant trip, with us talking and holding hands all the way. Kathy and I had enjoyed good healthy conversations on paper through our correspondence and in person one-on-one, our conversations were even richer and more interesting.

We would arrive in Gary around one in the afternoon and drive directly to my parole officer's location on Fifth and Broadway. My visit with him took only a few minutes and amounted to no more than a general introduction and reminder of the rules and conditions of my release and what was expected of me as a parolee. I knew the drill because it was not my first rodeo and I merely went through the formalities. Before concluding the meeting, I explained to the parole officer that I had a fiancée who lived out of state and requested a travel pass to go see her. Having no problem with my request, he took down the pertinent information, filled out the necessary forms, and sent me on my way. The travel pass was for two weeks. The parole officer handed me the slip of paper approving my travel with a word of caution to stay out of trouble and report in to him upon arriving at my destination. The meeting was hassle-free and I got the impression that as long as I did my part, I would incur few problems with the parole officer, which is not always the case when being under parole supervision.

Kathy was sitting in a small waiting-room area while I met with my parole officer and when I emerged from the meeting, her inquisitive mind immediately wanted to know how the meeting went. I informed her that everything went well and that I had received permission to spend two weeks in Minneapolis with her. Needless to say, Katherine was elated and a broad smile played across her face as we rode the old-style elevator down to the ground floor and exited the building.

En route to my sister Mary's house, who lived in one of the roughest and toughest project communities in all of Gary, Indiana, I warned Kathy to remain vigilant at all times. In her innocence and naivety, she replied that things could not be all that bad in Gary. I totally ignored her comment and reiterated my position. I feared that her ignorance might get her trapped in an unpleasant situation because she had absolutely no idea what the streets of Gary could be like. Kathy had never experienced anything similar to the neighborhood in which I grew up. She was the perfect example of a small-town girl with a small-town-girl mentality. In my old hood, she stood about a snowball's chance in hell of walking one city block without becoming a crime victim. I made it my sole responsibility to protect her at all costs and took her by the hand like a small child, as she had done for me in Minneapolis.

My sister Mary and her four kids welcomed Kathy with a warm embrace off the top. They genuinely liked her and it showed. The baby girl in the family and Katherine especially seemed to bond almost immediately and became inseparable. Every time I turned around, they were cuddled up together, giggling like two close and old friends. They seemingly had a kindred spirit and, from my perspective, it was a beautiful thing to watch.

While Katherine got better acquainted with my family, I made a call to George, the brother I considered my godfather. George had given his permission that I could live with him as part of the conditions of my release. I called him to bring him up to speed regarding my release and the moves I had made since coming home. As a kid growing up in Gary, George was the most supportive male figure in my life and would do anything to assist and help me. The brother was a pure intellect and this alone greatly influenced me in my early days as a youth. Talking to him on the phone following my release from prison, I found that I could now easily meet him on an intellectual level. In some ways, I had even surpassed my childhood mentor and godfather, sharing with him my knowledge of Islam and correcting his misunderstandings about the religion. The only thing of significance brother George would ever ask from me was a copy of The Holy Quran, and I gave him the personal one I treasured most.

As the conversation between George and I concluded, I told him I would be over to his place after visiting my sister and her family. He agreed to wait around for me. Kathy and I spent the night with George and were back on the road to Minneapolis the following day. By this time, I had lived in the South, on the East Coast, and in the Midwest, but the Twin Cities and the Land of 10,000 Lakes was definitely my kind of town. The winters were hard, yet beautiful, and the spring brought everything back to life, picture perfect. Being a natural-born

Aquarius, true to my nature, I loved being around the water and the Land of 10,000 Lakes had water and lakes everywhere. I decided then and there that I would make Minneapolis my city to start anew.

My brother David had lived in Minnesota for several years prior to my arrival, and being the people person I never was, he knew everyone. He educated me to the street life in Minneapolis and introduced me to all his friends, showed me all the popular hangouts, and schooled me on the different players and hustlers. My brother David knew me better than anyone else in the world, and although my intentions were to live the straight and crime free life, Dave knew otherwise. What my big brother did not realize at the time was that he was preparing me to eventually take the Twin Cities by storm and there would be no stopping me.

After my two-week travel pass expired, I applied for and received a second one, this time explaining to my parole officer that I wanted to lay the foundation for having my parole transferred to Minnesota. My parole officer agreed to this tentative plan, stating he would contact his counterpart in the Minnesota Department of Parole for the Minneapolis area to arrange the transfer from his end. The condition was that Minnesota would have to accept my application before I could make the move. My parole officer and I agreed that Gary, Indiana, was not an ideal place for a person in my position to get a righteous start if I sincerely wanted to stay out of prison.

I had no problem finding a job right away in Minneapolis, my criminal record never being an issue. Life and my future were beginning to look rather promising until one day, about a month down the road, I got a call saying my transfer had been denied and I had a week to report back to Indiana. Determined to keep my head up and struggle against the odds, I returned to Gary unsure of my direction from there but possessing enough fortitude to keep my confidence from withering. I had a place to lay my head with George, but other than that I stood on shaky ground. My money was limited and would not stretch very far and there were few job opportunities available. While staying with George was planned as a temporary arrangement, I knew I could lay my head there as long as necessary. Still, I did not want to wear out my welcome. With too much self-pride, I would not allow myself to fall into a situation where I had to depend on George for anything more than a place to live.

The only thing I can recall about my early days upon returning to Gary was how I walked from one place to the next, putting in applications looking for work, all to no avail. Every night, I went through the employment section of the newspaper and made a list of the places I would go the following day. One night, I ran across an advertisement for Kelly's Temporary Work Agency and decide to give them a try. I ended up getting a three-week job assignment working in the warehouse with Sears Department Store making minimum wage, a far cry from the millions I dreamed about while in prison. All my big prison dreams seemed out of reach at that moment.

Talking to Kathy on the phone one day, perhaps a month following my return to Gary, she informed me of her decision to relocate and join me. I was not crazy about the idea but reluctantly accepted her decision because it was the only way we could be together under the circumstances. When Katherine was ready to make her move from Minnesota, I went to my parole officer and told him I needed permission to go assist her with the move, asserting my position in such a manner that I was crystal clear that, with or without his permission, I was going, and my coming to consult with him was a mere courtesy call. My approach could sometimes be so defiant and aggressive when confronting those in positions of authority that my actions often questioned who was in charge. In prison, I had learned the art of subliminal manipulation of my keepers who were conditioned to take and follow orders. The most important thing to always remember is to leave them room to save face. My parole officer did his thing by giving me an empty lecture about it being the last time he would grant me a travel pass. I listened to his rhetoric knowing the man was just going through the motions. I had played this same game many times before in dealing with my keepers.

Given another one week travel pass, once again I headed off to the Land of 10,000 Lakes. The week would go rather quickly and before I knew it, Kathy and I were on the road with a loaded rental U-Haul and our old Mercury Monarch in tow. Little did I realize just how much moving to Gary would bring stress and disorder into our relationship,

nor did I realize at the time how psychologically and emotionally damaged prison had left me. I had trained and conditioned myself to live and
process things a certain way behind prison walls for so many years that
undoing my convict mentality did not happen quickly. Today, I still possess the vestiges of these behaviors that are a direct result of my prison
experience, only now I can better recognize them and keep them in perspective.

I do not recall what the first real argument and verbal confrontation
between Katherine and I was about or the circumstances surrounding it,
but at the time the psychological scars left from my prison experience
were raw and unchecked, instantly coming to the surface. I went straight
into my shell of seclusion and did not say more than a dozen words to
her for two whole days. On the third day, Kathy was packing her things
and ready to leave me. In prison, my sole defense against being hurt
emotionally was to completely close down. Arguments behind prison
walls could easily lead to a fatal confrontation, and many times I had
resolved such problems by cutting people off permanently. For years, I
walked right past individuals as if they did not exist once having heated
words with them, never compromising or apologizing for anything I
said or did. The years of practice and living this way eventually created
a man with dormant emotions and few communication skills when it
came to my feelings. Whenever I felt under attack or threatened, I auto-
matically closed down and could not be reached.

I remember taking Kathy out to the beachfront area of Lake Michigan in Gary, where I apologized for my behavior. I tried explaining to
her what I felt, yet at the time I did not fully understand the root cause
of my problem. Still, I attempted to share with her the inner struggles
with which I wrestled. Kathy encouraged me to talk with her so we
could work through our problems in the future and I agreed, but the
psychological conditioning I suffered had deep roots and could not so
easily be undone. If Katherine was not the loving and caring person she
demonstrated herself to be over and over again, I never would have
emerged from my bottomless shell. She gradually got me in touch with
my feelings by forgiving me and showing love. By example, she taught
me the essence of loving someone through the good and bad times.

Katherine and I got occasional work through the temp agency, but never enough to sustain us or keep us ahead of the bills. The job assignments were infrequent, low paying, and often short-term fill-in work. One night when lying in bed together pondering the never-ending task of how to make ends meet, we came up with the idea to sell candy door to door. As a highly decorated Girl Scout, Kathy confided that she had done very well selling such things. As I reflect back to those days, I see how Kathy and I were literally trying some of everything to legally make a few dollars. Taking our last money, we went to Chicago—less than an hour drive from Gary—and directly purchased an assortment of chocolates and candy bars from Brach's Candy Company. We returned from Chicago late in the day, having enjoyed the many sights and attractions the city of Chicago was known for, spending the day leisurely exploring this awesome and lively city.

The following day, we embarked on our new business venture, agreeing to let Kathy do the door-to-door work because of the neighborhood we selected: a middle class all-White community in Merrillville. I sat in the car while she made her rounds and from the start she appeared to be doing fairly well, making sales at better than half the doors she knocked on. Then suddenly, the Merrillville police mysteriously showed up, parking directly behind me. Both officers got out of their squad car, one staying just a little behind the Monarch I sat in, and the other approached the driver's side requesting my identification. I was calm through it all and immediately recognized the situation for what it was. No doubt, one of the neighbors, seeing a Black man alone hanging around in their lily-White neighborhood, had called the police. As the officer approached, I rolled down the car window and asked, before he could speak, if there was a problem. He replied there was no problem, but they had received a call and had to check me out. He went on to ask if I had some ID, which I produced and handed to him through the open car window.

By this time, I looked up to see Katherine hurrying in our direction as she witnessed the situation unfold from a distance. She arrived as a second squad car showed up on the scene. I just sat there with a growing sense of contempt and anger building inside. This incident was taking place merely because I was a Black man in an overly protective White community and we all knew it. Kathy pounced on them like a lioness, demanding that they explain what was going on. I could only half hear most of the conversation between them, but from Kathy's facial expression, I could tell she was not buying the bullshit they were trying to sell her. Kathy was furious, having reached the same conclusion as me regarding the cause behind the situation. I had never seen the mild-mannered Katherine become so angry as she related to me the verbal exchange she had with the officers. Of course they denied her charge of racial profiling and claimed, "they were only doing their job." The reality of this experience was new to Kathy and she took it rather hard, but this was the kind of White world I had known all my life.

We had to leave the area, they informed her, because it was against the law to sell our goods in Merrillville without a permit, which was a lie. When the scene finally played out, Kathy angrily walked over to the car and got in. One squad car had already driven off while the other waited until Kathy and I pulled away before following us a short distance, then turning off in another direction. Of course this obstacle did not discourage us. We simply went back to the drawing board and came up with another plan. By now, Kathy knew her way around the city rather well, so we decided to let her go out alone the next day.

At this point, I seriously wanted to lead a clean lifestyle. Although I occasionally hung out with old friends who were deeply involved in the flourishing Gary drug business, I resisted the temptation to get involved myself. Those who knew me best because of my reputation repeatedly offered me a seat at the table and an equal share of the profits. I would refuse time and time again, mainly because I was uncomfortable with the idea of selling drugs as a Muslim.

Kathy and I pursued our little candy-selling venture, yet the profits and turnover were not enough to sustain us. The little business was never meant to be a lucrative operation by which we could become rich and retire. For the most part, we were only doing something instead of doing nothing. Katherine eventually received a call for a new job assignment in Chicago. For her to get back and forth to work, I decided to sell a shotgun I had purchased for house protection. I had also purchased a small-caliber handgun for Kathy's personal protection soon after moving to Gary some months before. Owning or possessing a firearm was in direct violation of my parole, as well as against the law because I was a felon, but there was absolutely no way I intended to live in Dodge City Gary with no means of protecting Katherine and myself. That was the bottom line.

Contacting Jessie, a long-time friend and codefendant on the first case for which I went to prison, I made arrangement to sell the weapon. My boy Jessie and former partner in crime was still deep in the mix of things on the streets and knew where to go and who to see. But as fate would have it, I was arrested with the shotgun and taken to jail, charged with violating my parole. I was remanded back into the custody of the Indiana Department of Corrections. Perhaps a month after my arrest, I appeared before the parole board for a ratification hearing to determine if my parole would be revoked or reinstated. I remember having the kind of nervous energy I get when in combat mode, having nothing to lose but everything to gain. Spiritually, my confidence ran high. Subconsciously I knew the odds were stacked against me, yet my faith told me where there is a will there is a way; if the will is strong enough, the way will eventually open.

I had only one strategic game plan at my parole board hearing: tell the truth and play off the facts, and also play on the heart and empathy of the parole board members. I made my argument to the parole board all about protecting Katherine at all costs in the dangerous environment Gary was known for. Once again, I was in rare form, hitting timely punch lines and holding the full attention of the board members. These people had heard every story and excuse beneath the sun given by parolees, but my words were fresh and new. The move proved golden as the male members nodded their heads, approving of my position to protect Katherine under the circumstances, and the two female members appeared captivated in a romance story. Kathy would be called in front of the parole board as a witness on my behalf and her performance with real tears would seal the deal. Together, the two of us had accomplished what others would have given up on as being impossible. My parole was reinstated and I was ordered to be released.

12. Man on the Run

Before I was released, Kathy and I learned that my parole officer had petitioned the board to reconsider their decision, citing that the federal Alcohol, Tobacco, and Firearms Agency planned to indict me on weapons charges. Kathy and I found it hard to believe that my parole officer attempted such a back-stabbing move. Instead of helping me, he tried to undermine my release. I made a mental note to make an effort to change parole officers at my first opportunity because I feared the man would harbor a vendetta. I got out of prison on a Friday, went to visit an old friend still in prison on Sunday, and the following Monday my parole officer gave me 24 hours to turn myself in at the county jail. He was again placing me under parole violation and sending me back to prison for visiting my old childhood friend, Little Ant.

I vividly recall thinking to myself, "He got to be a damn fool; Who the fuck do he think I am." Telling me to go lock myself up was tantamount to telling me to place a loaded gun in my mouth and pull the trigger. Having an outlaw and gangster attitude since I was knee high, the catching had to come before the hanging was my final word. Kathy and I went home and packed everything we could fit into our car and hit the road for Minnesota that very day. While my parole officer was probably writing his report to have my parole revoked, I was already long gone.

In Minneapolis, I hit the streets where I immediately found myself hustling and reverting back to my old ways. Reluctantly, I traveled in the Minneapolis drug world until I raised enough money for Kathy and me to make a fresh start and get place to live. Yet, I quickly learned that street-level drug dealing definitely was not my forte or my style of hustle. In prison many years before, I had made a firm decision that if I returned to a life in crime, it would be on a totally different level. While incarcerated, I learned a great deal about white-collar crimes that were nonviolent and produced huge profits with low risk. I favored the finesse of a thinking-man's game over the rough hustle of being a petty street criminal, and my time had arrived.

Kathy and I relocated to St. Cloud, Minnesota, a small and low-key college town and a place I could hide in plain sight. We got a little apartment using a fictitious name and did the same with all our utility bills to cover our trail. I was a man on the run from the law and although the authorities had not started the man hunt for me, the heat was inevitably forthcoming, so we planned in advance for it. Our apartment was no more than a crash pad. We had no furniture and slept on an air mattress that folded in on us like a hot dog bun once the air leaked out. All that would suddenly change dramatically in a matter of weeks.

I eventually went to work putting together a bank-fraud scheme that extended from Minnesota to Maine and down south as far as Georgia. I sent Katherine off to St. Paul to find us another place because our apartment would be my starting point and ground zero when the dominoes eventually collapsed. In the beginning, I worked with what little I had and circled my wagons as best I could for damage control. Later, armed with a stronger bankroll, I put together more elaborate bank-fraud schemes the feds would follow to a dead end as planned.

For years, I had lived behind prison walls with my dreams of one day being free and enjoying the good life, living large and luxuriously. I was now well on my way to fulfilling those dreams and turning my prison fantasies into reality. Any time I went out to work my bank-fraud scheme, I scored no less than twenty thousand dollars a day, which was a great deal of money to me. But it was not even a fraction of the kind of money that would eventually flow through my hands as I established my position in the underworld as a street hustler and player on the streets of Minneapolis, Minnesota.

I made Minneapolis my power base and I carved out my territories with the same finesse and networking skills I employed while in prison. With a subtle approach, I imposed my style of influence in one of Minneapolis' more popular night clubs where all the drug dealers, players, and so-called high rollers regularly hung out. In building what would become a very lucrative criminal operation, I recruited Larome, the night club's head bouncer. Larome was born and raised in Minneapolis. He knew everyone and was a larcenist at heart. Yet my biggest coup came when I won the affections of Victoria, the head waitress. Victoria was a strikingly beautiful lady and every player in town wanted her, but she repeatedly rejected their advances. Seeing how others were in hot pursuit of Victoria, my strategy was to ignore her and pretend that I did not acknowledge her raw beauty. When I did make my move on her, I approached appealing to her intellect and the things that interested her. I often had lunch at the club. The club was my meeting spot and the club was where I hung out at night and did my business. I sat back and observed Victoria for weeks and got to know her, always showing respect and never pushing up on her. Once I had established the groundwork to distinguish myself clearly from all the rest, I turned on my southern charm and my polished class.

To a large extent, I believed my style and mode of operation was far superior to that of most street hustlers. I saw a weakness in the vast majority of them that indicated to me that they possessed a great deal of bluster but very little substance. Although I genuinely liked and was definitely attracted to Victoria, I pursued her mostly as a personal challenge to succeed where others had failed. The exceptionally beautiful curly-red-haired Portuguese was built like a model; she was the total package and my kind of woman. Larome told me I did not stand a chance with Victoria, telling me how he and others had tried to make moves on her, all of them being repeat failures. His opinion, as I perceived it, was a mere assumption that did not apply to me.

In the early days when laying the foundation for what would become my network of criminal activity, many thought I was a drug dealer. Having indulged in street-level drug dealing in the past, I had a strong aversion to selling drugs on street corners and I did not possess the mentality and unforgiving nature of a true drug dealer. My conscience troubled me and I felt a strong sense of guilt because, on the street level, I could clearly see the damage drugs were doing in the community. This created a major internal conflict for me. Yet, I was on the run from the law and was living in the dark world of the street life, which would eventually lead to dealing in drugs as well as other organized criminal activities.

I built my Minneapolis operation around the nightclub with Larome as my right-hand man and Victoria as my main woman. I moved through the club like I was a silent partner and received the celebrity treatment whenever I showed up on crowded nights. While I was surrounded by people vying for my time and attention, treating me like the man of the hour, I felt so alone and out of place. For the most part, I knew everyone around me had selfish motivations for wanting to get close to me, and I could trust no one. But more importantly, I was far from being happy or at peace with myself.

Katherine rented us a plush loft apartment in downtown St. Paul and furnished it throughout with brand new furniture. The apartment was perfectly located for a man on the run from the law in an obscure building one did not notice until they stopped to look it over. The building was newly renovated and converted into loft apartments with rather creative floor plans. Our apartment had three floors: the kitchenette was on the first level, the living room on the second, and the bedroom on the third. I could stand in the bedroom and look down on the floors below and the spacious opening of the apartment's design made it appear much larger than it really was. The bedroom also had a skylight directly above the bed, easily accessible to the roof and an ideal escape route. The classy loft apartment also fit perfectly in my prison dreams of being free and living large.

True, it takes money to make money, and I had accumulated enough financial resources to extend and improve my bank-fraud scheme. Taking my game on the road, I crisscrossed the country setting up dummy corporations and ripping them off like I had a license. I found it truly amazing how easy it was and how freely banks willingly accommodated me in executing my bank-fraud scheme. The banks made it so easy to exploit them that I became complacent and relaxed some of the safeguards I had in place. I put together a viable plan and it was working so well that I grew overconfident, to my own demise.

I chose bank fraud as my hustle and my cash generator because it rested less troubling on my conscience as a Muslim. I reasoned with myself, saying bank fraud was a victimless crime; they were insured and could easily absorb the loss. Because of my predisposition to a criminal lifestyle, I knew I was very susceptible to eventually embracing it again. Even as a criminal-minded individual, I had established principles by which I would govern and conduct myself. I would not rob, steal, or take malicious advantage of the poor and the helpless. My only targets would be the banks, financial institutions, and large multimillion-dollar businesses. I would openly refuse to participate in petty nickel and dime criminal behavior and activities. If you dropped your wallet, I was that guy who was more likely to chase you down and return it rather than keep it. I could be trusted with your life and your property and my word had iron and carried weight. Yes, I was living the American bad-boy life, and to a large extent, it was the hand life had dealt me and many like me. However, I was playing it according to my own dictates.

In the years to come, I traveled the entire United States and put in work with no misgivings about what I was doing. I had little or no respect for man-made laws because I saw too much hypocrisy in how they were applied. This was how I justified my actions superficially, yet deep down inside where it really mattered, I knew this was no more than an excuse to live as I was living. I would push forward by convincing myself that the end justified the means and somehow I could make things right by turning a negative into a positive by the end of the day.

Being a rebel at heart and no longer under the yoke of incarceration, I was both physically free and had the freedom and the bankroll to go anywhere and do anything my heart desired. I was not a materialistic person by a long shot, nor did I possess an unholy lust for the almighty dollar. I saw money as a tool to be used in a capitalist society where literally everything appeared to be for sale at the right price. To me, money served only one purpose; it provided real freedom to enjoy life to the fullest. Against all odds, I was determined to be one of the haves and not a has not. Many will question and fail to understand my thinking at that hour. Yet then again, I don't expect people to understand the path I have traveled until they take the first step on the same journey.

I dressed professionally in a suit and tie when out on the road taking care of business and when hanging out at the club. After purchasing a nice clean Cadillac Eldorado Biarritz, the only thing I really spent money on was clothes. I dressed to reflect success as well as to impress because I fully understood the power of the image and how to project my desired image on the streets. From all the reading I had done over the years while in prison, I developed a connoisseur-like appetite for the finer things in life. I had a natural inclination for being classy, having class, and demonstrating class in how I carried and conducted myself. Perhaps the only time my extravagant side came out was when going out to dinner and playing my role in the club. I ran up huge bar tabs in the clubs I frequented and dined at the finest restaurants in town as if money was not a thing to me. I had no concerns about the amount on my bill.

Everything was going beautifully and according to plan. I had a full-court press on the streets of Minneapolis and there was no looking back; I was deadly serious about my work because my survival and freedom depended on it. I did not acknowledge anyone as competition on the streets because I was operating on a totally different level and saw most of the street new breed of so-called players as fakes. As far as I was concerned, they were in the way, gave a black eye to the game, and had no real street credibility. To me, those boys were in my orbit playing checkers when in fact the game in play was chess. I thought of them as one dimensional; they could only sell drugs, and without drugs to sell, they would literally starve to death and never have a dollar in their pockets.

Once again, I was compelled to regroup and put a blanket of protection around Katherine after her freedom fell under jeopardy. Against my better judgment, I allowed Kathy to use my bogus checking accounts to go shopping prior to phasing out the account and moving on to the next one. The girlfriend of a business associate would take items back to the store for a cash refund Katherine had purchased. The authorities would follow the breadcrumbs straight back to her, and although she knew very little about Kathy personally, she told everything she knew and the threat came too close to home. Katherine had purchased hundreds of dollars of clothing and other necessities for the girl and her young daughter in exchange for driving Katherine around while shopping. Desperate for a taste of drugs, the girl back-tracked on Kathy and returned the purchases for drug money.

Uncertain as to how much damage was done, I would take no chances and moved Kathy all the way to the East Coast. Together, we travelled to Connecticut where my mother currently lived and began the process of finding another safe house. Neither of us wanted to live in Connecticut, so we made the short drive to Boston, Massachusetts to check out that location. I genuinely liked Boston as a beautiful flourishing city filled with potential and opportunity, but there was a thick and apparent racist element in the air that I strongly abhorred. After spending several days apartment hunting and finding nothing we both agreed was appropriate, I gave Katherine money to find us a place and left her the Caddy to get around. I got a flight back to Minneapolis. It was my job to clean out our loft and move us out. I had no reservations about my own safety at that moment because I had significant fake identity in my pocket. My driver's license was state issued and the police had to actually run my fingerprints to determine my true identity. Federal authority would later assert during a court hearing that I should be denied a cash bond because I could disappear on them and only by chance would I be apprehended again. True, I did have my disappearing act together and was an avid believer that the catching definitely had to come before the hanging.

Driving across the country alone proved to be good therapy for me. Not only did it give me time to do some serious thinking and soul searching, it also represented the epitome of freedom and being free to go wherever I pleased. Being deprived of my individual liberties for most of my life since my teenage years, I never felt freer than when driving across the country taking care of my business. Katherine had found us a new place in Portsmouth, New Hampshire, and I can vividly recall how free and in control of my own life I felt during my trip to reunite with her. My baby sister Geneva, who assisted Kathy with the apartment hunt, had told me I would love the New Hampshire state motto. She refused to tell me what it was and I remember being so eager to find out. Once I crossed the borderline into New Hampshire and read the state welcome sign, "Live free or die," my entire being exploded with laughter. My sister was right. I did love the state motto and it reflected my thinking at that hour. Being a man on the run with surrendering never considered an option and the state motto was truly my attitude: live free or die.

Katherine rented us a condominium in an upscale middle-class neighborhood with a stream running along the backyard. In general, the condo was a very likeable place and would serve our purpose, but it would be the fireplace that won me over. I would often build a fire in the fireplace and just relax, allowing my troubles to dissipate. Looking into the flickering flames of the fire and listening to the crackling of burning firewood, I would also plot and plan my next moves. Being what I call a mental person, I was always in the workshop of my mind, dissecting and analyzing all aspects of my life and making adjustments where proven necessary. On the street—no matter the foe—if you could not out-think me, then stay out of my way. This was my disposition in my business dealings in the dark world of the street life. It was the thinker in me and my innate clairvoyance to recognize potential danger that kept me alive in prison. The thinker stayed ahead of the game and kept the odds in his favor as much as possible: that was me.

I was forged in the furnace of the circumstances under which I had lived and my overall life experiences had produced what I had become. I had no complaints then and have no complaints now. To the contrary, I was living life my way. I was not a gangster, yet I had gangster in me from my youngers days. I was not a mere street hustler either. I was more like a businessman with no limitations in my tool kit on the streets as a hustler. Growing up in the red-light district of Gary, Indiana, my initial impression of a Black man being successful was what I saw in my environment. The only one seeming to be living large around me were the street players, and they left a lasting influence. With no one to tell me differently or redirect my erroneous way of thinking, my ambitions of being successful in the street life would settle and grow roots.

In my prison environment, those ambitions were fertilized and nurtured into full maturity and would eventually grow wings. All the elements were properly aligned for me to pursue a life in crime and I fully embraced the opportunity when the time came.

I was very fond of the twin cities, Minneapolis and St. Paul, but Portsmouth, New Hampshire would outshine them both. Located on the Atlantic ocean coastline, Portsmouth was a serene and naturally beautiful town. I found the people to be warm, friendly, and rather unbiased. I remember one occasion in particular when I stopped to buy firewood at a local garden nursery and the owner invited me to a cup of coffee and to meet his friends. I came to learn through our conversation that these men had been discussing me and were curious about who I was and what I did for a living. Being one of the very few African Americans in town, they somehow concluded I was an Air Force pilot with the Pease Air Force Base. When asked about my line of work, I informed them I was a private investigator. My cover story came across sounding more appealing and interesting than being a pilot and my little audience ate it up. The people in general treated me with decency and with respect. I often got the impression that I was a novelty of sorts who was warmly welcomed.

Katherine and I lived comfortably and stress free in Portsmouth, New Hampshire, yet due to the legal issues hounding us both, the threat to our freedom would continue to linger. I spent the next three weeks in New Hampshire, including Christmas. We invited my mother to spend the holiday with Kathy and me, spoiling her, showering her with gifts, and showing her a great time. A woman who never had much and whose entire life had been a struggle, I wanted badly to provide for her and make it possible for Mom to enjoy her later years. Having my mother with me that Christmas was also special because it would be the first time since age fourteen that we spent the holidays together and my first Christmas not incarcerated in over fifteen years. I went all out, dining at the finest restaurants in town and sparing no expense when indulging my mother's pleasures.

I hit the road again following the Christmas holidays to put in more work on my banks. I had several projects on the drawing board waiting to reach fruition and I was ready to strike them to replenish my bankroll. Before leaving town, I purchased Katherine a new Mazda 626 as a Christmas present. The vehicle was fully loaded and Katherine loved the car on sight. I was in the habit of counting my money in thousand-dollar increments and kept a cookie jar full of thousand-dollar bundles for household expenses, which I also left for Katherine's use. With Kathy situated, I caught a flight to the Midwest to further my bank-fraud schemes. While in Portsmouth, I also laid the foundation to execute my bank-fraud operation in Maine and Connecticut, setting up business accounts to rip off later. I currently had projects in the works in several other states, maturing simultaneously from Portland, Oregon to Portland, Maine. It was time to harvest the fruits of my bank-fraud schemes that were ripe for the plucking and I was ready to get back on the fast track of my paper chase.

Between bank-fraud missions, I eventually got involved in the drug-market business, buying cocaine in wholesale quantities to resell through the sources I cultivated in the Twin City area. I knew many people from Gary, Indiana, who used and sold drugs in Minneapolis and St. Paul, so the market was readily accessible and my bad-boy reputation on the streets made it easier to establish my game plan. In those days, my involvement in the drug business was no more than a matter of seizing an opportunity right in front of me. I was often asked if I had cocaine product for sale because many wrongly assumed drugs were my hustle to getting money. On one occasion in particular, during a cocaine drought in Minneapolis, no one could answer the call of supply and demand. I had strong connections in the drug underworld on the streets of Gary, so I reached out to them and got enough product to break into the Twin Cities drug market.

Generally speaking, my interest in selling drugs at that time was so indifferent that making a profit was of no real concern to me. My heart was not in it and I never fully embraced the idea as a positive move. The reality of being a drug dealer and the extreme damage drugs inflicted would perpetually haunt my conscience and vex my soul. Once again, I devised one excuse after another to justify my involvement in the drug business. I reasoned that people would continue to use drugs whether I sold them or not, so I might as well push the product too. I also entertained the concept that selling the untaxed drugs was not the problem; rather, the real issue was that people were abusing the product. These were all weak excuses with no true substance and subconsciously I knew it. Yet, my ultimate justification came in the form of using the drug myself, saying how could I sell a product to others that I myself would not consume.

I cultivated a tight clientele of customers who were mostly street hustlers and players like me who used cocaine recreationally, both men and women. My customers were found in the after-hour joints, in the illegal gambling houses, the strip clubs, and massage parlors. My clientele also included individuals from all walks of life, from professional businesspeople to low-level drug dealers. I would spend my nights moving through the streets checking my traps and club hopping, putting in work until the sun came up. Everywhere I went on my nightly excursions was like one continuous cocaine-snorting party. My clientele liked the way I handled business because I kept things drama free and provided quality and quantity with no trickery or games involved. I often heard my customers say they would rather wait for me than shop somewhere else because they appreciated my trusting approach to doing business.

The vast majority of my clientele were women: the women working in the strip clubs, massage parlors, and call girls. I did not intentionally design things to unfold as they did, yet by the same token, I found the arrangement to be very much to my liking. After being incarcerated and surrounded by men most of my life, the last thing I wanted was the company of another man. I thoroughly enjoyed the company and attention I got from the women with whom I dealt, especially the exotic dancers who all gathered around my table whenever I made my showing. Some would pursue me harder than I pursued them, making mixing business with pleasure inevitable. I was extremely picky when it came to the women I allowed into my inner circle or with whom I shared a sexual relationship. Still I had my share of flings and one-night stands. For the most part, a woman had to fit my stereotypical image of beauty to get my attention and possess a degree of intelligence to keep it. With

Katherine and Victoria in my life as my main two women, I already had a winning combinations and two of Minnesota's finest.

I continued to rotate in and out of the Twin Cities, staying put and moving while getting money hand over fist everywhere I went around the country with my bank-fraud game. Never staying in one place more than a few days, I was constantly on the move, putting in work and living out a prison fantasy to one day become ghetto rich and a street boss among my peers on the block. Relentless and driven to success by any means necessary, I possessed all the makings of accomplishing anything I put my mind to, yet used my talents in a self-defeating manner.

13. The Fall from Grace

Returning to New Hampshire after executing one of my bank-fraud scheme runs and exhausted from long nights of partying, drinking, and snorting cocaine, I rested for a couple of days before Kathy and I hit the road in her new Mazda 626, heading south for Alabama. I had promised my younger brother John and my mother that I would travel to Alabama to attend John's graduation. I could not miss this grandiose occasion under any circumstances because John would be the first of my siblings to attend college and graduate, and of course I was very proud of him. To me, John's accomplishments represented the power of perseverance, setting goals under adversity, and reaching them through determination. In my younger brother's achievements, I also saw another important element: a person can rise above poverty if they possessed the will to succeed. Born into a life laden with multiple disadvantages can still produce great minds, and a substantial education is the key to unlocking a promising future for African American youths struggling against the odds.

My brother John could easily have fallen victim to the negative environment of Gary, Indiana, as happens too often. He could have followed in my footsteps from the bad example I had set or surrendered to the many other darker influences that plagued our community. Instead, he discovered the strength and courage to resist and commanded the innate will within to rise above it all. I had two other younger brothers who would escape the many pitfalls of the ghetto and housing projects in which we grew up. My brother Kelvin would enlist in the Army and my baby brother Major Lee signed on with the Navy, both proving life was more about the decisions we made and not the unfortunate circumstances into which we were born. I knew very well the odds my brothers faced and were compelled to overcome. I applaud their fortitude and I'm proud of the men they emerged to become. During my incarceration, one of my greatest fears was the strong possibility that one day my brothers would join me behind prison walls. Today, I am elated and thrilled to the bone that neither of my younger brothers succumbed to the empty suggestions surrounding them that led straight to jail or an early grave.

My brother John attended Tuskegee University in Alabama and graduated as a promising electrical engineer, highly sought by General Electric and Company upon graduation. Tuskegee University is a well-known historically African American university, perhaps most famously known for the Tuskegee Airmen. Until I actually visited the university, I had a shallow and nonchalant opinion of the school because I considered Booker T. Washington to be an Uncle Tom and house Negro. Booker T. Washington was one of the founders of Tuskegee and I strongly disagreed with many of his positions after studying his status in Black history and his philosophy as an African American leader during that time. I got the impression that Booker T. Washington was attempting to create a class of professional Uncle Toms out of our people. In reality, and considering the totality of the circumstances, there was a sense of genius to Mr. Booker T. Washington's approach to elevating his fellow African American brothers through education. Regardless of whether I respected his personal philosophy or not, I had no choice but to respect the results of the work he put in when establishing Tuskegee University.

The miseducation of the African American, as expressed by the historian Carter G. Woodson in his book *The Mis-Education of the Negro,* was a real concern to me. To me, Mr. Woodson—considered the father of Black history—boldly asserted that African Americans lose their true identity when attending White institutions of higher learning. From personal experience, I found his assertions to be largely accurate. I have witnessed firsthand certain individuals I knew who went off to all-White universities and came back thinking they were too good to be Black, yet too Black to be White. Brain dead to their Black heritage and culturally deficient, they came home looking down on their humble beginnings disparagingly and harbored contempt toward the Black community.

Uncertain of what Tuskegee would produce, meeting some of my brother John's friends and fraternity brothers was another eye-opening experience. I learned that John was a member of his school fraternity, an order some perceived as an asinine group of college kids partying throughout their school days and being immature. Nothing could be further from the truth. Rather, these fraternal orders cultivated camaraderie and life-long bonds of friendship and loyalty with purpose. Hanging out with these brothers in Tuskegee, I witnessed a showing of brotherly love that humbled me and caused me to wish I had gone to college and been part of such a positive experience. The young men had their act together, were well-balanced, and had a real direction in life. I found myself thinking we would be properly represented in the days ahead if the African American future was in the hands of these intelligent and gifted young men. I say this mainly because I fully understood why it was once against the law in the United States to teach the African American slave how to read and write. I also fully understood the power of knowledge and getting an adequate education and those brothers were living examples of what a solid education will produce.

Mr. Bill Cosby would be the honorary Master of Ceremony for Tuskegee University's graduating class of 1991 and he conducted the affair with a rich mixture of seriousness and humor. He kept the audience laughing and lively without a dull moment, in a typical Bill Cosby fashion. Mr. Cosby had something amusing and clever to say to every graduating student as they approached the podium to receive their degrees. I remember one Caucasian student being called up to the podium and Bill Cosby playfully looked past him, giving the impression he expected someone else to appear. Finally, pretending to take notice of the White student standing in front of him, he said "You're a long ways from home, ain't you?" The crowd erupted with laughter and the White student seemed to enjoy every minute of being the center of attention. Mr. Cosby treated the young man like family and proceeded to address him accordingly and the audience would warmly embrace him as one of their own. As I recall, this young man was the only White student graduating in the 1991 class.

Like I said, Mr. Cosby had something witty and clever to say with each student receiving their degree. I don't remember the exact exchange between him and my brother John, but I vividly recall how well my brother confidently held his own. John had a sense of humor that was rare in the family and I remember him trading verbal comic jabs with Mr. Cosby that had the entire house in an uproar. The exchange, done with a good nature, ended with Mr. Cosby and John sharing in final humorous remarks as my brother received his degree and exited the stage. In that instant, I recognized that my younger brother was the total package and had a bright future in front of him.

Attending John's graduation was a very rewarding moment in my life because it defied all my false notions about young Black men. I had experienced life under the Jim Crow law and was part of the superficial school desegregation initiative in the deep South as a kid. In prison, I saw young Black men with enormous potential wasting away behind prison walls. The Tuskegee University graduating class of 1991 clearly demonstrated how well African American youths can excel when unimpeded and properly nurtured. The graduation ceremony was an overwhelming event and the students' excitement and energy was contagious. I was left with a natural high, proud of all the students graduating, and feeling reassured they would go on to do great things in life.

My natural high went up in flames as things began to unravel between Katherine and me. Twice, she overheard me talking to Victoria on the phone and finally called me out on the matter, demanding to know what was going on between us. I had a closet full of secrets I kept hidden from Katherine, both to protect her and to avoid hurting her feelings. My relationship with Victoria was one of those secrets and since I never openly or intentionally lied to Kathy, I told her the truth about the ongoing affair between Victoria and me. I apologized and tried to explain I never intended to hurt her, but the damage was done and Katherine wasn't hearing a word I had to say. The pain I saw in her eyes made me feel knee high, because the woman really believed in me and had supported me unconditionally, and my infidelity had destroyed it all.

No matter what I did or said, I could not reach Kathy. Her last words before totally dismissing my attempts to apologize and rushing off to the bathroom in tears were, "You've broken my heart." Those words echoed in the silent room and haunted me throughout the night. I understood how Kathy felt and I couldn't blame her for being so cold toward me in the days that followed. For all practical purposes, our relationship was over and I knew it. My every effort to communicate with her or seek forgiveness fell on deaf ears and was met with an indifferent attitude that put me on the defensive. I grew more nonchalant and stubborn as Katherine completely withdrew from me. I could not or would not beg her to consider reconciliation. After all, her conduct and behavior in the past was not without fault either and I had forgiven her infidelities.

I would go to a college function with my brothers, which Kathy refused to attend, only to return to find her packed and gone. I remember asking her several times to join us, but she refused, claiming she was not feeling well. I did not know how things would end between us, yet I knew the end was clearly in sight. Finding Katherine gone upon my return came as no real surprise. It was predictable that Kathy would move without a word, as it was something she had previously done. The one thing that disturbed me most about Katherine's vanishing act was that she took off with my remaining bankroll. This money was earmarked for travel expenses and to further my bank-fraud schemes while in the South.

I understood she was angry with me and emotionally wounded. I did not mind her taking the car because I considered it hers, nor did I mind her leaving me somewhat stranded because I was resilient enough to regroup without missing a beat. But taking all my money with her was an unconscionable act that thoroughly pissed me off and was completely unacceptable under the circumstances. My life was complicated enough being on the run from the law. The last thing I needed in my life was more unwanted drama.

Later that night, Kathy called to lecture me about my affair with Victoria, stating the damage I had done was irreversible and she could not stand to be with me any longer. I offered no argument on the matter because by this point it was a dead issue for me. I only asked what she thought she was doing by running off with all my cash. She replied, "You can get more money and you will be okay." I tried to reason with her to no avail and the smug undertone in her voice served to further infuriate me. I snapped at Katherine in a fit of rage in a manner like never before. She countered calmly saying it was over between us, not to try to find her, and hung up the phone.

No sooner than hearing the phone hung up, I was on Kathy's trail like a bloodhound, locating the hotel where she was staying within minutes. Mad to the point of being out of control and harboring a wicked disposition, I had my brother Kelvin and his wife drive me there. Once in the hotel parking lot, they convinced me to allow my sister-in-law to comfort Kathy, fearing I might go off on a tangent and lay serious hands on her. My sister-in-law went into the hotel and came back with a message from Kathy saying she did not wish to see me. I sent her a message right back saying, take whatever money she felt she needed and send me the rest or I would be in to see her one way or another to deal with the matter. I made it perfectly clear that I did not want to see her either, and she could push on without me. Just get my hard-earned money back to me immediately.

A couple of days after Kathy's departure back to New Hampshire, I began to lay the foundation for my next bank-fraud move. I was in Savannah, Georgia at the time, a peaceful little town with few bank branches connected to the bank I had targeted. However, the bank also had multiple affiliate branches in the greater Atlanta metropolitan area and that's where I planned to execute my play. I was ready to move out the following morning and get back to my road hustle. That night the phone rang with my mother on the other end. It was urgent that she speak with me. Answering the phone, I instinctively knew something wrong was in the air. Katherine had made a three-way call through my mother to reach me and the news she delivered was all bad.

Answering the phone, Kathy's voice greeted me sounding tense and under tremendous stress. My guard immediately went up and a subtle concern crept into my heart. The shocking news she revealed was like a gut shot below the belt. Katherine was in jail, arrested the day after returning to Portsmouth, New Hampshire. Kathy explained that the

Portsmouth police were in the apartment the day before, when I had called to make sure she had arrived home safely. She informed me that the police somehow thought I was a big-time drug dealer and also had connections in the Middle East as a weapons supplier. Being a Muslim with a pending federal firearms warrant out against me and having an ongoing criminal history, they obviously jumped to a hasty conclusion. Kathy said they knew I was currently in Georgia and suggested I move out as soon as possible.

I would exhaust my brain power analyzing all the probable scenarios that led to Kathy's arrest. The cover we created was airtight, and only one or two individuals knew about Kathy and her predicament of being on the run, and my situation was a well-kept secret. Yet someone had enough information to expose Katherine and me and I did not like the small number of suspects I could list. The personal problems in our relationship suddenly became insignificant as we joined forces to deal with the more threatening situation confronting her. Kathy was being held on a five-thousand-dollar cash bond and regardless of the fight between us, there was absolutely no way I would leave her in jail. The woman was there for me every step of the way and in turn, I would be there for her with no reservations. Telling Kathy to give me a few days to maneuver, I would raise the necessary money to get her out. I hung up and began to ponder my options.

My sister Doreatha, the most independent of all my sisters, and her boyfriend came up from Atlanta the following day to pick me up. Doreatha lived in Atlanta and like all my sisters and brothers, she had my back without a lot of probing questions. I spent Sunday night with them and while they slept, I took out my map of the greater Atlanta area I had purchased earlier in the day and began studying it. The city maps and the local phonebooks were my two essential tools when executing a fluent bank-fraud scam. I did not have to know anything about the many cities I hit. With a phonebook, I easily located my intended targets and with the city map I located each bank branch on my hit list. The more branches a bank had, the better, those with fifteen to twenty branches within striking distance being my primary choice. When finished with my preparations, I had a map covered with check marks revealing the most convenient route to reach each target. Adhering to the rules of my game plan, this bank-fraud scheme was practically air-tight, yet my overconfidence would later betray me.

This money came so fast and so easy that I began to neglect the principles and governing rules on which I originally established my bank-fraud schemes. Banks have so many flaws and are unbelievably susceptible to fraudulent scams like the one I perpetrated. I found it in-credible. My ultimate mistake was in becoming so complacent that I would abandon the safeguards I had in place. Using some checks from a previous bank job, which I should have destroyed long before, would prove to be my downfall. Violating my own rules and mode of operation left me wide open to a one-way ticket back to prison, and that inevitable event came soon enough.

Using the same checks I had already worked on two previous occa-sions, I set out to score enough money in Atlanta to get Kathy out of jail and replenish my dwindling bank roll. After a couple of hours working my scam, the bottom fell out when one bank manager made a follow-up call to verify sufficient funds for a check I had cashed. I had already left the bank before this call was made, but the bank manager put out an alert to all associate branches to be on the lookout for me; my scheme had been revealed. I stayed one step ahead of them, not knowing the authorities were hot on my trail. Some branches told the bank manager making the calls that I had already been there or had just left the build-ing. The other branches would lay a trap while waiting for my antici-pated arrival, and sure enough, I walked right into it.

I was arrested on the spot and taken to the Peachtree Detention Cen-ter, where I was held on an informal charge of fraud. At first, I refused to say a single word to the detectives attempting to interrogate me; I didn't give them my name, divulge where I resided, or say anything else about myself. The detectives demonstrated unusual interest in who I was and I realized that not giving them my name would compel them to con-duct a more thorough inquiry into my true identity. Finally, I told them my name was Roy Jones and that I lived in Atlanta. The detectives did not buy my story and stated they would have me checked out. I knew what I was up against and my immediate concern at the moment was my fingerprints, which would instantly reveal my entire criminal history and true identity. I tried sanding my fingertips on the concrete bench in the holding tank without drawing attention to myself, hoping to retard them enough to render a negative reading, but it is nearly impossible to actually alter fingerprints unless it is done surgically.

Hours passed and I spent the whole day in the booking holding tank, restless and contemplating the odds of getting out of jail on bond. By 8 o'clock that night, my keepers set a two-thousand-dollar cash bond for my release and I quickly made a call for someone to rush down to pay the bond before the brief opening closed. I remember it being close to 10 o'clock when a jailer came for me, saying my bond had been posted. My personal property was returned and the jailer escorted me to a common area to await the completion of my release documents. Inside, my adrenaline pumped over time with the building excitement of slipping through another crack in the system.

Perhaps thirty minutes later, the booking officer came over to where I sat waiting to be released and began to ask such questions that would totally deflate my confidence. She had my real name and a printout of my criminal history in a folder that she frequently accessed as she asked me several questions. Her first question was, "Do you know a James Edward Faison and did you ever live in Indiana." Of course I replied in the negative, yet had to acknowledge to myself that the false pretenses were over and I was going nowhere fast. Then the booking officer asked if I had a tattoo on my chest of a black panther. I said no. She asked me pull up my shirt so she could take a look for herself to confirm my denial. I pulled up my shirt as far as possible without exposing the tattoo high on my upper chest of the black panther. She reached out to push my shirt up further to make a thorough inspection of my entire chest. Seeing the black panther tattoo standing out as bold as day, she turned and walked away without another word being said.

At my preliminary hearing, I was formally charged with forgery and passing fraudulent documents and ordered to be held with no bond as a potential flight risk. The day I went to court, all eyes were seemingly on me as if I was a notorious criminal and one of America's most wanted outlaws. The officers transporting the group of prisoners from the jail to the courthouse evidently received some sort of instructions regarding my posing a serious security threat because they watched me like a hawk the whole way. I was kept separate from the other prisoners, who were shackled together, ankle to ankle and wrist to wrist, while being transported. The different level of treatment was so obvious that the other prisoners began to mumble among themselves and cast inquisitive glances my way. The questions started once we reached the courthouse and were placed in holding cells where we all waited to see to the judge. I brushed them off with one liners, claiming I had no idea why I was arrested or what was going on. People getting in my business never appealed to me and from experience I knew jailhouse talk could create problems. I knew of guys who got themselves into uncompromising jams by talking about their case with complete strangers in jail who would take the information they learned straight to the enemy as jailhouse informants, seeking leniency from prosecution.

An older African American bailiff came for each prisoner scheduled to appear before the judge. When my turn came, two Caucasian bailiffs suddenly appeared, dismissing their coworker with an authoritative air of arrogance saying, "We will handle this one." The submissiveness of the brother, relinquishing his duties with no protest and drooping his head like a defeated house Negro, made me sick. The man's ego was bruised, which was plain to see, and the manner in which the two Caucasian bailiffs dismissed him was belittling and without tact. My own pride instantly surfaced in full force as I watched the episode unfold and I vowed to step straight through my escorts with a show of arrogance that reflected my contempt toward them.

Handcuffed and shackled down, I pulled away when one of the bailiffs attempted to take me by the arm and lead me toward the courtroom entrance. In a provocative expression saying it was not necessary for him to be touching me like he was gay or something, his complexion turned a beet red; if looks could kill, I would have been dead right on the spot, but he did not touch me again. As I hobbled past the Black bailiff, I could see a subtle grin playing across his face. In the courtroom, the two White bailiffs posted upon each side of me as I stood before the judge to hear the formal charges brought against me by the State of

Georgia. I would plead not guilty to the multiple counts of forgery that the judge informed me was the charge. Over the objection of the state prosecutor, the judge ordered that I be held on one-hundred-thousand-dollar cash bond. The prosecutor argued that I be held without bond due to being a flight risk. Yet, the judge concluded that even if I made the outrageously high bond, I still had pending warrants from Indiana that would prevent my release. The judge further ordered that my case be transferred to Georgia Superior Court for future prosecution and that I be transported to the Fulton County Jail to await my trial.

The two bailiffs proceeded to escort me from the courtroom, now talking trash. One made a comment, "Now you're playing with the big boys, coming to our city with your criminal bullshit." I sharply replied with a smirk, "Playing with the big boys all right. It's more like playing with a bounce of hillbillies." This degrading remark drew a rough shove in the back just as I was about to step out the door to exit the courtroom. I anticipated further abuse once we reached a secluded area and were alone. From past experience, I knew this was how these people worked. Catching the two bailiff completely off guard, I suddenly turned and dashed back into the courtroom shouting loudly, "Your honor, they're trying to beat me up." The court was still in progress and had a full audience of spectators and my outburst drew everyone's attention. My move caught the two bailiffs by surprise. One finally regrouped and told the judge that there was no problem. The judge looked from one bailiff to the other with a long firm look and told me, "If you are mistreated in any way, young man, you are to notify me immediately." Once outside the courtroom, the two bailiffs again tried their hand at verbally intimidating me, only to face a verbal assault in return that defied free speech using my bad-boy grammar.

At the Fulton County Jail, I found life under the yoke of incarceration to be the same old routine. Being a seasoned convict by this time in my life, I had no problem fitting in and commanding the respect of everyone in the unit to which I was assigned. I transitioned back into convict mode like it came second nature and before long I moved around the jail with the same finesse that served me behind prison walls. Exercising my constitutional rights as a prisoner, I had my keepers dancing to my tune using the power of the pen. I was under a great deal of pressure and had no room in my life for games from anyone and made my position crystal clear. Indiana and Georgia would not be the only two states seeking retribution for my past criminal activities and I had no idea how long I would be locked up behind bars. I only found solace in knowing that I made enough money to get Katherine out of jail on bond before they caught up with me. When arrested, I had no money in my possession. It was all safely stashed away and retrieved later by someone I trusted with my life. With Kathy free, I focused my undivided attention on my own legal battles.

Perhaps a week after being held at the Fulton County Jail, I appeared before the Georgia Superior Court. Prior to seeing the judge, a lawyer came to see me and explained he would be handling my case as a court-appointed attorney. He introduced himself and read the indictment of charges against me, and it all sounded bad. He also advised me that the Secret Service had expressed an interest in my case. For some reason I only half heard him and paid little attention to the comment. For the most part, my mind was still on the indictment and how ugly things were looking.

At my second court appearance, which came a short time later, the state prosecutor would offer me a six-year plea agreement, meaning I simply would plead guilty to the charge for a six-year prison sentence instead of going to a jury trial. I informed my lawyer I had to think about the plea agreement before committing myself to such a deal. Once again, the lawyer reiterated that the Secret Service had an interest in my case. This time I heard him loud and clear but gave absolutely no credence to his statement. I actually thought the Secret Service talk was no more than a pressure move to force me into accepting the plea agreement offer made by the state prosecution. I truly got the impression they were rather eager for me to accept to plea offer. I instructed my attorney to request a continuance on my behalf, which was granted under the condition that I either accept the plea deal at my next appearance or be prepared to face a jury trial.

I remember telling Katherine about the Secret Service issue over the phone and we both agreed that it had to be a mere scare tactic. Neither of us believed the federal agency would be concerned with me or a criminal case like mine. I had a limited understanding, thinking that the Secret Service job was designed only to protect the president and other high-profile government officials. Thinking the Secret Service had no real jurisdiction in my cases, I pushed the thought aside and began to consider my options regarding the plea-agreement offer, which I had to accept or reject soon. Of course, I was in a no-win situation and my best move was to engage in damage control. Forcing my keepers into a jury trial was not only foolish, but would have been suicidal and indicate I was a glutton for punishment. Reluctantly, I had to go with the flow. I conceded and accepted the plea deal because there was no sense in fighting a losing battle that would compound my troubles and add years to my prison sentence.

When called back to court, I asked my lawyer to see if he could negotiate for a better deal and get the number down to three or four years. He informed me that the state prosecutor was firm in the six-year offer and there was no room for negotiation. Persistently, he wanted to know if I was going to accept the plea offer. To him, my case was just another case among his many public-defender cases. He wanted to quickly dispose of my case and move on to the next. Finally, I told him yes, I would take the deal and, like a ghost in the night, he was off to finalize the plea agreement. I recall sitting there thinking to myself how I was about to sign away six years of my life to the State of Georgia, and how that was only the beginning of my legal problems.

My attorney returned a short time later, not with a plea agreement to sign, but with news that someone from the Secret Service was there to see me. The wheels in my head immediately began to spin at full speed. What did they want? Why did they get involved in my case? The questions crowded my head, but no answers came forth. There was one way to find out though and that was to consent to the interview, which my lawyer advised I could refuse. Common sense told me refusal to consent to the Secret Service interview could only invite more trouble, plus my curiosity would not let me refuse. My lawyer, now with a new sense of importance in his attitude, rushed off to deliver my message of consent.

A deputy sheriff came to escort me to a conference room where a Secret Service agent waited. He instructed the deputy to uncuff me and politely asked that we be left in private. He introduced himself as the deputy exited the conference room and his first question when we were alone was had I pled out to the charges against me yet? I answered "no." He replied that was good because the government was assuming jurisdiction over my case. I then voiced my opinion and belief that I thought the Secret Service's function was to protect the president. The agent corrected me, saying they also handle bank fraud, counterfeiting, and credit card cases when either showed the potential to be an elaborate scheme that was capable of offsetting the economy in the slightest. The agent then asked if I minded the government taking over my case. I countered by asking if I had a choice in the matter; he said "no." We talked a few more minutes before concluding the interview and the talk was professionally conducted in a manner that left a good impression, considering my prior dealings with law enforcement. Before leaving, he again advised me not to accept the state's plea-agreement offer.

That evening, back at the county jail, I called Kathy and told her about the new developments and she was astonished. Kathy still loved me and was concerned about my situation and welfare. We never spoke about my affair with Victoria and for the most part, all that drama was behind us and we were a team again. I was not sure in what direction things would go with the Secret Service but had enough foresight to see it was to my advantage for them to take over my case. Relaying my thought to Katherine, I tried to ease the stress I clearly recognized she was under and repeatedly instructed her not to worry about me because I would land on my feet after all was said and done.

Two Secret Service agents came to visit me at the county jail prepared to do battle with a hardened criminal. Reading my criminal history on paper depicted the image of a bad man who was deceptive and dangerous. I'm certain they had already drawn an impression of me based on what they discerned from my criminal record on paper. I totally disarmed the two agents with my direct and honest response to every question they asked and before the interview was over, the two men were my biggest supporters. I did not lie, make excuses, or downplay my involvement in the crimes I committed, taking full responsibility for my illegal actions and deeds in a way that demonstrated remorse and won the agents' respect. I came on strong, speaking openly and freely to such an extent that the interview flipped from being an interrogation to a friendly discussion between three men. Most importantly, the agents wanted to know how I learned about the bank-fraud scheme I executed and where my information and knowledge came from. My answer was unexpected and caused both men to look at each other, mystified and surprised. "From reading books while in prison," I told them, which was the truth.

The interview lasted perhaps two or three hours and at every point, I felt in control without being in control. Many would have thought I was telling on myself, but in fact, I was looking way ahead to minimize the damage. The agents had a stack of photographs from banks I hit, checks with my signature on them, and they knew everywhere I had been and everything I had done. My cooperation, to a large extent, was no more than a matter of confirming what they already had the evidence to prove. I could only help myself by cooperating with them, which later proved to be a fantastic strategy on my part. As a result, the agents agreed to combine all my cases into one and write a favorable report on my behalf. Hearing this was like music to my ears because, in Georgia alone, I almost pled to a six-year prison sentence with at least five other states waiting for a piece of me.

The following day, an African American female agent came to visit me with a few additional questions. She was very polite and sympathetic toward my situation and prison history, saying she found it amazing that I emerged from my prison experience without the bitterness she saw in others, especially considering how young I was when I went in. In particular, she wanted to know if I had done anything else in Georgia about which I had not informed them. I answered "no" and the rest of our conversation was mostly about me and my life. Like the other two agents, she too promised to make favorable mention in her report of the remorseful attitude I demonstrated and the level of cooperation I provided. She also advised me that within the next few days I would be taken into federal custody and transferred to the Atlanta federal penitentiary. The visit concluded with her wishing me well with my case and cautioning me not to worry because things were not as bad as they looked.

Like clockwork, the U.S. marshals came for me a couple of days later, taking me to their headquarters in downtown Atlanta to register me as a federal prisoner. From there, they took me directly to court for an initial court appearance and detention hearing. To my surprise, Alcohol, Tobacco, and Firearms had an outstanding federal warrant pending against me in connection with my parole violation in Indiana. This unexpected news caught me off guard and I remember thinking, "this bullshit keeps getting deeper." Now the court had to decide was who would get me first. The judge ruled that the State of Indiana had prior jurisdiction and issued a court order that I be sent there to stand trial on those charges. The judge then explained the court's decision regarding the matter of jurisdiction and asked if I understood. The judge further explained that I had the right to contest the decision if I so desired. I told him I understood the procedures and did not want to contest the court's decision. Once again, this proved to be a fantastic move on my part because I would never return to Georgia to face prosecution.

From the courtroom, the U.S. marshals took me to the Atlanta penitentiary where I was held without bond pending my transfer to Indiana. The prison was still under reconstruction when I arrived following what became known as the Cuban Riot, when a large portion of the prison was destroyed and went up in flames. Close to a hundred years old at the time, the older section deteriorating from the foundation up looked prehistoric and like something from an old silent movie. Famous for housing American gangsters such as Lupo the Wolf Saietta, Jimmy the Gent, and Scarface Al Capone, the prison was now housing me: a contemporary gangster and outlaw. Right away, I had to upgrade my convict mentality because the tension in the air seemed so thick that unchecked violence could erupt at any moment, but I knew the art of survival in such environments. I grew up under the same conditions and was a product of the elements that surrounded me. I projected the image of a man to be taken seriously, saying very little and quietly minding my own business. The Atlanta penitentiary was a real killing ground and no one had an absolute right to come out alive. During my stay in Atlanta, I would walk straight past the fights and stabbings I witnessed, not due to being coldhearted but according to my own convict rule to mind my own business.

My departure from Atlanta came by way of what the government referenced as the airlift on a Boeing 727 used to transport federal prisoners any and everywhere in the United States. Prisoners were handcuffed and shackled with an additional chain connecting the leg and hand chains together. The security at the airport left nothing to chance and the U.S. marshals were all business. The entire area was under armed guards and sealed off and the plane was completely surrounded by marshals, heavily armed with shotguns and automatic weapons at the ready. Once everyone was aboard, a marshal walked the length of the plane telling each prisoner what was expected of them during the flight. We were instructed not to leave our seat for any reason or under any circumstances. I soon learned they meant what they said because one prisoner "attempted" to get up to use the bathroom while the plane was in flight, and they were all over him like white on rice.

The whole day was spent landing and taking off from different airports, picking up prisoners and dropping them off, until we ended up in Oklahoma. FTC Oklahoma, the Federal Transfer Center, was the main hub for transporting male and female federal prisoners and the last stop of the workday for the marshals. The following day proved to be the same routine. The only thing that changed was the faces and places. My airlift ride was an unsettling experience I never again wanted to endure. I have never felt so helpless and completely at the mercy of my keepers. Around midday, the marshals dropped me off at the Terre Haute Federal Prison, another deadly joint with a bad-environmental reputation for violence and killings.

The metropolitan correctional center was my final destination, located in Chicago, Illinois: a twenty-eight-story building in the heart of downtown Chicago. I would spend approximately fourteen months at the MCC before accepting a plea agreement for bank fraud and being an ex-felon possessing a firearm. MCC Chicago was a laid-back joint, stress free as far as trouble and mischief were concerned, and everyone demonstrated a mutual respect for each other. I found myself in the company of major crime figures, guys I had heard about over the years and gangsters I had read about in books. I met individuals who moved cocaine and heroin by the ton: millionaires who could buy any and everything except their freedom. I was on the same floor as mob bosses, gang leaders who controlled entire sections of Chicago, and doctors and politicians who went bad. Most everyone incarcerated at the MCC during this time was considered a major league player in the criminal world with the exception of a few bank robbers and me, but this would soon change as the federal government began to indict low-level drug dealers and gang bangers.

Once again, my natural ability to get along with everyone put me in a good position. By this time in my life, I was completely colorblind and truly accepted each man based on his own merits and how they accepted me for the man I represented. The Italian mob on the floor embraced me because they liked my style, saying I had real class and was not a loudmouth like my fellow brothers. The Mexicans who seemed more prejudiced than most White people broke their tight little circle and let me in because they thought I was cool. The Blacks saw me as a strong independent leader they turned to for counseling and advice because they saw me as being the real deal with the history to back me up. Establishing myself among these guys all across the board was no more than a matter of being myself and speaking through my actions and deeds in how I carried and conducted myself.

My spiritual light as a Muslim was beginning to burn bright again as I applied myself to practicing and studying more diligently. An old Muslim brother once told me that Allah would sit us down so we could hear and receive the message if our hearts inclined toward being a believer. I found a great deal of truth in his words because when Allah sat me down in prison, I would experience my biggest growth and development. I found Islam while incarcerated, and while in the free world, I gradually strayed until my spiritual light got dimmer and dimmer. Now I was back on the straight path, spiritually powering up and building further on the foundation I had already laid. One of Jeff Fort's lieutenants would ask me to take over as the Imam because I was the most knowledgeable brother at the MCC and I agreed. Jeff Fort was the leader of the El Rukans, a major street gang in Chicago who was serving a life sentence in federal prison. His lieutenant was still awaiting trial on the same conspiracy indictment with which Jeff was charged.

I never met Jeff Fort personally, but I knew most of his crew who were indicted along with him. Jeff was tried and convicted before I arrived at the MCC. I did get to know Larry Hoover—the leader of the Gangster Disciples—and Willie Lloyd, the leader of the Vice Lord Nation. At the Friday Muslim services, I had El Rukans, Gangster Disciples, Vice Lords, and Latin Kings all attending and feeding on my teachings about Islam. These guys were conditioned from a young age to obey and follow leadership as gang members. If I had bad intentions or provided corrupt instructions to pursue my own selfish gains, they would have followed my lead. I was always conscious of my position and influence, so I did my absolute best to properly represent the truth in my teachings and the message I delivered. Perhaps I did not set the ideal example to follow, but I was one of them and could communicate in a language they understood. Also, I saw these brothers were searching for guidance as I once searched for guidance. I knew how Islam had elevated my thinking and wanted to pass this on to them.

I would cultivate many friendships and future business associates during my long stay at MCC Chicago. n Italian buddy name Sammy would become a lifelong friend, and we're still friends to this very day. Sammy's case reflected how ruthless and merciless the U.S. government can be when prosecuting organized crime. Considered the biggest bookie in the Midwest, Sammy was a professional gambler charged in a conspiracy indictment along with several high ranking and well-known mob figures. Sammy would be tried and convicted of gambling, extortion, and conspiracy, for which he received a twelve-year prison sentence. Everyone in Sammy's family with the exception of his mother would be charged and sentenced to prison time. His father received twenty-four months and his brother, brother-in-law, and two sisters all received eighteen months for illegal gambling; to my understanding, no family member had so much as a prior traffic ticket. These harsh and severe penalties for first-time offenders were meant to punish Sammy for refusing to flip and testify against codefendants.

Although Sammy was Italian and had strong Mafia connections, he was not what they called a "made man," meaning he was not a member of the syndicate family. Most notable among his affiliations were Dominick "Tootsie" Palermo, a legend in the Mafia underworld, and I was told his criminal history went all the way back to the Al Capone days. Dominick would embrace me like a son and even helped me make my bed one day when we were transferred to the transit floor after being sentenced. Then you had Rocky Infelise, the Cicero mob boss, and Harry "The Hook" Aleman, the most feared enforcer in the Chicago mob who was famously known as Harry the Hitman. Harry, Rocky, and I were the only three men on the floor who had already served serious prison time and were cut from the same cloth. Books have been written mentioning both men. Harry was a quiet man like me who dealt with very few people, but he gravitated toward me for some reason and we became cool. Rocky was a huge fellow, standing about 6' 5" and weighing nearly 300 pounds. He would later introduce me to mob guys from New York, jokingly saying I was his Black Sicilian brother from Northern Sicily. We were in the joint by this time and the guys from New York were curious about seeing me hanging out with the Italian crew.

Sammy had the connections, but he was absolutely nothing like the other guys; he was neither violent nor a killer. He was just a stand-up guy who could hold his own: a very likeable person, highly intelligent, and a man you could not afford to underestimate. Really, Sammy did not have to be a tough guy because Dominick and Rocky Incorporated had his back. Sammy, was a professional gambler and bookmaker, was a natural at his work, and was a prized asset to the family. Sammy made the kind of money for the family that made him a boss without being a boss and you did not mess with the mob's golden goose and lifeblood of the family. Sammy and I became friends and then got super close as card partners, playing pinochle against the other mob guys on the floor. The hyperactive Sammy would come to my room walking fast and swinging those arms of his like the Energizer Bunny, saying, "Taz, my Man, I need you." Probably ready for a break from reading all day, I would put down my book and accommodate my friend. Not only did Sammy and I get close, but I also became friends with his entire family.

Eventually, my day in court for sentencing came and I was truly ready on all fronts and prepared to enter the lion's den to meet my fate. Having thoroughly studied and researched the law pertaining to my case and charges, I had a pretty good idea as to where I stood. All the bank-fraud charges were consolidated under my plea agreement, and although I faced a thirty-month prison sentence on those charges, the court could enhance this sentence due to the multiple cases I had in other states. The maximum penalty for the weapons violation was twenty-four months. Viewing my situation from the worst possible perspective and outcome, I deduced that I would not receive less than a four-and-a-half-year sentence. Yet, I had one final move up my sleeve: my statement to the court prior to sentencing.

My court date came during the holy month of Ramadan when Muslims all over the world fast for thirty days from sunup to sundown. The fast was, perhaps, in the last ten days when I appeared in court for sentencing. I could actually feel the extraordinary spiritual power with me like never before. Totally at peace with myself, I knew nothing could go wrong this day. I did not pray asking God to get me out of the situation I was in or to keep me from going to prison. My prayers were always asking God to guide me, to protect me, and to keep me safe from those who might attempt to oppress me or cause me harm. I was ready to face the consequences of my actions because that was how I lived and the results came with the territory. Still above all my personal faults and shortcomings, I overwhelmingly felt the presence of God surrounding me and knew that I would prevail against the odds.

When the judge asked if I had anything to say on my own behalf before sentencing, I said "yes" and stood up to command the undivided attention of everyone in the courtroom as I spoke for about half an hour. For weeks I mentally rehearsed the topics I wanted to expound upon in my statement to the court. Not only was I in rare form, I was in the zone of a completely different stratosphere. I heard what I was saying but could not believe the words were coming from me. The experience was so surreal that I felt consumed by a natural high for days afterwards.

When I concluded my statement to the court, I didn't know if my audience wanted to cry or applaud. The courtroom fell silent for several moments as the judge seemed to collect his thoughts and the stenographer struggled to regain her composure while fighting back tears. Finally speaking, the judge cleared his throat and said rarely had a defendant come before him and expressed themselves as eloquently and articulately as I had done. Such a compliment coming from this particular judge struck every court official present as unusual and out of character, yet they all seemed to nod approvingly at his words. The judge went on to sentence me to the lightest term of imprisonment he could impose by law, concluding by wishing me well in the future. I received handshakes all around from my lawyer and the court probation officer handling my case. Even the government prosecutor gave a thumbs-up sign. In my heart of hearts I knew God was in power and in full control that day, aiding me in speech and guiding me through, his protection shielding me from the greater harm.

From the Chicago Metropolitan Correctional Center, I was transferred to a federal joint in Oxford, Wisconsin. At FCI Oxford Federal Correctional Institution, I spent approximately eight months serving out the remainder of a very lenient two-and-a-half-year prison sentence. Like always when I hit the compound of a new joint, my first move was to establish myself and project my image of a man to be reckoned with and to be taken deadly seriously. At FCI Oxford, I showcased my boxing skills on the heavy bag to demonstrate how lethal my hands could be, a classic move that often worked like a charm. My paramount reason for doing this was to cast doubts and hesitancy into the hearts and minds of anyone considering trying my hands one on one. I recall the first day on the prison yard asking one of the guys who routinely worked out on the heavy bag if I could use his bag gloves. I received a cold welcome from these guys initially until they saw my work. I fully understood what was going on. To them, I was an outsider and perhaps a novice who knew little or nothing about boxing. Yet curiosity would cause them to check out my work and measure the skills of the new kid on the block. In my mind, I thought "Let me put together some flash and dash for these guys." Once again, I made the desired impression and intended impact, which was obvious from the comments of surprise and approval I overheard from the onlookers as I transformed into a beast in action on the heavy bag. From that point on, I was not only rendered the utmost respect in the boxing corner, but the guys sought me for training. Being good with my hands got me instant respect at Oxford; it also made people not want to fist fight with me. To me it was all about gaining the psychological advantage and keeping the odds in my favor as much as possible under any given circumstances, something I had been doing since age 15 behind prison walls.

FCI Oxford was an easy, laid-back joint to serve time and the class of prisoners incarcerated there was of a different caliber altogether. These guys were mostly bosses and shot callers: millionaires and former millionaires. They came from every part of the country and represented the finest U.S. criminal minds. Rocky and my man Sammy would also be shipped to FCI Oxford and I knew quite a few other convicts there so it did not take me long to create alliances while remaining an independent operator. The Muslim brotherhood at Oxford was exceptionally strong and far more advanced than me, and I found myself being a student again instead of a teacher, a role I preferred. I only encountered one altercation with another prisoner during my stay at Oxford: a Cuban guy called me out only to back down later once he could get no help or support from his fellow countrymen to come up against me. The Cuban was a talker not a fighter, and a coward at heart; I could see straight through him. I literally grew up with violent men and real killers. I knew the character, I knew the behavior, and I could speak the same language. This Cuban had no idea.

14. Back to Indiana

My time at Oxford was like a stress-free walk in the park for a seasoned convict such as myself, having already served hard prison time. The eight months I had left to serve on my two-and-a-half-year sentence went by fast and before I knew it, my release date had come. But there was no going home for me because Indiana had an outstanding warrant pending against me for parole violation. By law, my keepers could no longer hold me at FCI Oxford so they released me into the custody of the local authorities in Friendship, Wisconsin. I was then taken straight to court for an extradition hearing where I had the option to either contest being extradited back to Indiana or waive the extradition proceedings. Once again, carefully picking my battles, I opted to waive my rights to an extradition hearing and put the burden on the State of Indiana to immediately come for me. Personally, I thought Indiana had no interest in me, especially since my keepers at Oxford had sent them several requests regarding the matter and received no detention orders. Waiving the extradition created a situation where Indiana had to promptly claim custody or the authorities in Wisconsin would be compelled to release me. The judge issued a court order for Indiana to claim custody within fourteen days. I asked that they be given seven days, arguing that Indiana had sufficient time prior to my scheduled release to make the necessary arrangements for my extradition. The judge agreed with my argument but told me it was standard procedure to allow them fourteen days to act. If they did not respond according to his orders, I would be released.

My stay at the Friendship jail was all dead time with nothing to do but read and sleep. On Day 12, Indiana came for me, chartering a small four-seater plane for the trip to and from Friendship, Wisconsin. As stingy and cheap as Indiana is well known for when it comes to spending money on prisoners, I could not believe those idiots went so far as to charter a plane to secure my return. The mere fact that they went through such trouble for a parole violation spelled bad news for me on the Indiana end upon my return. With more than fifteen years under my belt in dealing with my keepers in Indiana, I had never ever heard of a situation where they chartered a private plane to retrieve and transport a prisoner. For a fleeting moment, a grey sense of depression and despair enveloped me. Then, I shook it off as an unacceptable notion to even ponder as the fighter in me emerged and I turned my attention to plotting my next move. I heard one of my most valued philosophies echoing in my mind: "Where there is a will, there is a way, and if the will is strong enough, the way will eventually open up and come into sight." From years of struggling against all odds, I amassed the will and the fortitude to overcome adversity and I vowed to exploit every means available to once again regain my freedom.

When the plane landed in Indiana, I was transported to the Indiana Diagnostic Center. IDC is the central clearing headquarters where prisoners are evaluated by some ludicrous standard and designated to different penal institutions throughout the state. I would spend approximately three or four days there before being transferred to the Correctional Industrial Complex, the first privately owned prison in Indiana and perhaps one of the first in the country. CIC was located practically next door to the Indiana Reformatory, the prison of my initial debut behind prison walls at the age of 16. I quickly discovered that my reputation in the Indiana Department of Corrections proceeded me, and staff and fellow convicts knew of me or heard of me already. Now, in my older age, my name appeared to be attached to the list of legendary convicts transitioning in and out of the Indiana penal system. I never saw myself in the same light as others did, nor did I feed on or subscribe to the identity with which I was being associated as a hardened convict. To me, I was just another prisoner doing my time and making the best of a bad situation, and my reputation was no more than a by-product of how I lived over the years behind prison walls.

My people, those I knew and had served time with, held good positions in the joint at CIC and before long, I had everything within reason to make things as comfortable as possible while I awaited my parole-violation hearing. Some of my ties and connections went back to the early years at the Indiana Reformatory at age 16; other affiliations went back to my Indiana State Prison debut at age 19. A close friend and fellow Muslim brother from my Michigan City days was the Imam and the leader of the Muslim community at CIC who had practically free run of the joint. Upon learning of my arrival, he sought me out immediately, embracing me with a big bear hug on sight. I remember extending my hand in greeting, which he totally ignored and said, "No, my brother, you gotta give me a hug!" Lifting me off my feet, Brother Amir embraced me with a demonstration of brotherly love that we both had shared from Day One. Built like a prized bull at approximately 5'10" and 250 pounds of solid muscle, Brother Amir had little trouble seemingly snatching me up effortlessly. A true force to be reckoned with, Brother Amir had a black belt in the martial arts, was a bad man when provoked, and someone neither staff nor fellow convicts wanted a confrontation with.

I spent close to three months at the Correctional Industrial Complex and once again it was nearing the end of the holy month of Ramadan, the month of fasting in the Muslim world. My greatest victories when fighting for my freedom always seem to come during the fasting period or immediately following Ramadan. I would appear in front of the Indiana parole board toward the end of the month-long fast and spiritually I felt the powers of being invincible again. Deep down inside, I had a reassuring sense of confidence that I would prevail despite the obvious odds against me. I had no real legitimate grounds to stand on in support of my request to have my parole reinstated, but my mind continued to work the angles until I decided my best approach was an emotional appeal. From there, I began mapping out a mental plan of action that included my hardships as a child living with a physically abusive stepfather and erroneously being misled into a life of crime by the unhealthy influences I absorbed over the years.

Lucky for me, I drew a female member of the parole board council to hear my case and once again my oratorical skills were seemingly enhanced, hitting a profound peak. I had the perfect audience for my strategic approach, a female chairwoman along with two female assistants. I spoke truthfully and from the heart, although I may have exaggerated on a point or two for effect. I sincerely meant everything I said. It was not my sole intention to manipulate the emotional element in the female nature in relating the sympathetic side of my life story. I knew it was necessary to touch them from the heart for them to feel me and to feel my personal struggles and pains. I concluded my story by expressing great remorse for the lifestyle I had lived, apologizing for the suffering I caused my family and others, and suggesting the board members turn me over to the three years of federal supervised release I still had pending on my federal prison sentence. I saw the emotional impact of my statement on the faces of all three board members and one in particular was openly shedding tears.

When I finished my lengthy speech, I was asked several questions by the parole board members pertaining to my release plans, all of which had favorable implications. The chairwoman then advised me that any recommendation she made would be subject to review by the full body of the parole board committee. She wished me well and with a subtle wink, told me not to worry, indicating she had my back. I left the parole hearing feeling very positive that Allah would once again bring me safely through yet another self-created storm. Later, I would learn the decision to discharge me from my state parole and turn my case over to federally supervised release went through a big in-house contention with the board member approving my release, taking a firm stance on my behalf. Few people understood how I could be so fortunate under the circumstances. A great deal of money had been spent chartering a plane to bring me back to Indiana only to release me. I understood what was going on though; simply put, I plan and people plan, yet God has the power and is the best of planners. After approximately three months,

I walked out of the Correctional Industrial Complex a free man once again, in accordance with God's plan.

I left CIC under the escort of a correctional officer assigned to transport me to the bus station in Indianapolis, which was perhaps thirty minutes away. At the bus station, I made several phone calls to friends and family to let them know I was out and on my way home. I also called the chairwoman of the parole board to thank her for the overwhelming support she extended me in regaining my freedom. Coming out of prison in 1993, my attitude was positive and so were my future goals and objectives. My religion had me mentally and spiritually stronger than ever before and I felt deep within that God had a purpose and a mission in life for me that I was yet to fulfill. However, my education from the school of hard knocks was a long way from being over. The negative elements of the street life began to lure me in within a few weeks of being out of prison, and soon I found myself compromising my principles and again thinking I could take short cuts to succeeding in the things I wanted to accomplish in life.

Returning to the economically depressed city of Gary, Indiana, where jobs were few and far between did not help my cause in transitioning back into the free world and pursuing a meaningful income. Being an ex-convict with absolutely no work history would also put me at a total disadvantage in the job market. Once again, I went all over town putting in job applications until I began to feel like a beggar looking for a handout instead of a hand up. I fail to comprehend the laws that allow employers to openly discriminate against ex-felons. It seems as if those laws were structured in such a way that an ex-convict could not get a job washing dishes or even as a garbage collector. I further fail to understand how you can refuse to allow an ex-felon the opportunity to work and earn a living and still expect them to lawfully provide for themselves. I am inclined to directly associate the prisoner recidivism rate with society's refusal to employ ex-convicts in general. I know from personal experience that the closing of the job market to those with a prior criminal record is ludicrous and merely invited future bad conduct by those striving to get on track following time spent behind prison bars. My past and the past of those similarly situated made us unemployable according to the status quo, and that alone was a discouraging factor with which I had to live with constantly.

When released from CIC, I remember having a job interview with a car dealership after seeing an advertisement in the newspaper. The ad was for a car salesmen and mentioned no experience required, and the company would train new employees. During the job interview, I explained to the junior manager handling my application that I had a criminal record and was recently released from prison. The junior manager responded positively, saying my criminal record was a thing of the past as far as he was concerned and I should come in the following day to start my training. He then left the room for what seemed like hours. He was gone for so long that I thought he had forgotten all about me. When the junior manager finally returned, he was accompanied by another car salesman who was obviously the big boss and the real shot caller. The very first words out of his mouth were, "I do all the hiring here." He then went on to say he would further consider my application and get back to me. From the tone in his voice and the nonchalant attitude he reflected, I immediately discerned the junior manager's decision to give me the job had been overruled.

The open hypocrisy and blatant discrimination revealed during this job interview caused me to face the reality that I would never out live my past. No matter the extent of my good intentions to go straight, society would not be so forgiving and extend the benefit of the doubt. In that instant, my total disposition flipped and I concluded there was no longer room in my life for trying to compromise or cooperate with those wanting me to live righteously, yet hindered my efforts to do so. I remember leaving the job interview with the decision already made to revert back to my street mentality and my natural inclination to survive under any conditions and under any circumstances by any means necessary was again in full force. A different man left the job interview, and just like that, I walked straight back into the street life. It seemed as though I transformed in an instant into the person I was fighting against becoming.

A hardness enveloped me and my thinking turned keenly serious. My focus was incredibly intense as I embraced my decision to go gangster once again. I had a plan of action taking form with each step I took as I left the car dealership, now driven by an unhealthy mixture of anger and raw determination to live my life according to the hand life had dealt me. I immediately went to work laying the foundation for my next street hustle venture in the criminal world, where I was accepted with honor and without question. My people on the streets knew I was a relentless go-getter and were excited to learn I was back in play because everyone on my team made money and ate well. Tapping into my street resources and working my network, I had a game plan in play before the day was over.

Later that night, I met up with a brother named Sampson, a former enforcer for the notorious street crew known as The Family that ran the Gary underworld in the early '70s. Sampson was the one brother in all of Gary who had my utmost respect on the streets; he was a brother I considered a true friend and someone I could trust with my life and beyond. Sampson had a strong reputation throughout the city of Gary. Contrary to the false hype I found in most others, Sampson actually lived up to his reputation; he was a classy brother as smooth as silk, a lady's man, and a player with the heart of a gun-fighter, like me. Perhaps ten years older and far more experienced on the streets of Gary, Sampson became my mentor and someone I could talk with about absolutely anything. We were so much alike in our approach to the street life, both moved as independent operators, and were both completely color blind in our networking and with the people we embraced. In my opinion, Sampson was the most popular, most liked, beloved, and highly respected brothers in the mixture of things on the streets. In our dealings, we complimented each other rather well and we both stood firmly on the honor system of our word.

I first met Sampson a few years earlier following my last release from prison. With no introduction, I approached him straight up and told him who I was. I laid out my street credentials revealing my criminal background and the individuals we both knew who could vouch for me and my reputation as a stand-up brother, true to the game. I remember Sampson looking at me with an astonishing gleam in his eyes. Here I was, a complete stranger approaching him about advancing me the product to get started in the most clandestine and closely guarded illegal enterprise on the street: the illicit drug business. After hearing me out, Sampson replied to my request for a starter kit saying, "Brother, no one has ever come to me like this and I don't know why, but I'm going to do this thing for you." That was the beginning of a long-lasting bond of friendship and very profitable business relationship.

I met up with Sampson at his nightclub, The Mirage, an upscale club that catered to the affluent, the bourgeoisie, and high-profile drug dealers, hiding in plain sight as legitimate businessmen. The Mirage was a plush night club lavishly decorated with black and gold trim. Sampson spared no expense in totally remodeling the entire building and converting it into the most popular club in the city and in every aspect, the club reflected Sampson's image. He would spend all his savings on getting the club up and running, adding an extravagant touch to every inch of the nightclub. I remember showing up for his grand opening to find my brother struggling financially and his bankroll nearly depleted. I was coming from executing one of my bank-fraud schemes when I arrived in town for the grand opening and learned of Sampson's financial predicament. As we talked, he revealed his money problems and without hesitation, I escorted him to my car where I counted him out five thousand dollars in hundred-dollar bills. Sampson happened to peep into my briefcase where I kept my cash and said, "I need to be doing whatever you're doing. This don't even put a dent in your bankroll." I merely replied with a smile and a wink. With his nightclub up and running successfully, Sampson was back to his full strength on the streets and was more than happy to assist me in any way possible. As a major street player in those days, Sampson had access to cocaine by the kilo and I could get as much as I wanted with no questions asked. On this occasion, I only wanted enough product to get in the game to see where it would lead. Once again I say, I was never a true drug dealer at heart and Sampson was the one who pointed this out to me one night while hanging out at the club talking long after closing until the sun came up. He said, "Little Bro, you're not a real drug dealer man because you're not ruthless and aggressive enough. You're just an opportunist who knows how to take advantage of the situation from the business angle." At first,

I thought his comments were meant to disparage, but in fact he was right. I possessed a compassionate and very giving and forgiving nature that ran contrary to that of being a true die-hard drug dealer, and this I knew. I would work around my weaknesses and navigate my way throughout the drug world with finesse and a self-serving calculated approach.

Although there was money to be made on the economically depressed streets of Gary, Indiana, the competition was far more violent and deadly, so I decided to take my game on the road and headed to the Twin Cities where there was fertile ground and the cash flow was definitely more plentiful. Katherine was living in Minnesota at the time and we eventually got back together, putting the past behind us and never mentioning my affair with Victoria. The flames between Victoria and me faded while I was incarcerated and I only saw her a few times following my release from prison. On one occasion in particular, immediately after getting out, I traveled to Minneapolis to see her and to pick up several firearms I had left with her for safe keeping. From there we gradually drifted apart.

I consider this moment in my life to be the days of justification and rationalization; I justified and rationalized how I was living and getting money and told myself if I did not sell the drugs I put on the street, someone else would answer the call of supply and demand. Using cocaine myself to medicate my own guilt did not ease my conscience either, as I attempted to justify my actions. The deeper I got into the drug game, the more cocaine I snorted to numb myself and retreat further into denial regarding the destruction my hands were causing.

It did not take me long to get things established, and I was up and running strong within a few months. Still on federally supervised release, I was not allowed to leave the state of Indiana, but I was moving around between Minnesota and Indiana as if I had a green light to do as I pleased. My every move was in direct violation of my supervised release and it was only a matter of time before it caught up with me and I found myself on the run from the authorities once again. Violating the conditions of my release by testing positive for drug use, my probation officer filed to have my supervised release revoked and I be sent back to prison. I managed to talk my way out of being taken into custody on the spot by contesting the test results and insisting my urine sample be sent to the lab for further testing. I would leave the probation office and immediately hit the highway for Minnesota without looking back. The dye had been cast and the days of my remaining a free man would be numbered.

In Minneapolis, I could more easily operate beneath the radar and become invisible. I had several legitimately issued state identifications and driver's licenses in my survival kit for being on the run to hid behind. I immediately slipped into one of my false identities and circled my wagons to put the odds in my favor as much as possible against the pending attacks I knew were forthcoming. Little did I know, my biggest threat at the time would emerge from among those around me who festered with jealousy and envy and those harboring what I call the crab-ass mentality. On the streets, jealousy and envy emerge when a person casts the image of success and doing well above others. The individual with the crab-ass mentality is the one who pledges false loyalty while trying to drag the next man down, often to save his own ass to escape his own self-made problems.

The first sign of trouble came one morning while I was out making my final rounds, picking up money owed to me before hitting the road to purchase more product. I remember vividly cruising down the now seemingly peaceful streets of Minneapolis that early morning. I was out and about far earlier than usual and most of the city was still asleep. I believe it was a Saturday morning, but there was still some lingering action from the previous Friday night to be found if you knew where to look. Before leaving home that morning, I had already made my travel plans, packed my travel bags and counted my cash to see how much I would be working with. Until this very day I still have a picture in my head of seeing the doors to my safe wide open and the fifty thousand dollars I made laying in plain sight. As I left my bedroom, something told me to close the safe and lock it, but I said to myself this was not necessary because I would be right back.

I was gone less than an hour when Katherine paged me with our 911 emergency code and I rushed to find a phone to call her. Katherine answered the phone sounding slightly nervous but under control and informed me the police had just left the apartment looking for me. She told me one detective kept her in the living room and asked her questions while the other detective looked around the apartment to assure I was not present. Remembering how I had left my safe open, I told Kathy to check it. She came back on the phone line with the dreadful news that my safe was now completely empty and my fifty thousand was gone.

My emotions were mixed, elated that I had dodged another bullet and remained a step ahead of those who pursued me, yet angry as hell that the police stole my money, knowing there was absolutely nothing I could do about it. The money, per se, was not the issue because I will trade fifty grand for my freedom without giving the matter a second thought. The fact that these two detectives were tracking me down due to my criminal conduct while all the time their conduct was equally criminal, now that's what had me pissed off. I would have to charge the loss to the game and keep it pushing, and I remember thinking to myself that they had revealed how close they were and I would use it to my advantage. A few hours later, I was on the highway heading south to Atlanta, Georgia, after collecting enough cash to put as much distance as possible between me and my beloved Twin Cities.

By midday, I was in another time zone heading south, putting the Twin Cities behind me and leaving my pursuers a cold trail to follow. As I drove and settled into the long drive ahead, my thinking turned to the events that started my day. The number one question troubling me was how the police tracked me down and how they learned about where I lived. Who was the source of their information? There was no doubt in my mind that it was an inside job and someone close had betrayed me. One name continued to stand out no matter how I looked at the facts. Only four people in all of Minnesota knew where I lived and also knew the particulars of my situation, being on the run from the law. I had circled my wagons so tightly that my brother David, who lived in Minnesota, did not know where I stayed or laid my head and I could trust him with my life. But due to the circumstances, David and I understood the importance of my being invisible to hide in plain sight. Yet, on the other hand, I used the wife of a business partner of mine as a reference when leasing my apartment. The business partner, who was locked up in federal custody at the time, his wife, Katherine, and I were the only ones who knew about my very private hideout. You could not follow me home to learn where I stayed because I lived in my rear-view mirror and made several maneuvers before reaching home to detect being followed. Over and over, I would replay the scenario as a I drove, only to reach the same suspicious conclusion.

I drove straight through the 1200 miles from Minnesota to Atlanta, only stopping for gas and an occasional break to rest my eyes. Upon arriving in the city, well known as a major organizing center for the Civil Rights Movement, I located my brother Kelvin and proceeded to his house to crash and get some much-needed sleep. My retreat to Atlanta only lasted a few days until I collected my composure and decided on my future plan of action. Eventually, I circled back to the Midwest where I got a place in Chicago approximately a thirty-minute drive from Gary where I would continue to put in more street work. During this time, I would also get my first introduction to the highly lucrative heroin business.

Like my man Sampson had stated, I was not a true drug dealer. I simply knew how to take advantage of the open opportunity to make money in the drug trade. By chance, I got involved in dealing heroin following one of the occasional cocaine droughts that hit the area. Living off the short money I had in my pockets upon my hasty departure from the Twin Cities, it was not long before I was down to my last few dollars. Talking with Sampson one day, he suggested I try my hand at moving some heroin and gave me several ideas on how to proceed. I took off from there as if I had dealt in heroin all my life. My mind seemingly digested and understood the intrinsic of producing a good product that users sought and demanded. The key was in the cutting and mixing of the drug. A bad mix will ruin even the best and purest heroin, leaving it worthless. Like a scientist, I created my own recipe and formula for cutting and mixing heroin until I became a mix master.

I would set up my operation in my old neighborhood on the border, once a thriving area filled with action 24/7 and the heart line to all illegal activity in the city. As a paper boy many years before, the entire border was my district for delivering the daily newspaper and I always thought about the players, pimps, and hustlers working the streets who were the only Black men living the good life. What was once a ghetto metropolis flourishing from tax-free dollars due to illegally gotten gains was now blocks and blocks of abandoned buildings and vacant lots. The border was not even a minute reflection of its former self, but people still came from every corner of the city to purchase drugs, especially heroin.

After laying the foundation for my heroin operation on the border, I decided to sneak back into Minnesota because I still had money on the streets there I wanted to collect. Leaving things in the hands of my right-hand man, a gang leader in the Black Gangster Disciples, I flew out to the Twin Cities. Instead of staying at my old apartment with Kathy in St. Paul, I got a hotel room close by and had her join me there. A couple of days later while out making my rounds, I stopped by the house of a friend and business partner who owed me money and while there, my guy in prison called. Talking to this brother on the phone, I remember him asking me several peculiar questions that I did not give much consideration at the time. Later, our phone conversation only added to my suspicions about who was behind putting the police on my trail initially. Soon after talking with him, I began to feel uneasy and kind of claustrophobic as if things were beginning to close in on me. Katherine had dropped me off and returned to the hotel to check us out and also to pick up some things for me from my storage unit. I had forgotten to give Katherine the room key, which she had to come back for, and the chain of events that followed would get her charged in a federal drug conspiracy.

While waiting for Katherine to return for the room key, someone came by to give me money. Kathy came through minutes later for the room key. All the time we were under police surveillance and I remember having the uncomfortable feeling of being watched from afar. Later, the authorities would claim I gave Katherine money from a drug sale instead of the hotel room key. They would follow her to the hotel, to our apartment, and then to my storage unit where they thought the motherload was stashed. The police stopped following Kathy from the storage unit, thinking they hit pay dirt and it was more important to investigate what was happening at the storage unit than to continue following Katherine.

My feelings of being watched were so intense that when I eventually met up with Kathy later in the day, I had her take me straight to the airport to get a flight out of town and back to the Midwest. Sure enough, the following day, the FBI raided my partner Foster's apartment, taking him to jail on drug-conspiracy charges. They would also arrest Katherine and charge her with drug conspiracy in the same indictment, along with Foster, a brother she did not know and with whom never so much as exchanged a word of greeting. Katherine had absolutely no involvement in my drug-dealing activities and never saw so much as a grain of cocaine. The indictment against her was so frivolous and absurd that the court would dismiss the charges in a matter of months after realizing she had no role. What the federal agents really wanted out of Katherine was information leading to my apprehension and her cooperation as to my illegal dealings on the street. Katherine pretended to be the naïve girlfriend who I occasionally visited and she had no way of contacting, except by paging and waiting for my return call. As a matter of fact, Kathy handled the pressure of the situation far better than some hardened criminals I know, holding her ground and saying very little that would incriminate me or lead to my apprehension.

Back on the block in Gary, I found myself getting more entrenched in the notorious heroin trade until I had a strong hold on the border, with no contenders. The few who initially challenged my presence and operation on the block were met with street diplomacy, which implied either peace or a street war, and they engaged me at their own risk. I had a deadly crew riding with me on the streets, but more importantly, I was the one who bore watching and represented the true threat. I had a personal arsenal that would instantaneously turn me into a one-man army and I had no reservations about using these weapons to protect myself and my business interests on the streets. Never one to start trouble, I believed strongly in being in a position to alleviate such issues immediately and without hesitation.

Among the tools in my war chest were twin AK-47s with extra clips, an M-16 converted to fully automatic, two .44 caliber handguns with 8-

inch barrels, bulletproof vests, and even a crossbow. But my weapon of choice was the Colt .45 automatic. Although I had an assortment of handguns in my war chest, that .45 had the stopping power and I could count on it as reliable protection. While living and hustling on the street of Gary, under no circumstances would I leave home without my .45 as a companion. The lifestyle I was living placed me in a very dangerous world, surrounded by deadly and often bloodthirsty individuals. My main deterrent to becoming a victim of predators and foes in the world I lived was in making it crystal clear that me and my .45 did not run and did not hide from any man.

The streets of Gary were no playground and life was sometimes cut short, yet always held cheap. Living the gangster and outlaw lifestyle was proving to be less glamorous than I was once led to believe. Carrying my .45 every day as a traveling companion was not how I wanted to conduct business, but I was in the game and I was playing for keeps and therefore embraced my role. The stress of staying ahead of the police on the block, with the U.S. marshals and other federal agents dogging my trail as well as the stick-up men, kept me constantly watching my back and my rearview mirror with every move I made. I would find no glamour in knowing I could trust no one and one bad move could easily lead to my own death or to spending life in prison. I was under no illusions regarding how violent and deadly things could get on the streets of Gary, Indiana, and I readily acknowledged I was not the only bad boy on the block and was no exception to being a victim of the violence that came with dealing in drugs. Against all odds, I was determined to prevail and be among the last players standing when the dust settled at the end of the day. I was in true survival mode with one overall objective: staying alive and remaining free at all costs.

I stayed out of the spotlight and maintained a low profile to avoid drawing attention to myself; however, my business enterprise grew so fast and word quickly got around that I was putting out some of the best product on the streets, until my name began to ring out of my control. I continued to put in work, never staying in one place and never revealing my movements, staying a step ahead of potential enemies and the authorities who pursued me. The more my reputation as a drug dealer grew on the streets of Gary, the more I had to hide and be invisible. Many would know and repeat my name, yet very few would know me personally or recognize me on sight, and this would also include the local police. With each passing day, my wiggle room got less and less until I would no longer be one of Gary's best-kept secrets. Just being out on the streets placed me in imminent jeopardy to all my lawful foes and my natural adversaries on the block.

Constantly thinking in terms of self-preservation, I decided to move out of my apartment in Chicago. This decision was partly due to paranoia, but mainly because I did not feel safe or comfortable living there. The apartment actually belonged to a brother named Prince, a major Nigerian heroin distributor and my main heroin connection. While I trusted Prince to the utmost, I did not know what kind of unforeseen illegal baggage was entangled in his operation. I had my own legal problems to address and by no means did I want to get ensnared in someone else's legal drama.

I found a place in Gary not far from the beach in the Miller area of town that was incognito and perfect for addressing my concerns for a safe haven to rest my head. Putting together a completely new identification package, I reinvented myself with a fresh identity to lease my new apartment. When filling out the rental application, I used Broadway Auto as my place of employment. I knew the owner, a sister named Miss B., and asked her to vouch for me in case the rental agent called to inquire about my employment status. We also had a common friend: "I had no idea she was still very much in touch with my guy in federal prison".

Miss B. was a closet party girl who snorted cocaine but kept it hidden from those on the outside looking in, so I often saw her for business reasons. I remember talking to her a couple of days after asking her to cover for me if the rental agent called. During our conversation, she happened to mention receiving a call from my guy in prison and a numbing feeling instantly hit me, yet I brushed it off. The brother in prison was eager to get in touch with me, Miss B. said, and wanted to know how and where I could be reached. I am pretty certain Miss B. divulged to him more information about my movements than she led me to think; how much, I did not know.

Perhaps a week after submitting my rental application, I received a surprise message from the apartment manager saying they suddenly had a vacancy ready and available. Upon originally submitting my application, I was told it would be at least a month before an opening came up. Someone had canceled their lease agreement, he said, and asked if I wanted to take a look at the now-available apartment. I agreed to stop by later in the day to check out the apartment; the thought never crossing my mind that I was being set up to get arrested by the U.S. marshals.

As I pulled into the apartment complex later that evening, I remember quickly scanning the parking lot and seeing nothing suspicious or out of place. I prided myself on being aware of my surroundings and being vigilant at all times and it was not easy to sneak one in on me. But the game the marshals executed when arresting me was a move I never saw coming. One marshal, pretending to be the maintenance man, offered to show me the apartment to make sure everything was satisfactory. As we walked to the back side of the complex, U.S. marshals appeared, seemingly out of thin air. Two marshals had me on the ground before my mind could process what was going on. I would look up to see marshals with weapons drawn and taking dead aim at me. Someone kept repeated, "Where's the gun? Where's the gun?" as if they anticipated me being armed. I had left my forever present Colt .45 in the car but it was clear someone had informed the marshals to expect me to be armed and they came prepared in case I wanted to put up a fight.

Once subdued and handcuffed, the U.S. marshals seemed to express a sigh of relief that the event was over and ended peacefully without any gun play. With me secured and under their full control, one marshal made a useless attempt to question me and got absolutely no response. I would not utter a single word. For the first couple of days I remained totally uncooperative and said nothing at all to my keepers. When asked basic questions like my name or age, I simply looked at the marshals like they were stupid or ignorant. They knew perfectly well who I was and did not need to confirm this fact. To me, it was the same old games that law enforcement plays to get a criminal suspect to open up and start talking in hopes of gathering additional information. I knew the score, but my understanding upon being arrested was zero and so was my willingness to cooperate or compromise with the U.S. marshals. I had only one question on my mind that crowded out all the other immediate concerns: how did the marshals track me down and who informed on me?

Once again, I found myself incarcerated at the Metropolitan Correctional Center in downtown Chicago. Charged with violation of my supervised release, possession of a controlled substance, possession with the intent to distribute, and being an ex-felon in possession of a handgun, the judge would order that I be held without bail, citing I was a flight risk and danger to the community. On paper, my criminal history cast an intimidating portrait of a violent, gun-carrying hardened criminal and ex-convict who could no longer be trusted to roam freely in society and who was beyond reforming. I knew I would be locked down for a while and accepted the reality of the fact like the man I had become: a man willing and ready to live with the consequences of his actions.

I spent the first couple of weeks at the MCC Chicago resting and thinking. Physically exhausted and my body demanding relief from all the drugs I had consumed, I slept like a baby for the first time in months. I had been under tremendous stress living on the run, ducking and dodging the local police on the block as I put in work, finessing my way around the many death traps on the streets, and surviving against all the odds I faced. When not asleep, my mind was obsessed and entirely preoccupied with how I got caught. This Judas was deep in my inner circle and my inner circle was very small. No matter which way I viewed the episodes leading up to my eventual arrest and my previous close calls in Minnesota, one name repeatedly surfaced. In each situation, my guy in prison was the only individual who could have provided the kind of inside information federal agents were getting. The mere thought of him trying to crawl out of prison on his knees with my demise did not make me angry. It only further confirmed to me that the old school code of silence was no longer honored and had grown obsolete. This would be the turning point in my unconditional loyalty to the street law and my overall respect for those claiming to be stand-up guys in the game. The times of bad boys carrying their own weight were gone and it clearly appeared to me that the name of the game had changed to every man for himself. In every direction I turned, I saw individuals informing on one another to get out of jail, and the crab-ass mentality was in full effect everywhere I looked.

In a matter of weeks, I reestablished myself at the MCC with my old convict approach to doing things, which included winning and commanding the respect of my fellow prisoners. I was in my mid 30s at the time with half my life already having been spent behind prison walls and fences, so I was in familiar territory, having been practically raised in a prison environment. In contrast, those around me had little or no experience with the prison system. Like cream rising to the top, my convict character and how I carried and conducted myself would distinguish me from all the rest and put me in a unique and strong position. My criminal history, prison experience, and bad-boy reputation would be a badge of honor among these guys and room was made for me at any table.

In the beginning, my legal predicament looked like a mountain that was insurmountable, but once the picture became clear and I learned the extent of the evidence against me, I felt confident I could manage a favorable outcome. It is said in the profession of crime and punishment that there is no such thing as the perfect crime. By the same token, I believe every criminal case has flaws and weaknesses that can be exploited to the defendant's advantage. My case had significant elements and missing facts I could and would manipulate when my day in court eventually arrived. I spent hours in the MCC law library researching the law and studying every aspect of my case until I had a complete understanding as to how I could best use the law to once again regain my freedom. The countless hours I spent in the law library surrounded by law books, reading one legal decision after another, would pay off with huge dividends when the time came. Knowing and comprehending how to apply the law gave me a real fighting chance and also provided me with a viable battle plan.

My strategy was simple: damage control by minimizing the evidence against me. There was no doubt in my mind that I was going to do some time locked down and my objective was to keep the numbers as low as possible. When arrested, my .45 was found in the car I was driving and they found heroin on me. I had violated my supervised release and walked a very thin line from being charged as a career criminal, which carried a thirty-year sentence alone. A felony conviction for either the gun or the drugs would make me a career criminal candidate and I knew this in advance. My battle plan centered around denying and fighting the firearms allegation altogether, and contesting the drug charges, arguing it was only a misdemeanor possession. Yet one miscalculation and I would be doomed to decades in a federal prison.

It took exactly one year for me to have my day in court and during all that time, I prepared and refined my defense until I had it air tight. Although I had a court-appointed attorney representing me, he was just there for show and to handle the formalities of the proceedings. I would fight my own fight. I was very well prepared, but more importantly, I had more precise knowledge and information about the case than anyone else in the courtroom. It would also play in my favor that the U.S. attorney handling my case showed up overconfident in the outcome, totally underestimating me and not prepared in the least to defend against my attack on the government's case. Everything came together perfectly for me to execute my game plan and defense with only weak opposition from the U.S. attorney side.

I remember getting up early that morning in a very pleasant mood and thinking to myself, "Here we go again; it's showtime." My day in court had come and I had patiently waited and thoroughly prepared myself for it, and like a prize fighter, I was going in for the knockout. The U.S. attorney strutted into the courtroom with a self-assured air about him, as if he knew the deck was stacked against me and he was certain that he held the winning hand. After the judge took the bench and went through the formalities of explaining the purpose of the hearing and my rights to contest the allegations against me, the U.S. attorney made his first move. Addressing the court, he requested that my probation and supervised release be revoked and I be sent back to prison for being an ex-felon in possession of a firearm. The judge looked over in my direction and asked how do I answer to those charges.

The mere fact that the weapon was found in the car, and if I knew it was in there, and also had ready access to the weapon would be enough to find me guilty of constructive possession. Nowhere in all the legal documents did it say where the gun was found when I was arrested, so I would place the weapon safely out of my reach. I remember standing up to answer the judge, speaking in a matter-of-fact tone of voice saying, "Yes, Your Honor, when I was arrested a firearm was found in the glove compartment of the vehicle I was driving." I went on to explain that the car belonged to a friend and I had only used it that day to run a quick errand, and with a subtle edge to my words, I added "by no means did I search my friend's car for weapons prior to borrowing it and had no idea it was in the vehicle.

The judge would turn to the U.S. attorney asking if the marshals were present who executed my arrest and he replied "no." It's rare that federal agents appear at such hearings as mine and I absolutely counted on that because this provided no evidence to contradict my story. Seeing the weapons charge implode and lose its punch, the U.S. attorney told the judge he wanted to dismiss it and proceed forward with the drug-possession charge. Once again the judge turned to me and again I stood up to take the floor. "Yes, Your Honor," I said, "drugs were found in my possession, not to sell, but for my own personal use." After being asked several more questions by the judge, to which I provided plausible answers, the judge seemed to think for a minute and then suddenly ruled the matter to be simple possession and a misdemeanor.

The U.S. attorney leapt to his feet as if someone had set off a fire-cracker in his back pocket, exclaiming, "But Your Honor, the government intended this charge as possession with intent." His words came out sounding rather rude and challenging and the judge would reply with the sound of authority echoing throughout the courtroom saying, "I have ruled" and his words sounded final. The judge would also conclude that with the time I had already spent in jail, I should be released immediately with time served. Upon hearing the judge issue a court order that I be released, the U.S. attorney exploded with rage and stormed from the courtroom like a madman out of control. I had accomplished my objective but made an enemy in the process who would abuse the law while claiming to enforce it.

After my court hearing, my lawyer came to visit me before the marshals transported me back to the MCC with a message from the U.S. attorney. The message came in the form of a threat that I plead guilty to the criminal charge of possession of a controlled substance or he would indict me on additional drug charges. The events that followed would demonstrate to me that if one cannot fight the legal fight as a criminal defendant and hold their own, then do not start the fight. The U.S. attorney was angry because I had cunningly outmaneuvered him during my probation-violation hearing and I heard vindictiveness in this message. My revocation hearing was held late in the day on a Friday, so the paperwork for my release could not be processed until the following Monday. I would spend the weekend hopeful that I could squeeze through another crack in the legal system, but I was under no illusion about the U.S. attorney's mischievous intentions.

Instead of being released that Monday, I was taken back to court and formally charged with a misdemeanor drug possession offence, a charge the U.S. attorney would file just to keep me in police custody. He needed to convene a grand jury to indict me on felony drug charges and the clock was running against him. I understood the law in this situation as well as he did and would stay one step ahead of him as I anticipated his every move. At my preliminary hearing on the new possession case, I would totally surprise everyone present by promptly pleading guilty to the charge. From Day One, a simple possession was what I was fighting for to get my legal problems reduced to, and the U.S. attorney had handed me that victory through his threats, made in anger. The message the U.S. attorney sent me through my lawyer to plead guilty to possession quickly came back to repay him as his attack on me became more devious and vindictive.

Perhaps a week after pleading guilty in the drug-possession case, I was unexpectedly summoned to appear in court again. I had no idea what the hearing was about or that I was even on the court docket to appear before the judge. Once the court proceedings began, I would learn that integrity for the law in my case had been thrown out the window. The U.S. attorney would dismiss the simple possession charge to which I had already pled guilty and formally charge me in a three-count felony indictment. This was a highly irregular and very uncommon move on the part of the U.S. attorney and I knew right away it had the smell of being unethical if not outright unconstitutional.

Subconsciously, I knew the U.S. attorney was not about to walk away and allow me to prevail at his expense without striking back. But I was truly astonished as to the extent to which he was willing to go in bending and redefining the law to accomplish his objective. Once again, the U.S. attorney had underestimated me and my capabilities to research the law and properly apply it. Having been raised in the system, I learned at an early age that if I could not afford justice and if I wanted justice, then I had better learn how to fight for justice, and I learned how to fight. It would take me another year of courtroom battles to walk the U.S. attorney back down to the misdemeanor charge to which I had already pled guilty. When the dust from my legal problems finally settled, I walked out of the MCC a free man.

15. On the Block Again

Black, broke, and unemployable, I was firmly convinced that the only way for me to get ahead in life was as a street hustler. The conditions were perfect to influence and encourage me to pursue my livelihood on the streets. Upon my release from the MCC Chicago, I would pick up where I left off prior to my arrest and put down a full court press on the hustle game in the steel city. Still torn between what I call my two personalities, the natural good guy who wanted to go straight and the bad boy created by life circumstances, I would yield to my lower self. Society had made it clear that I could not outlive my past for the remainder of my life, being considered a social reject disenfranchised from sharing in the American dream.

From personal experience, I had lived through and witnessed the mass incarceration explosion that entrapped and snared the poor, those considered White trash, young African Americans like me, and all those looked upon as expendable, starting with President Reagan's get-tough-on-crime campaign during his race for the presidency in the '80s. This was followed by President Bush's war on drugs during his tenure, which added fuel to the mass-incarceration explosion. Whereas President Clinton would catch the blame for the exploding prison population, his super-predator crime bill merely accelerated the conditions. All these factors would contribute to my decision that it always would be a me-against-them situation. Those on the outside looking in, who never faced the oppression I have faced or lived under the oppressive conditions I have lived under and the environment in which I grew up, cannot judge me until they have been where I have been.

Suppressing my moral convictions between right and wrong and seeing my realities in the secular world surrounding me, I continued to grow more and more indifferent to man-made laws. In my view, I saw lawmakers and those charged with authority to be worse criminals than myself and they had the track record and history to prove it. If it was not for the deep roots the religion of Islam had taken in my spiritual being, I would have had no compass at all by which to find my way back home from where I had been and was about to go. I openly admit that I had my share of misconceptions and my life experiences had created a beast that only the religion of Islam could tame, hold in check, and eventually eradicate.

In full rebellion mode, I took to the streets following my release from MCC Chicago and worked my way around the Midwest, hustling and having absolutely no regard for the law or the consequences of my actions. I tapped into my connections on the streets once again and got heroin and cocaine on consignment based on the strength of my word alone. My word carried enough weight to literally get anything I wanted from my resources. With a power base in Indiana and Minnesota, I would spread my wings in the drug world until it inevitably caught up with me.

One day after returning to Gary from a trip to the Twin Cities, I arrived in town to learn that the local police and a federal task force was on the hunt for me. This was in the mid '90s and at the height of President Clinton's notorious super-predator crime bill. To my understanding, the federal task force GRIT (Gary Response Investigative Team) was in town on orders from the President. These federal task forces were established throughout the country pursuant to the President's crime bill to combat the violent drug-related criminal and gang activities plaguing communities. I would get caught up in this federal-task-force dragnet and subsequently be charged in a federal drug-conspiracy indictment.

While on my way to deliver a package to one of my workers, I was arrested in my old neighborhood on the border and taken straight back to MCC Chicago. My legal battle this time around would be my most tenacious fight with the U.S. government of all my legal battles. I was charged with conspiracy, distribution, possession, and possession with intent to distribute a controlled substance. Charged in a conspiracy indictment {alone} with no coconspirators or unindicted coconspirators was a completely bogus and impossible crime. It takes two or more individuals to constitute a conspiracy and one person alone can never be accused of conspiring to do anything legally or illegally. My court-appointed attorney knew this, the district court judge knew this, and the U.S. attorney filing the charges knew this, yet the case would proceed. The charge was unlawful and we all knew it, but no one would defend my rights to fairness and justice but me, so once again I was on my own. To me, I was facing and dealing with the only kind of justice that was available to someone like me, and I expected no more from my adversaries and keepers.

Back in the MCC again, the first thing I noticed in the short time I was gone was how much things had changed. Those incarcerated and awaiting trial were now far younger, African American, and all gang members. During my previous stay at the MCC, the Chicago street gang known as the Vice Lords and their leaders were locked up and taken out of circulation. Now, the Black Gangster Disciples and the Latin Kings, a nationwide Puerto Rican street gang, were all being held at the MCC. I was considered an O.G. (old gangster), a title of respect among gang members, acknowledging that I had put in creditable street work and was worthy of the utmost respect. They would all gravitate toward me to seek legal advice, to settle personal quarrels, or to be the peacemaker on the floor when different gang members clashed. Everyone would embrace me as I reestablished myself at the MCC once again on the floor to which I was assigned in the 28-story building. I was able to secure a very unique position because I was not bound by anyone's rules or gang laws and stood on my own. The environment of incarceration was a place I had come to know very well over the years and I became skillful at managing the elements around me as a matter of self-preservation, a skill I would refine over the years since age 15.

I was at the MCC for perhaps six months when a young brother named Little Frank arrived. The officer on duty that day called me down to his desk and asked if he could put Little Frank in the room with me as a roommate, since my room had the only bed space available. I had enough juice on the floor with the officers that I could pick and choose who they put in my room. I could have easily told the officer no and have him move someone already on the floor into my room who I knew and was cool with. Frank was only 19 years old and the officer wanted me to take him under my wing as a roomy more as a favor than just throwing him in with me. Most fights at the MCC were between roommates who could not get along, had nothing in common, and were entirely incompatible. The officer on duty knew me and knew my history. He also knew very well that putting a young gang banger in the same room with a seasoned convict could be like trying to mix oil with water.

Little Frank was a Black Gangster Disciple and, to my understanding, was one of Larry Hoover's most trusted and loyal soldiers. Frank's position was more or less a buffer between the gang leader who was incarcerated and the other gang members. King Larry was sentenced to 150 to 200 years in Illinois State Prison in 1973 for allegedly killing a drug dealer and would receive six life sentences in federal prison while still incarcerated. Larry would still command the Black Gangster Disciples from behind prison walls and Frank, when visiting Larry, would receive orders that were passed on to other gang members. Little Frank also picked up Larry's money from his street taxes owed by those governing territories on the streets of Chicago, according to Frank and the legal documents I read.

Little Frank was a very likeable guy and I treated him like a little brother from Day One. To him, his incarceration was a badge of honor and meant he had finally arrived at the top as a gang member. We would talk late into the night and on one particular occasion, he told me something shocking and disturbing. We were discussing his future when the young brother told me he did not want to live past age 21 because anything beyond that was too old. All his friends were dead before 21, he told me, and he wanted to go out the same way. Frank's words saddened my heart and left me questioning what in the world our young Black men have been reduced to, and I vowed to work on Little Frank to straighten out this crazy idea he had about life and dying young like his friends. I do not know if I said enough to Frank to alter his thinking, but when I inquired about him a few years later, I learned he was killed in the streets shortly after being released from federal prison. The social conditions that produced Little Frank's mentality, and that of many others like him, would also produce my mentality.

I spent about 15 months at the MCC awaiting trial and during that time I studied and researched the conspiracy laws. Although I had become familiar with these laws over the years, I had no reason to study them in depth until I myself was charged with conspiracy. I would go all the way back to the insertion of the conspiracy law enactment and work my way through the maze of pertinent decisions until I had a complete understanding. I had a very good head for the law in general and would have made a fantastic lawyer. By the time I was finished with my research, I felt confident I could compete with any attorney defending a conspiracy charge. Once again, it would dawn on me that the power of knowledge truly distinguished those who walked in darkness from those who walked in the light.

It was absolutely necessary for me to do my own legal footwork because my court-appointed attorney provided no assistance at all. No lawyer worth his license to practice would allow his client to be charged in a conspiracy indictment as a sole conspirator without challenging the allegation, and my attorney said and did nothing at all. No one would believe how the United Snakes were prosecuting me for the crime of conspiracy and it was obvious that I was being railroaded into a conviction and a long prison sentence. There was only one problem with this scenario: I would not go away quietly and without fighting to the bitter end. I was so confident in my abilities to represent myself that I would fire my attorney after growing totally disenchanted with his lack of effort and elected to represent myself at my trial. In the legal profession, they have a saying: "He who represents himself has a fool for a client." I might have had a good understanding of the law and knew how to find supporting case law, but was out of my league going up against an experienced prosecutor in a jury trial.

The U.S. attorney prosecuting my case turned out to be the same one who had handled my last encounter with the law and he was out for blood and revenge. He made several ridiculous plea-deal offers to keep the case from going to trial, but I rejected them all. I knew where I stood with my case and could not be intimidated into pleading guilty even when the U.S. attorney issued empty threats of charging me with being a career criminal, a charge on which he could not legally stand. I had the criminal history of a career criminal but was outside the federal sentencing guidelines to make the charge stick. Against all odds, I was ready to go toe to toe with the U.S. attorney and let the chips land wherever they fell.

On the first day my trial was scheduled to begin, I fired my court-appointed attorney and informed the judge I wanted to proceed *pro se* and represent myself. The U.S. attorney would claim I was engaging in stall tactics to avoid going to trial. I assured the judge that I was ready to move forward with my trial without further delay and the U.S. attorney was incorrect in his assumption. The entire mood and atmosphere of the courtroom suddenly changed as I proceeded to pick my jury and set the stage for my trial to begin. Everyone from the judge to the U.S. marshals escorting me to and from the courtroom seemingly treated me like I had leprosy from that point on, as the proceedings continued. Picking my jury would take up the whole day and I can recall the subtle hostile attitude everyone had toward me as the first day concluded. To me, the handwriting was clearly on the wall that I had jumped out of the frying pan straight into the fire with my decision to represent myself.

True enough, he who represents himself has a fool for a client and by no means was I a foolish man to the extent of playing Russian roulette with a loaded gun. There was no way my keepers would allow me to represent myself and win because it would set an unwanted precedent and others might follow my lead. I would be subjected to being made an example to discourage such a move. I was a dead man walking if I continued my course of trying to defend myself as my own attorney, and I knew it. Therefore, seeing my situation for what it was, I wrote a letter to the judge saying I felt it was in the best interest of all parties concerned that my former attorney be reinstated to handle my case. The judge had already ordered him to remain at my defense table as a standby attorney and putting him back in play was no problem.

I wrote my letter late that night, unable to sleep and fully understanding I was in over my head with how things were unfolding. The next morning, before appearing in court, I had one of the marshals hand deliver my letter to the judge: and just like that, we were all friendly, courteous, and peaceable again. The judge would start the proceeding that morning when I was called into the courtroom by joking with me and being unusually polite, and everybody else followed suit. I think my actions shook things up enough to let it be understood I was a fighter and was willing to fight for myself if my attorney would not do his job in representing my cause. The beautiful thing about all this is that my every move was a part of the court records and open to future review.

My trail took three days and the word *conspiracy* only came up when reading my indictment to the jury, as the judge told them of the crimes with which I was charged. At the conclusion of my trial, he would grant a judgment of acquittal on the conspiracy charge and the jury came back with a guilty verdict for possession and possession with intent after approximately five hours of deliberation. I would later learn that the real conspiracy was between all the court officials, including my attorney, who was in on the deal from Day One. It eventually came to light that the federal task force GRIT was under tremendous pressure to produce results after being in the Gary area for several years and having no impact on reducing the drugs and violence overwhelming the city. In town under the orders of the President and considered a vital law-enforcement unit, they faced the threat of being disbanded, so a rally cry was made to secure as many convictions as possible to save the existence of the task force.

I would be sentenced to only thirty-three months in prison for my crimes, and once again, the judge did something highly irregular and had my trial records sealed so no one could see what transpired in handling my case. To cap things off, I was told that if I appealed my conviction to the Seventh Circuit Court of Appeals, additional charges would be brought against a girlfriend of mine name Val and me. They threatened to charge us both with money laundering, a charge that was like a catch-all. Using one dollar of drug money to pay even a light bill was enough to be accused of money laundering. Val was my main woman in the Gary area. Her house was raided following my arrest and drugs and money were confiscated, which put her in legal jeopardy, and I could not allow that. Cutting off my losses at the knees, I would honor the threat and never appeal my conviction. The question lingered: Why did the court not want me to file an appeal? The answer was obvious. They did not want the higher court to see the travesty of justice I received.

Ordered to serve my time at FCI Milan in Milan, Michigan, I left MCC Chicago counting my blessings, knowing that I had dodged another bullet intended to be a direct head shot. Unto this very day, I believe God was protecting me from my own rebellious behavior and from the diabolical intentions of my keepers and their unfair brand of justice. My plan was to defy man-made laws to the bitter end because the scales of justice were so unbalanced when applied to someone like me. My keepers' plan was to lock me away for the rest of my life and throw away the keys. Yet God also had a plan for where my life would eventually lead me and God was the best of planners. No one could intervene, not even me.

16. FCI Milan

I spent a little more than a year at FCI Milan and by this time had over 20 years of incarceration under my belt at the age of 39. When the judge sentenced me to prison, he made a statement about me being con wise, but that was the understatement of the century. I had been attending crime school behind prison walls since age 15 and for all practical purposes, as a result of my experience, held a Ph.D. in criminology, a Ph.D. in criminal injustice, and a master's degree in survival under adversity as a convict. Intellectually, I trained myself to become a man who the judge and men like the judge would consider beyond conforming or rehabilitation. True enough, the judge's image of me as a con-wise defendant was only a mere reflection of the real man who lived within. My contempt for man-made laws had no boundaries and I could see only hypocrisy in those who prospered while claiming to uphold them. It took years for me to deprogram myself from this way of thinking once I walked away from the street life and totally submitted myself to following God's law as an upright man and Muslim.

My time at MCI Milan went by quickly and for the most part, all I did was work out every day and mind my own business. I got a laid-back job in the prison library with the help of a Muslim brother who had some influence in the joint, and like always, pretty much did as I pleased under the circumstances. Being able to move in many circles, I cultivated connections with brothers from New York to California and all points between. For some reason, people trusted me without question, I believe because they found honor in my word and respected how I carried and conducted myself. I did not portray false pretenses. I was not a liar at heart and was honorable in all that I laid claim to in words and deeds, all of which I believe others recognized and admired. Even as I lived the lifestyle of an outlaw, my principles and values as a man were grounded in the teachings of Islam. Millions of dollars would flow through my hands because I could be trusted to fulfill my obligations based on just my word alone, and many doors opened for me that were closed to others.

When I was finally released from MCI Milan, the dye was already irreversibly cast for me having no intentions or desire to be a so-called law-abiding citizen. Society had clearly demonstrated it was unforgiving toward me and I took it rather personally and found no reason to cooperate or compromise. My resentment was real, my bitterness had deep roots, and I was determined to do things my own way regardless of the consequences. I would be driven by my ambition to be successful in life and felt I had no choice but to play the hand I was dealt, and the hand I was dealt put me at a disadvantage from Day One.

Upon being released from Milan, I was required to spend an additional three months at a halfway house in Michigan City, Indiana. Given a bus ticket and seventy-five dollars, I was dropped off at the local Greyhound Bus Station with instructions to report in at the halfway house within 24 hours. My girl Val and my sister Gin would pick me up at the bus station once I reached Indiana, and after spending the day with them, we drove the short distance from Gary to Michigan City, where I checked in. They would allow Val and my sister to stay for a couple of hours to visit with me and after that the halfway house director called me into his office to lay down the law as to what was expected of me during my stay there. I did not like the director's attitude off the top, and at one point when he mentioned sending me back to FCI Milan if I did not follow the rules, I looked him straight in the eye and said, "Don't do me any favors; do your job." That would be the beginning of a contentious exchange between the director and me until I left the halfway house.

All federal prisoners were required to spend at least ninety days at a halfway house when released directly from prison as part of the Bureau of Prisons reintegration program. We were supposed to go out and find gainful employment in a job market that rejected ex-convicts and openly denied them equal protection of the law to secure a decent paying job. Unless you knew someone, an individual with my criminal background was left with scantily paying employment that offered no future and made it impossible to live a substantial and meaningful lifestyle. As for me, I had absolutely no interest in a dead-end minimum-wage job and instead of going out each day looking for work, I went out to lay the foundation for my future criminal enterprise.

Once freed from the halfway house, I immediately put my plans into action. A Nigerian brother from Chicago who I'd met at Milan was a major heroin dealer. The brother put me in contact with his people and instructed them to show me love. I would do business with a brother named George, starting with a mere five grams of China white heroin and worked that up to a hundred grams a week in less than a month. By the time I expanded my operation to the Twin Cities area, I was moving nearly five hundred grams every two to three weeks. My operation continued to grow until I reach over kilo a month, which was not bad business by any standards in the heroin market for a one-man game that kept it moving. I would again move around the Midwest, quietly putting in work and staying beneath the radar of federal and state authorities. Reinvesting every dollar I made as I climbed from the bottom to the top, one day I had a pile of drugs and no money and the next day a pile of money and no drugs. This cycle continued until I was able to start squirreling away a no-touch personal stash of cash.

Not only was I living in the fast lane, I also made some bold and aggressive moves to accomplish my objective, which some would consider crazy or imprudent. Rather, in my opinion, I simply had the courage and the balls to do what the next man did not have the nerves or heart to do. My boldness was not a reflection of stupidity but a reflection of my strong will to achieve my goals. Although I did not live life recklessly at the time, I do acknowledge that I was living life close to the edge and was flying very close to the sun. In my thinking, I stood alone, just as I seemingly had stood alone for as long as I can remember and had nothing or no one to keep me grounded. If I went back to prison, I would go alone and do my time alone and would not be missed. If I was killed in the streets, my family could only mourn for a stranger and the mere shadow of the person I was before life behind prison walls produced the rebellious outcast and outlaw I would become.

I recognized a tremendous void in my life and in my heart that needed to be filled with more than myself and my dreams to be rich and free to go and do whatever I pleased. I fully understood I was more of a threat to myself and my freedom than all the law-enforcement agencies combined, and needed to make adjustments. I decided to marry a young lady named Betty to fill the void in my heart and create an anchor to keep me from living so close to the edge. This was a conscious decision on my part and a very good one because it made me think twice about every move I made and think again before making it. Betty had a young daughter about five or six years old who was like my own. I was at the hospital when she was born and showed up with everything a newborn needed when the baby came home. Betty and I were very good friends long before we got married and today I think perhaps we should have stayed just friends, but Betty was my kind of woman: educated, very attractive, neither naïve or overly streetwise, and most importantly, she was a woman I could trust with my closely guarded secrets.

When Betty and I first became lovers, the father of her daughter—a Gary police officer—had blood in his eyes and wanted my head and me dead. Although Betty put an end to their relationship after learning the guy had fathered one and possibly two other children while they were together, he was stuck on stupid over Betty and wanted to have his cake and eat it too. Many of my friends told me to leave Betty alone because this police officer was bad news and I could not win going up against him. But I too was stuck on stupid when it came to another man trying to bully or intimidate me, even if they had the entire Gary police department behind them. The conditions were perfect for a potentially deadly situation to erupt on any given day. We were two extremely deranged individuals in conflict with each other, one being a hardcore ex-convict and convicted murderer and the other a corrupt police officer under federal investigation for a double murder. The only thing that prevented him from eventually killing me or me from killing him was the federal authorities arresting him on murder and drug-conspiracy charges.

Married with a ready-made family was a real stabilizer for me and I embraced the responsibility of being a husband and father with gratitude. I felt obligated not only to make it safely home at the end of each workday in the streets, but also make it home at a reasonable hour. Betty and my step-daughter became the anchor I needed to provide substance and significance in my life at the time, keeping me from living carefree and being so nonchalant about the consequences of my actions. As a direct result of accepting my duties and commitment to being a family man, I would stay out of prison for a good eight years. Not since age 15 had I spent more than a year on the streets without going back to prison or being on the run from the police. Prison life was finally beginning to gradually fade into a distant memory, and with each passing day I grew to feel more invincible to the curse of incarceration that had left a permanent scar on my inner being.

One day while visiting my baby sister Gin, she told me a brother from California had called and left a message for me to get in touch with him. The caller turned out to be a brother named Stephen, a major cocaine connection I had cultivated while at FCI Milan. Stephen was out and wanted to do business, he informed me upon returning his call. We talked, mostly feeling each other out to see where things stood since we both were now on the streets and back in the game. Our conversation concluded with Stephen inviting me out to San Diego with the promise that he would make the trip worth the long drive to California from Indiana. Within limits, I trusted Stephen and his word when it came to whether he could produce, yet had not determined the degree of mischief in his heart versus his loyalty to a friend. Scheming and conniving for self-serving gains ran rampant in the drug world, some being more shady and black-hearted than others, and Stephen was no exception.

Playing it safe, I took a hundred thousand out of my stash and headed for San Diego to meet up with Stephen to see where our business plan would lead. If everything went according to plan, I would be returning with a load of cocaine. Knowing that anything could happen during my travel to and from California, I had a cover story ready in case I was stopped by the police. I had accumulated a great deal of expensive professional photograph equipment over time and decided being a photo journalist would make an excellent cover in travel. My advance planning and preparations paid off with huge dividends on my return trip heading home because, sure enough, I got pulled over by the Utah state police.

I spent three days in San Diego waiting for Stephen to get things together, which was my first indication that the brother warranted close watching. He had assured me he was ready to serve me before I had left Indiana, but once I arrived, he made one excuse after another as to why I needed to give him additional time. I was certain Stephen was working some sort of angle to secure cocaine for me but I did not like the idea of being sold an empty dream. Say what you mean and mean what you say was how I did business, and I made it clear to Stephen that in the future he had to keep things straight if he wanted to deal with me. Sitting around waiting for days was not part of my game plan, and it had me off balance because I was a strong believer that everything worked best when I stayed inside the parameters of the game plan.

Stephen eventually came through with ten kilos of cocaine after giving him a 24-hour deadline to produce or I would leave and all bets were off. He wanted fifteen thousand per kilo, which was a good number because in the Midwest the numbers ran as high as twenty-two thousand a kilo at the time and even higher during a drought. I gave Stephen the one hundred thousand dollars I came with and we agreed I could send him the other fifty once I got back on my end. Stephen smiled with a look of surprise playing across his face when I took the gun from the bag the money was in before handing the bag to him. Sliding the weapon beneath a pillow on the bed, I pretended not to notice how Stephen watched my every move, but little did he know I had my trusted Colt .45 at the ready, concealed under the loose-fitting tee-shirt I was wearing, as real protection.

Stephen and I discussed future business plans and engaged in general small talk for several more minutes before he announced he had to leave. I recalled him asking when I intended to depart for my trip back to the Midwest, and I intentionally replied with a vague and ambiguous response, saying I was uncertain and perhaps I would get a good night's sleep and leave early the following day. It was my practice to limit the information I shared with others regarding how I moved when riding dirty because the less they knew, the less they could convey that could possibly jeopardize my safety. I never told anyone how or when I was moving when making a drug run, and I packed my bags and prepared to leave as soon as Stephen was gone.

I immediately slipped into my photo journalist character, putting on a nice Armani suit and spreading my photography equipment around in plain sight on the passenger seat of my truck. With my cover story well-rehearsed and the professional image I wanted to project in place, I hit the road moments after Stephen's departure. I would drive nonstop to put as much distance as possible between San Diego and me until I reach Las Vegas later that night. By sunrise I was pushing my way through the state of Utah, enjoying the serenity of the early morning and watching the sun lighten up my surroundings to fully reveal the beauty of the vast natural landscape for which Utah is known. The scenery was so picturesque and intriguing that I draped a camera around my neck and started taking photos. The thought was impulsive and seemingly appeared from out of nowhere. I recall feeling as though hanging that camera around my neck and assuming the role of a photo journalist was synonymous with putting on a bullet-proof vest.

Driving right along and genuinely enjoying the beautiful and rugged scenery of the seemingly virgin terrain flashing past as I drove, I suddenly spotted a state police car sitting on the overpass of a bridge up ahead, monitoring all oncoming traffic. Instinctively, I felt the police officer would fall in behind me as I approached his location and sure enough, he did. Foreseeing what was most likely to unfold next, I quickly collected my photo journalist composure and prepared myself to give a freedom-saving performance. I knew the drill very well. I knew the things a well-trained police officer looks for when making a random stop, how they read reactions and body language. I was ahead of the game that would eventually play out once the officer pulled me over for a random traffic stop after trailing me for several miles.

The speed limit was perhaps 70 or 75 and I was approaching an eighteen wheeler traveling at a lesser speed. With the police car directly behind me, hot on my trail, no doubt running a check on my vehicle, I decided to maintain my speed to see if the police officer would go around me and push on. After a few miles of the cat chasing the mouse game, I accelerated and smoothly shot past the semi and continued on, the police car behind me like a shadow, following my every move. The police officer would pull up beside me as though he was about to pass me by, then glancing my way, our eyes made contact and he suddenly fell right back in line behind my vehicle. I got the impression that the police officer, seeing a Black man behind the steering wheel of the classy and very stylish vehicle I was driving, had decided to further pursue an interest in my presence on the highway.

I was driving the first edition of the Harley Davidson F-150 pickup truck, a real look-at-me vehicle that was rich in character and commanded the attention of admirers wherever I went. I rarely drove my Harley when at home because it drew so much attention; I only used it for long-distance road trips. I purchased the Harley Davidson F-150 off the showroom floor with only fifteen miles on it as a Christmas and birthday present for myself. Buying the Harley was something I felt compelled to do as a selfish act for myself after seeing how everyone else was enjoying the fruits of my labor while I neglected my own wants and needs. I spent money on others and helped others constantly every single day, assisting people with rent payments, utility bills, groceries, and even funerals. I spent very little on myself and rarely purchased the material things that street players buy to boost their street image. Buying the Harley F-150 was a matter of rewarding myself and doing something for myself, putting me first for a change over gratifying the wants and needs of those who acted like my generosity was endless.

It came as no surprise to me when the state police officer hit me with flashing lights and pulled me over for what he called a routine traffic stop. It was no more than I expected. I had grown accustomed to the racial-profiling tactics of the police and preconditioned myself to be prepared for what would unfold. I believe the police officer pursued me out of mere curiosity because very few of the limited edition Harley

Davidson F-150s were on the road when they first came out. The Harley F-150 had an extraordinary appearance that made a person want to follow it and further adore the beauty of the vehicle, and the police officer was no exception. However, intrigue would fade into something more cynical once the officer saw a Black man driving the F-150.

When the Utah state trooper got out of his car and appeared at my driver-side window, I greeted him with a big disarming smile that said I had absolutely nothing to hide. In a non-defiant manner, the smile also implied that I knew very well the reason I was being stopped. As the officer asked for my driver's license, he would claim he pulled me over because my tires touched the white line and I was driving under the speed limit. His ludicrous statement should have produced an indignant response on my part; instead, it produced an even broader smile to play across my face. Without saying a single word, I allowed the frown in my eyes to say for me, who's fooling who here? We both knew why I was being pulled over, but what this officer did not know was my entire plan anticipated such probabilities as police stops during my journey, and I trusted my plan. The officer was also totally unaware of who I was, what I was, or from whence I came as a man.

The trooper then asked where I was coming from. He posed the question in such a way that it sounded like he was only warming up for his opening act. Yet, sudden doubt and hesitancy enveloped his demeanor upon hearing my reply. "From a photo journalist seminar at the MGM Grand in Las Vegas" I answered with a subtle hint of confidence and self-importance. My answer had the desire effect, a well-placed gut shot that caused the trooper to retreat to a more neutral position. I could clearly see in his eyes and in his change of attitude that he was thinking whether it was a feasible idea to compromise my civil rights, as the police are notoriously known for doing when dealing with the African American community. The photo journalist character I was portraying created enough separation to imply that things had the potential to get out of control if mishandled. For all practical purposes, as a journalist I could have connections and resources to fight an unlawful police stop and the trooper obviously wanted no part of such probabilities.

My overall objective was to prevent the Utah state trooper from asking or wanting to search my vehicle, a common occurrence when profiled as a likely drug dealer. With ten kilos of cocaine in a suitcase on the back seat and two firearms in the vehicle, I gave no excuses or lawful reasons for a vehicle search. My composure was perfect, revealing no sense of nervousness. I provided direct and thorough answers to his question while maintaining the appearance of a professional at my craft. The trooper looked around the inside of my Harley F-150, seemingly sizing me up one final time, and then, handing me my license back, told me to have a good day and walked back to his squad car.

My plan worked as designed, saying just enough to indirectly convey a message of being above reproach. I simply reversed and applied the same form of psychology the police are trained to use, but left the trooper room to gracefully choke himself out. From personal experience, I knew an African American man driving a nice new automobile made him highly susceptible to a random police stop on any given day. I was occasionally stopped and questioned by the police for no other reason than driving while Black. It came with the territory in the life I lived. For those who think racial profiling is exaggerated, I am compelled to ask, when was the last time you were randomly stopped because your car tires touched a white line or for going approximately four or five miles under the speed limit in a 70- to 75-mile speed zone? Even more simplistic, when was the last time you heard of someone being pulled over for such a trivial and purely asinine reason?

Back on the road again, I was able to exhale and allow the tension in the air to gradually dissipate as I continued to push on toward my final destination, which was Minneapolis, Minnesota. My connection with Stephen would prove to be the beginning of my climb to the top as a major cocaine distributor in the Midwest. Selling most of the ten kilos in wholesale quantities, my first shipment was gone in less than a week and with prior arrangements already made to keep the product coming, I was off and running against all odds.

17. Where Mistakes Are Made

I was a loner and an independent operator in my business dealings in the streets, and although I had several individuals on my team who I considered trusted friends, I had no partners with whom I shared my decision-making. I preferred being a solo act over being part of the crowd or a member of a gang. I had no real inclination for partnerships or for having a partner in crime connected to my hip like a twin, without whom I could not move. My early experience with having codefendants and crime partners had already proven to me that police pressure often produced betrayal. I would carefully pick and choose those with whom I established a business relationship and I also had an uncompromising criterion as to those I welcomed into my inner circle.

As I powered up for what I was planning to be an eventual subtle takeover of the lion's share of the cocaine market in the Midwest, the Old Man would show up. The Old Man was out of prison after serving approximately twenty-eight years on a life sentence for a contract murder and word reached me that he desperately wanted to hook up with me. The Old Man was a pure intellect, a true alpha male, and no doubt one of the deadliest men I have ever met. The Old Man was also an absolute capitalist. We shared a mutual respect, and although many in our prison environment had no real love for him, the Old Man and I had an unspoken bond. The same capitalist who seriously worshipped his money but gave me an interest-free loan while in prison together now wanted to be on my team on the streets.

Not only was the Old Man back on the block, but many brothers with whom I grew up in prison as teenagers were now out after serving twenty or more years on life sentences, and they all sought to join forces with me on one level or another. My inner circle would comprise primarily these brothers, individuals who had been tested and proven and had distinguished themselves as stand-up men. I literally grew up in prison among them. They were men I could trust and embrace as friends. In prison, no one can hide their true identity. If people were weak and soft, lacking the fortitude to represent themselves as men, they would inevitably be exposed. My guys were original bad boys who could not be bought or sold, who did not compromise or cooperate under pressure and, like me, said what they meant and meant what they said.

I dealt with Stephen for perhaps six months before the Old Man came into the picture. Our business relationship began with me giving him a kilo of cocaine on consignment, which the old man returned a week later because he had not worked up to a kilo clientele and did not want to break the kilo down and sell it in pieces on the streets. Upon returning the kilo of cocaine, the Old Man hit me with a proposition I had to seriously consider. Admitting street-level drug dealing was not his forte and he had no real desire to operate on that level, the Old Man went on to explain that he had been taking flying lessons with a young pilot he met and cultivated as a potential asset. Before our conversation was over, I had the answer to the forever perplexing and present problem of moving product and huge amounts of cash between the Midwest and the West Coast.

I had a rather uncomfortable arrangement with Stephen where we were sending drugs and money back and forth through the mail, a suggestion I agreed to reluctantly. For twenty-five thousand dollars per round trip, the Old Man easily convinced me to allow him to handle my transport issue. Leasing the plane, paying the fuel cost, and compensating the pilot with twenty-five grand was a no-brainer if it meant making my life less complicated. But not only would this proposition solve my transport concerns, it also infused my overall game plan with a new component that took things to another level. By air, I was able to move larger amounts of product at a faster pace with far less exposure to law-enforcement traps. Stephen also loved the idea when I informed him that I was taking my transport operation to the air. He locked in on the idea immediately and wanted to employ the service of my newfound connection to further his own business venture from his end.

The deal I negotiated with Stephen would work out perfectly for me because every time the plane moved, the Old Man and I made money. My number per kilo was reduced by a thousand dollars, the Old Man would receive two percent of all cash being moved around, and we split the thousand dollars from each additional kilo transported, designated to other locations. To further secure my twenty-five-thousand-dollar investment in the plane trips, I insisted I receive no less than twenty-five kilos each time I sent my people on a run. No one saw me coming as I maintained a low profile and operated beneath the radar as the underworld's best-kept secret on the streets. In no time, millions began to flow through my hands until my personal bankroll rapidly pushed past a million dollars. Yet as Murphy's law implied, "whatever can go wrong will eventually go wrong."

The first indication of trouble looming on the horizon came in the form of Stephen revealing his true nature as a greedy, self-serving individual and user of people. Money has a way of revealing a great deal about some people and I quickly recognized the change in character in Stephen and the Old Man as the money and the operation grew. Stephen had a greedy and selfish nature at his core that I soon discovered. The Old Man was a true boss, used to dictating how affairs went. Although he praised me for what he told me was giving him a chance to live his dream in the drug world, I forever remained conscious of the fact that he resented being considered second man, following my instructions. With the exception of my real inner circle of those proven true and loyal, everyone else bore constant watching, including Stephen and the Old Man.

It was perhaps during these hours that I began to see, acknowledge, and begin to feel a sense of guilt in how I was using my God-given talents. I built a very lucrative organization from the ground up, which directly contributed to the spread of death and destruction. This thought continued to stress my conscience to the limits. Yet I would press onward to build a criminal network where everything revolved around me. Without my presence and energy, things would immediately fall completely apart. I designed my game plan from Day One in layers where only I had the full picture of how my operation functioned, and keeping the left hand from knowing what the right hand was doing, made my invaluable position golden.

In my dealings on the streets, I came in contact and conducted business with a multitude of unsavory and devious personalities. Jealousy and envy ran rampant in the drug world more than in any other aspect of the criminal lifestyle I lived. The player haters, paper tigers, and those on the block perpetrating a fraud as bad boys, seemed too busy watching the hole and not the doughnut. My thoughts were in what I considered to be a totally different dimension from the rest of the pack and although most of them were playing a mere game of checkers, I was playing chess and thinking several moves ahead of everyone in the game. Here again, I used my unexplainable and uncanny gift as a natural organizer to turn foes into friends, bringing peace between adversaries, and bringing together men who functioned harmoniously only because I was the sole common factor.

I would acknowledge that I was blessed with something special. I would also acknowledge that I was using my gifts in the worst and most wasteful ways possible. Yet, standing on my mountain top looking down into the valley, I could see it all and I was too far gone to turn back. With skill and finesse, I would manage the egos and conflicting personalities and my innate abilities to dissect and read human nature served me well. My true test in keeping all the players in their proper place of play came between Stephen and the Old Man attempting to move without first consulting me. Stephen's selfishness and greed would collide with the Old Man's ego to make decisions independent of me. As a result, when things went badly, the original bad boy and solo street gangster in me emerged to resolve the troubles that followed and, in the end, my word would prove final.

I can vividly recall that first trip to the West Coast by plane before turning all transport over to the Old Man who truly loved the work he was doing. The Old Man's ambitions and aspirations revolved around being a major drug smuggler and I put him in a position to live his dream, according to him. Coming from the same penitentiary school of thought, I knew I could trust the Old Man to handle business. He was a man of his word and lived by the honor system shared among seasoned convicts. No one could intimidate him and no one would knowingly attempt to strong arm the Old Man because the brother possessed an extremely lethal side. Our first trip by air in the twin-engine Cessna we leased would be my first and last. I found the flight so uncomfortable, with all the bouncing around in the little plane, that I happily delegated the responsibilities to the Old Man.

From what the Old Man told me and from what I was able to discern using my instinctive habit to listen and process everything—including those things said and those left unsaid—I got a clearer picture of our young pilot and what he was about. The young pilot was a former member of the U.S. Air Force and currently worked for a major airline. He was a young African American brother, perhaps in his mid-30s, married to an older high-maintenance and very materialistic wife. The brother had a pleasant demeanor about him and I genuinely liked how he carried and conducted himself. His focus and professionalism would expel any doubts I had about flying in the small plane with him for the first time. I also quickly recognized that the young pilot was definitely out of his element in dealing with two hardened criminals like the Old Man and myself.

I would not fly back with them on that first trip due to a weight issue. In working up his flight plan in preparation for our departure, our pilot, in calculating his flight weight, concluded we were a little overweight for a safe take off. I happily suggested they leave me behind to take a commercial flight home. Without my few little pounds calculated into the equation, the weight was right and they were good to go. I remember standing there on the tarmac watching them take off, relieved I did not have to take the small bumpy plane ride back. The Old Man, on the other hand, was purely elated with a grandiose sense of self-significance and adventure upon being given full responsibility to assure the shipment's safe delivery to our home base in Chicago. I fully understood what the Old Man was doing. He wanted a meaningful position in taking my operation to a higher level and wanted to demonstrate himself to be a valued component in doing so, as well as accomplishing his own objectives to become a major player in the game through my operation.

I could literally trust the Old Man with every dime I had. I could even trust him with my life, but I knew well in advance, I could never completely control him and could never trust him with too much power. The West Coast operation ran smoothly until Stephen and the Old Man decided to make plans and moves without first consulting me or getting my green light to go. The total collapse of the business arrangement between Stephen and me came when I sent the Old Man to pick up a shipment out West for me and he ended up all the way out East, in New Jersey, on a drug run for Stephen instead. I was not informed of this deviation until the Old Man and the pilot were already in midflight and well on their way. By this time, I had discovered that Stephen possessed a tendency to use anyone around him selfishly to gratify his greedy nature. I recognized Stephen as that guy who thought everyone was less intelligent and gullible enough to do his dirty work. On more than one occasion in the early days of our dealings, he tried me until I put him in his proper place by telling him, "Man, I am not your damn foot soldier."

He would also misread the Old Man when thinking he could outfinagle that ruthless and shrewd businessman, mistaking the Old Man's eagerness to be a power player in the game as a weakness to be exploited. I sent the Old Man to the West Coast with seven hundred thousand dollars cash and when he did not return on schedule, I made the usual inquiring calls. Unable to reach the Old Man, I eventually learned from Stephen, to my sudden and shocking surprise, that the Old Man was not en route to Chicago but on his way to New Jersey on a run for Stephen and his Mexican connection. My raw irritation was clear upon learning about this. I was definitely pissed off and Stephen felt me. Yet, for the most part, I did not panic and held my composure until I heard from the Old Man, who I was certain moved with a reasonable purpose in mind.

I got a call from the Old Man a little after midnight, after they landed in New Jersey, and they were having problems already. The Mexican connection was supposed to have taken a commercial flight, meeting the

Old Man in Jersey, and take charge of the shipment. The Mexican was nowhere to be found and neither the Mexican guy nor Stephen were answering their phones. The following morning and throughout most of the day, they still had no word from Stephen or the Mexican guy. When I finally made contact with Stephen, I did not hold back or pull my punches, clearly expressing my disapproval about what happened and how things got to where they were. I would verbally chastise him for putting my people in jeopardy by leaving them hanging in limbo while riding dirty, and advised him to make things right before things got worse. My inner bad boy had emerged, a side of me of which Stephen was totally unaware and unprepared to address. Before the dust settled, I would be the last man standing and all the odds would be in my favor, with the Old Man following my lead.

Stuck in New Jersey loaded down with thirty-two kilos and my seven-hundred thousand, I instructed the Old Man to be airborne and on his way to Chicago by nightfall if the planned rendezvous had not taken place by then. Needless to say, they failed to meet the deadline and the Old Man followed through with my instructions. Some hours later, my phone began to ring off the hook, first Stephen calling and then the Mexican. They both wanted to know where the Old Man and the pilot were. When I nonchalantly informed them "My people were on their way home after being stood up on a dummy mission" the conversation would become rowdy and turn confrontational. I remained cool through it all until the Mexican guy called me, claiming I was kind of responsible for the shipment. "Kind of responsible!" I shot back with an angry smirk laced with venom, and then softly added with obvious finality in my words, "Man, don't you fucking call me again, ever." I hung up on the Mexican and proceeded to call Stephen and relay the very same message to him, saying they cut their little side deal without me and now they had to solve their conflict without me.

Stephen, being greedy, money hungry, and a petty miser at heart, always had his hands out for the money due him, yet was slow to grudgingly pay his tab. He owed the Old Man a substantial amount of cash. Compensation for the flight from the West to the East Coast had to be accounted for, plus my twenty-five grand for the original trip West was on the table. The Old Man and I agreed nothing would move another inch until these issues were addressed and satisfactorily resolved.

Once again, Stephen would reach out to me seeking my assistance, at first asking if I would arrange for the shipment to be transported forward to Detroit. I told him I had no intention of moving or touching the shipment, period, and that the Old Man refused to move until he got paid. I suggested Stephen call the brother because they created the issue and the issue was between the two of them. Stephen then asked if I would secure the shipment until he could send someone for it. Thinking I could solve everyone's problems and also maintain the peace, I offered to take care of the Old Man and just pay for the thirty-two kilos. His answer totally baffled me and immediately fired up my suspicions. "No," he flat out stated. "That's gotta go somewhere else." I remember reaching the conclusion on the spot and at that very moment that the shipment would never make it somewhere else. I did not know what sort of conniving Stephen was up to, but as far as I was concerned, all bets were off and every man had to stand on his own and represent his own interests from that point onward.

Where mistakes are made in street life, somebody must pay. Mistakes will often cost a person their life in the drug world in particular. Always security conscious because I had a family to protect, I stayed invisible, appearing and disappearing on the scene accordingly. I was not a creature of habit and could never be found in the same place at the same time and on any given day. But most importantly, absolutely no one knew where I lived and kept my wife and daughter. To keep my family safe and have a peaceful zone to escape to, I would relocate my family every time I felt one too many of my potential enemies knew where I lived.

Now the Old Man, on the other hand, would pass out his personal information like handing out his business card in his reckless zeal to cultivate connections through my network; thus, it came as no real surprise when I got the call one evening from the Old Man saying he had visitors and needed to see me right away. Assured he was okay, I asked no questions and simply said, "I'm on my way." The Old Man lived in Chicago, a good forty-five minutes away. I probably reached his doorstep in thirty. I showed up with complete urban gorilla combat gear: two bullet-proof vests, an AK 47 equipped with fifty round drums, an M-16 with extra clips, a 12-gauge Mossberg shotgun loaded with deer slugs, and of course my forever present Colt .45.

Upon arriving, the Old Man handed me a piece of paper that I quickly read as he related what had just happened at his home. Two Mexicans approached the door pretending to be a package-delivery service and made a move to subdue him. The Old Man threw one assailant over the balcony of his stairs and wrestled the gun away from the second one and began to shoot at both men. The two Mexicans apparently misread the information on the slip of paper they lost and left behind during the scuffle. The piece of paper had the words Old Man written on it, followed by an address. Those of us who acknowledged this brother as the Old Man did so as a token of respect creditably earned, and definitely not because he was an old man. In fact, he was far from being what anyone would perceive to be an old man. The two Mexicans learned what we already knew: approach the Old Man at your own risk in the game of life and death. The brother actually had a serious body count under his belt of those who have tried him and failed. In fact, when I decided to welcome the addition of the Old Man into my operation, I did so primarily for two reasons: I knew I could trust him and live with the results of his overzealous business-instinct tendencies, and I also knew for a certainty that I had a known killer on my team, ready to quickly eliminate any hostile opposition in the air and match me bullet for bullet against our common enemy if proven necessary.

The failed attempt to strong arm the old man, abduct him, or do whatever they had intentions of doing would be the last we heard from those boys on the West Coast. Where mistakes are made in the dope game, someone must pay. Violating or deviating from one's word and introducing bullshit into the game counted not only as a mistake, but as a gross insurmountable error on Stephen's part. Stephen and his Mexican connection paid royally for their mistake. I settled with the Old Man with a two-hundred-fifty-thousand-dollar cash payout and the thirty-two kilos were mine at a cost of less than ten thousand per kilo and a drug dealer's dream price.

18. Back to the Drawing Board

Safe continuous product flow is the Achilles heel for every drug dealer, no matter the level. With my West Coast connection no longer in play, my immediate concern was finding a distributor to answer my growing call for supply. Back at the drawing board, I came up with a plan to explore my options in Texas after carefully pondering how much of the same border the state shared with Mexico. To anyone seriously involved in the cocaine market, it was common knowledge that the vast majority of all cocaine smuggled into the United States at the time came by way of clandestine routes through states that ran parallel to our southern borderline with our neighbors in Mexico.

I would reach out to another one of my prison confidantes, D.R., the most dynamic pure leader I met during my prison experience. D.R. also served more than twenty years on a life sentence in prison for his involvement in a triple robbery-homicide case. Out of the joint and living in Dallas, D.R. knew I was a legit go-getter and without question agreed to join forces with me to uncover a new connection. D.R. should have been a ten-star general in the military because he was a natural-born leader who was capable of turning a mere kitty cat into a ferocious lion. I respected D.R. and felt we shared a unique bond of brotherly love, being loners and leaders and both being giants in our own right from prison to the streets. While incarcerated as teenagers, I would flip D.R. from being just a gang leader to becoming a gang leader of a small army behind prison walls, getting money, smuggling drugs and other contraband into the prison system. The one thing I appreciated most about

D.R. was the brother's quickness to fight his own battles when others were willing and ready to defend him with their lives. Unlike most gang members I met and knew who only had courage when running in a pack like hyenas, D.R. possessed valor and commanded killers.

Most would say I was playing with fire in how I executed my first venture into the Texas drug market. With three hundred fifty thousand dollars cash and a clear mission in sight, the Old Man and I set out for Dallas, fully armed and ready to defend. The move was not only highly dangerous, but also unconventional. Entirely too many unpredictable variables came into play when attempting to purchase large amounts of cocaine on this level. Between the stick-up men and the police, when strangers are dealing with strangers, they can never be certain who or what might turn up. For the most part, one cannot simply take three hundred fifty thousand dollars and go shopping for drugs as if you're going grocery shopping; things just do not work that way! In a land where no one trusted anyone, the stakes were uncompromising and the risks involved were potentially life threatening. Yet, I remained confident I could masterfully negotiate and manage the situation by mentally staying one step ahead of all opposing forces. My mental game was my best weapon.

After three days on the hunt, we got lucky and scored twenty-one kilos following two false meetings with individuals who I strongly believe were attempting to set us up for a robbery. I had pre-planned for all such possibilities and showed up at those meeting in full force with our fire power on full display, as an intimidating deterrent. Heavily armed, the picture was crystal clear that we came prepared to protect and defend our invested interest. The picture was also crystal clear that very serious-minded men were behind those guns, men who would not hesitate to use them in decisively dealing with any troubles confronting them. No doubt, my crew of hardened ex-convicts who played for keeps when called into action can make things end rather quickly for any would-be or want-to-be adversary.

We made several trips to Dallas, sometimes scoring a load and sometimes returning home frustrated and empty handed. Then on one trip to Dallas, when managing to purchase only a partial amount of what we actually came for and needed, our strategy would change. D.R. had a young Mexican protégé under him who had a family with drug connections in Mexico. The Old Man, being the adventurous one, volunteered to travel into the land of the drug cartel with the young Mexican, intending to secure us a more consistent source. I would agree with the Old Man and give him the unspent cash I had left and send him on his way. I returned to the Midwest with the product we already scored, having absolutely no interest at the time in crossing the border into Mexico because I was once again on the run from the authorities for violating my parole. No one knew I was on the run and though I continued to play past the police during occasional traffic stops by using my fake identities, I did not want to chance crossing the border into Mexico.

My operation was growing so rapidly that I could not supply the demand and a reliable Mexican cartel connection would serve me well. The cocaine I got would be gone literally before I purchased it, and considering the territories I could reach into, I projected my future target range to be a ton a month. I needed and wanted a Mexican cartel connection to further my objective to dominate and put a full-court press on the Midwest. The Old Man was in his element in pursuit of that connection as well as being a man highly capable of making things happen. I was ready to fulfill my childhood ambition of not only being a major street player, but also outshining everyone in the game as one of the very best who ever contributed to the Gary gangster chronicles.

As a kid, I grew up heavily influenced and infatuated by my surroundings and what I perceived as the images of success in all that was around me. There were no physicians, attorneys at law, or other professional people in my surroundings to provide an image contrary to what I lived and breathed. It would be the pimps, players, and street hustlers who cast the image of success I aspired toward. My ambitious drive to one day become a true force to be reckoned with on the streets inevitably became a reality. The same neighborhood in the red-light district of Gary that I once controlled as a paperboy and observed the activities of the street life from a distance was now under my full control as a drug dealer. I would sit at the round table with men who were giants with well-known reputations as gangsters on the streets, yet I was the giant everyone looked up to. They did not look up to me as their leader, but as a man with a plan they were willing to follow. My reputation itself as a legitimate bad boy was well documented and recognized. Those in the know wanted to be on my team and those who eventually learned of my works were eager to connect with me.

Again, staying beneath the police radar and keeping my business dealings closely guarded, I quietly amassed a strong army of men who could take over the entire city and the drug market. I'm talking about a crew the National Guard would have to be summoned to confront if we went on an open rampage. I was the boss of bosses and I fully understood how much power I commanded. Knowing how such power can corrupt, I would vow to never abuse my position or become a war monger or a senseless spreader of wholesale death and destruction. Over the years I had witnessed how heartless gang leaders who were drunk on power perpetrated horrendous acts of violence against others with no thoughts of remorse and I loathed the practice. My philosophy was simple; I wanted my mob to prosper as I prospered because at the top there was room for all and the need for senseless violence was absurd. From my Italian brothers, I learned violence was truly bad for business and to never take business personal.

I had everything going my way and it appeared that there was no stopping me. I felt invincible to a large extent and believed I could continue to outsmart and out-finesse the player haters and the police on the streets indefinitely. The Old Man had made significant progress in Mexico and had several shipments delivered to me already. My goal to reach a ton per month was a rather extravagant proposition, but I could clearly see my objective coming into fruition. One thousand kilos was a lot of cocaine, yet I had the crew to move the product throughout the Midwest with little to no opposition. The paper chase was about to get real serious real fast and all hands were on deck. At least that's what I thought during my ephemeral moments of glory and street prestige.

No man could dethrone me and I was thoroughly convinced that no man would. When the day inevitably arrived for me to face the God-consciousness that lived within me, I would respond with defiance. I would acknowledge God's presence one day and be reminded of the human destruction to which my hands were contributing. In my state of defiance, I instructed Allah to stand aside and allow me to do my thing, openly saying out loud, "Let me do this and see if I can make this turn out right!" This was not a silent discussion. I spoke these words aloud as if speaking directly to God. I vividly recall the moment and how I felt like a disobedient child going against the profound wisdom of a very wise parent. My defiance did not come by way of unchecked arrogance, but by way of trying to reason and bargain with God to justify what I was doing.

This talk with God came when I was alone one day, waiting for the Old Man following a recent trip to Mexico. Contemplating my life in general, I found myself thinking about the many excuses and justifications I had given myself for being a drug dealer. Being a Muslim and considering myself a conscious-minded Black man, at my core I opposed drug dealing. I had told myself my involvement in the drug business would be short lived and once I made enough money to do some positive things, I would walk away. My talk with Allah was regarding that very pledge, on which I appeared to be reneging, because at the hour my personal bankroll was close to two million strong with perhaps another half million on the streets still in play, and I had no intention of quitting.

In essence, my talk with God about my criminal activities amounted to me asserting that my plan was better than God's plan. My obvious delusion that I knew more than Allah and possessed a superior enlightenment only reflected how blind and darkened my heart had become. Tell God, "Let me do this and see if I can make things turn out right" was like telling God to take a break and let me govern my affairs. In that very instant it seemed as though I had spoken my own demise as a drug dealer into existence because my criminal empire began to crumble from the foundation up. Later, after all the damage was done, I did not view my demise and downfall as a form of punishment or chastisement; rather, it was a matter of being saved from my own self-destruction. No man would dethrone me. I believe with all my heart and soul that God would be the one to knock me completely off my square before I reached the point of no return.

My internal conflict between my God consciousness and following my worldly aspirations and appetites of the flesh were compounded when I met with the Old Man. He returned from his latest trip into Mexico bearing positive news of the ground he had covered and the contacts he had made. As I listened to the Old Man relate his adventures and speak in his typical authoritative manner. I heard him reveal a great deal more than his words conveyed. The Old Man wanted to be king and conducted himself in Mexico in the grandiose style for which he was well known, and no doubt projected himself as being the boss of bosses. In listening to him, I heard a number of subtle things that concerned me and in that moment, I felt it was highly probable that I would one day have to aggressively eliminate the brother.

More strongly, that voice in my heart spoke again, telling me now was the perfect time for me to gracefully bow out of the street life altogether. I continued to quietly listen to the Old Man narrate details of his Mexico exploits while mentally calculating his severance pay and pondering the words to tell him I was stepping down. By no means was the Old Man a dummy. He was both clever and a shrewd operator and seemed to read my every thought. When I was about to speak, the Old Man abruptly cut in and said, "Little brother, please don't say what you're about to say. Let's not do that, man!" His plead seemed to come from a place of sudden humility and submissiveness that totally caught me off guard because the Old Man was too arrogant to bend his will to another man. He had sensed that I was about to end things between us and, without me, the entire operation became unglued and every man had to fend for himself. The Old Man also knew that if I decided to step down, there was absolutely nothing he could say or do about it. The fact was well established that I was my own man and an independent thinker who could hold his own. The Old Man also personally knew many of the lethal bad boys rolling with me and on my command they would not hesitate to put him to sleep permanently. Most of them did not like the Old Man due to his arrogant attitude and only dealt with him because of me. On more than one occasion, it was suggested that we keep our guard up and be prepared to swiftly deal with him if and when the time arrived.

Going against my better judgment and ignoring the inner voice that told me to give up my lifestyle as a street hustler, I agreed to send the Old Man back to Mexico to carry on with his mission. My heart no longer fully behind the move and my enthusiasm to grow my operation was reduced to a mere flicker of a flame submerged in darkness. In that moment, the recurring battle between my good and bad intentions had me seriously questioning myself and the spiritually unhealthy moves I continued to make. The dueling characters that lived within had finally collided and there was no room for the two to coexist. My soul was deeply troubled and I suddenly lost the determination or necessary drive to pursue my objective as a notorious drug dealer. Not only did I lose my driving force, but I also seemingly lost my Midas touch.

From that day forward, my criminal lifestyle began to gradually deteriorate as the evidence became crystal clear that no man can serve two masters. To succeed at anything in life, one must be all in, have a total sense of commitment, and possess a relentless pursuit of the objective. My heart was no longer in it; my total commitment and relentless pursuit were no longer present. Things started to go badly with my business dealings on the legal and illegal fronts and I really did not care. I believe, subconsciously, I had already decided to destroy the beast my hands had created before that very beast consumed me. The one thing that would remain razor sharp through it all was my astute survival skills, along with my fortitude to be the last man standing, no matter what happened.

The Old Man would cross the border again into cartel territory, this time taking a million dollars in cash. No doubt due to his arrogance, the fool would be robbed and abducted and transported to a secluded location to be killed. The Old Man, the young Mexican, and two other guys would untie themselves and escape from the back of a truck in which they were being held and manage to get away. As soon as I learned the news, I immediately thought about something the Old Man said to me, which caused an inward frown. Mexicans are docile and used to taking orders, he said, blatantly disparaging and underestimating all Mexicans. I recall when he made the statement, I thought to myself that his attitude would one day be his greatest downfall. I believe the Old Man got robbed, but there were wide gaps in his story in describing to where the whole million disappeared. By street law, the Old Man should have come home and faced certain death. When my rude boys in the crew learned about what happened, they questioned the Old Man's loyalty and asked for a green light to lay him down. Yet I gave the brother the benefit beyond a strong doubt because I knew his character so well. Also, if anyone was going to lay the Old Man down, it would be me and he would never see it coming.

I got back on the road again for Texas, charging the Mexican loss to the game, because truly, someone must pay where mistakes are made. Suffering a million-dollar hit took a lot of wind out of my sails and after sitting down for over a year, I had to get back on the fast track once again to make up for the loss. Reestablishing things with D.R. was no problem, but I grew complacent in thinking things would continue to run smoothly without my constant hands on guidance. Granted, D.R. was definitely a dynamic leader, but not nearly as advanced as me in business sense in the drug game, nor did he possess my foresight in how to keep the odds in his favor at all times. The first time I left my brother to handle things, he purchased twenty-five kilos of cake mix for three hundred fifty thousand dollars.

Things continued to decline from there until I was using more drugs than I sold. In every way imaginable, I lost money until one day I was ghetto rich and the next day I was flat broke. It only took perhaps six months from the time I instructed God to stand aside because I was the better planner for all my plans to vanish into thin air. Throughout the following year, I spiraled out of control, engaging in self-destructive behaviors and medicating myself daily with drugs and alcohol in an attempt to hide from my personal reality. When the dust finally settled, Betty and I were divorced, I was financially devastated, and psychologically my purpose in life became more elusive. The world in which I lived took more than it gave and where mistakes are made, someone must pay.

19. Where Do I Go from Here

I was a falling star, having an out-of-body experience, seeing myself falling out of my personal and spiritual orbit, yet unable to direct my course. Constantly, I questioned myself, asking why my life was filled with such vicissitudes of adversity and trials that troubled my very soul. I could not understand why my existence held any real significance, but deep within, I felt my life held a purpose greater than me, a purpose that seemingly eluded my comprehension. I remember feeling as though I was deprived of the right and privilege to govern my own life because of bad management and was relegated to the position of being a passive observer. Giving a bird's eye view looking down on my life as it unfolded, I saw my self-destructive pattern and knew I had to experience whatever lay ahead, willingly or unwillingly. My wings had been clipped and where I could once fly higher than an eagle and see far and wide with clarity, I was now as blind as a bat and had the wings of a barnyard turkey.

My first step in existing the criminal world and the life of crime I lived was to leave every bridge into the lifestyle burned to ashes. My reputation on the streets as a stand-up guy was my badge of honor, respected by friends and foes. I intentionally and knowingly annihilated that reputation by putting myself and my family above my loyalty to those in the game who had no apparent loyalty to me. One brother in particular, named Cook, was working a devious plan to double cross me and I saw him coming. Cook was what I considered a bottom feeder who did not have the teeth to eat steak: a dog with a furious bark but only tried to bite you when you turned your back. What Cook did not realize is I knew his history very well. As a teenager he testified against his childhood friend in a murder trial; that friend received a life sentence. I also knew he had made incriminating statements to federal authorities in connection with a major drug case. I dealt with Cook from a comfortable distance and never trusted him. I simply found him useful at the time. We had a five-hundred-kilo-shipment deal in the works between us at no cost to me other than providing a drop-off location on our end. The shipment was arriving by way of semi and I had the perfect location. I owned a diesel-mechanic shop in the industrial part of town, surrounded by about five acres of land with a Quonset hut large enough for four tractor-trailer trucks to fit inside. Everything about my shop made it a perfect location to hide in plain sight and govern my illegal business, and to accommodate the five-hundred-kilo shipment.

Before the shipment arrived, I would be arrested and subsequently taken into federal custody for violation of my supervised release. I had been on the run for more than five years, a fact about which very few were aware of and a subject never mentioned. I woke up one morning in jail after partying all night at the gambling boats parked on Lake Michigan. I was so loaded on my drug cocktail mix and cognac that I kept nodding off at the wheel as I drove home, coming dangerously close to crashing on the highway at a speed of sixty-five miles per hour. The last thing I remember was pulling off the highway and stopping in a nearby residential neighborhood. Being so loaded was nothing new to me; rather, it was a normal part of my day just to cope, but the sudden slumberness and my total inability to fight it was new and it also sort of frightened me from a strange place deep within. Never before and never since has such an occurrence happened to me in such a mysterious and phenomenal way, leaving me feeling dumfounded and insecure.

Suffering through the pains of withdrawal from a dealer's drug habit was always brutal and merciless, but I bounced back resiliently, clear headed in a matter of days of being locked up. On the streets, I would often crawl into a hole for two or three days to kick drugs out of my system and get my act together. I spent my first couple of days in jail focused on getting myself together before giving any attention to my pending legal issues. When I finally came around to considering my new legal predicament, I immediately reached the conclusion that I should be down for the count for at least one year for violating my probation, and I remember thinking, "There's no real pressure here. I can serve a year standing on my head."

Things would begin to unfold differently once the FBI learned I was in custody and sent agents to interview me at the county jail where I was held. The interview lasted long enough for the agents to introduce themselves and for me to tell them I had nothing to say without my lawyer present. They would angrily storm out of the interview room, leaving me sitting there alone, only to return a week later with a more aggressive approach. The second interview came with explosive news that "my drug shipment" had been intercepted. Their words implying the drug shipment was mine got my undivided attention and I put on my listening ears to hear every word the agents spoke or left unspoken. Quietly, I sat and listened and the more the agents talked, the more they revealed; the more they revealed, the more I learned about what I was actually up against. The shipment was busted and the dominoes were already beginning to fall with the rats running for cover, making statements minimizing their involvement for a promise of leniency. The picture was emerging that I was the alleged kingpin behind the whole operation and the agents were there in an attempt to connect the dots.

As the agents presented their allegations against me, I heard them relating information that could only come from one or two individuals, and Cook came to mind with a convincing impact. Everywhere I looked and in everything I heard, it all led straight back to Cook in one way or another. Once again, the interview concluded with me telling the FBI agents I had nothing to say without my lawyer present. During the first interview, I requested my attorney because I knew it would terminate the meeting on the spot and I had no desire to talk with them. But from the second interview, I learned information that put me in full defensive mold and my request to have my lawyer present was genuine, and came only after I heard them out.

Back in my jail cell, laying on my bunk replaying everything the agents said to me, I suddenly recalled an exchange with Cook. One of his close running buddies had been arrested by the feds for drug possession with an attempt to deliver and cooperated with the authorities to free himself. He told Cook about his new strategy to play both sides of the fence and work with the feds on the down low and invited Cook to do the same. He mentioned using signals to alert close associates not to say anything incriminating when they came around wired for sound if the intended target was a friend. I remember getting the impression that Cook informed me of what was going on simply to see if I would approve. Only after I spoke out in total opposition did he claim the scheme to be ridiculous and unworkable, yet there was very little conviction in his words and I heard the lack of sincerity in them.

The FBI agents would pay me a visit for the third time and it was obvious they wanted either my head or my cooperation. They came with my attorney and with a fight plan that put my back against the wall, producing a mountain of circumstantial evidence that pointed incriminating fingers in my direction. One African American FBI agent in particular would address me in a straightforward down-to-earth manner and got my full attention for some reason. He started by flatly saying "Man, haven't you had enough yet, my brother?" His words seemingly came from a place of real concern and were not laced with negative criticism. He continued on to explain the feds were prepared to hit me with everything they had, including charging members of my family and my wife Betty with money laundering and conspiracy if their investigation revealed I spent a single dollar of drug money on them in any way. Technically, they had a point about the money-laundering charge, and although it was a weak allegation with a slim chance for a conviction, the legal battle itself would be costly in more ways than one. By design, I had kept my family and Betty far removed from my street dealings to keep them from being placed in jeopardy, and under no circumstance would I compromise my position. No matter how or where I landed, the decision was already made that my first loyalty would forever be to my family, regardless of my personal loss.

An array of photos lay on the desk of different individuals I knew or with whom I did business. I knew they were placed there for dynamic effect. The trained agents no doubt read my reactions loud and clear when the Black agent began tapping a finger on a mug shot of Cook and looking me straight in the eyes said, "This man here, he don't mean you any good. You can protect and defend him if you want to!" I could not contain my anger and contempt and it had to be written all over my face. The agent went on to remind me of a traffic stop where forty-seven thousand dollars and a Mercedes-Benz I had only driven twice was confiscated after paying Cook a visit. Of course I was on the run at the time and Cook was one of the very few who knew this. I managed to finesse my way out of the traffic stop by slipping into one of my forever-ready identities that no one knew about but me. Cook owed me three hundred thousand and I was leaving his place after picking up forty-seven grand as his first payment when out of nowhere, the Indiana State Police and the FBI stopped me for an alleged traffic violation. You got to be completely ignorant to believe both the FBI and the state police are interested in a routine traffic stop. I walked away from the encounter, but I was getting heat and there was no doubt in my mind where it was coming from.

The agents wanted to hear me speak because I had a long history of being a man of my word and if I happened to break and tell what I knew, all the dots would suddenly be connected. I made the decision then and there that my first responsibility was to protect my family from any form of suffering and then protect me and my crew. I agreed to talk with an understanding that neither my family nor my crew would be touched, no matter what I said or revealed. My street reputation would take a severe hit, a reputation I spent a lifetime building and a reputation I no longer aspired toward. I went into the agreement knowing my criminal life was coming to an end. I merely slammed the door behind me. My exit came with compromises and cooperation and I was cool with that.

After spending approximately three months in the county jail awaiting the disposition of my probation violation, I was released. I returned to the streets of Gary, Indiana, to hear rumors that an open contract was out on my life. Instead of running for cover, I armed myself and hit the streets, going everywhere people said I could not go. To anyone wanting to collect on the contract, I made it perfectly clear that I was not hard to find. I rode around the city freely with my bad-boy attitude on full display, carrying two handguns on me and having enough fire power in my truck to start a small war. Bodacious and daring, I welcomed my enemies to confront me whenever and wherever was convenient for them. I felt strongly that I made the right decision under the circumstances and was willing to defend my position to the utmost, even to my last breath.

I was a man who could not be threatened, but by the same token, I was not foolish enough to think no man could reach out and touch me with a bullet. With the scent of death all around me, I refused to leave Gary until my ego was satisfied and my enemies bowed like cowards, wanting none of the drama I promised to surely bring to the streets. The prison beast I had locked up in my private dungeon was on a rampage, a beast with a bad understanding who spoke the language of violence very well. That beast was running loose and he was ready to increase the death toll significantly, if proven necessary. My brother David would plead with me to leave Gary and come back to Minneapolis where he lived. I would finally take his advice after realizing I was in a no-win situation. Had I continued roaming the streets of Gary looking for trouble, eventually trouble would have found me and right now I would be dead or in prison for the rest of my life.

Back in Minnesota, things still did not improve when it came to my involvement in dealing drugs. The handwriting was clearly on the wall that never again in my life would I succeed in the dope game. I knew this to be true at the core of my very soul, yet resisted accepting this fact until the darker days that followed forced me into total submission. In the past, Minneapolis was fertile ground for me and I believed getting a fresh start in the Twin Cities would put me back on track. Joining forces with my partner, Tony, who was like a brother by another mother, we made a drug run to Los Angeles and were arrested in Nevada on our return. I would spend approximately three years incarcerated in Las Vegas during which time it dawned on me that prison life was a life of empty dreams. It was not a matter of doing hard prison time. It was more a matter of finally opening my eyes and seeing clearly what my blindness had previously failed to comprehend. I grew up among strong men who could hold their own: men who commanded respect in the world in which we lived and who stood on their word of honor. During my incarceration in Las Vegas, I found myself surrounded by inmates rather than convicts. An inmate is no more than a person residing under similar conditions. I found most of them to be weak and without honor, all talk and no action.

For years, I watched the convict mentality change face until only traces of reflection were left. From my personal experience, I consciously observed the convict code of silence become totally obsolete. Beginning with my first crime and imprisonment, my codefendants would betray me. In the years that followed, the convict code of silence would be replaced with the inmate code of every man for himself: you are not hip until you flip. I watched the prison system itself evolve into human warehouses and into one big business venture with no interest in the concept of rehabilitation. Petty crimes received harsh prison sentences and produced a growing prison population of individuals deemed social rejects. All over the country the business of crime and punishment fed off the flesh of the unfortunate ones caught in its dragnet. Once again, the man in the mirror was compelled to acknowledge the need to change his position in life. He himself must change his own thinking and the position in his heart.

I would serve my prison sentence at High Desert Correctional Facility, where everyone was so self-segregated along racial lines that there was no cross mixing of inmates. By this time, I had been incarcerated in prison systems or jails through the United States and never had I seen the likes of what I saw at High Desert. My Las Vegas prison experience would be the final straw to break the back of my illusions regarding an inclination toward criminal conduct. Either I had outgrown what I perceived to be a glamorous lifestyle or I simply had enough of running down the same dead-end street and facing the exact same results. Either way, my decision would be absolute and final, yet the journey ahead would prove to be the greatest challenge and the most psychologically turbulent period of my entire life.

During my stay at High Desert, not only did I feel as though I was a man alone on an island, but I also felt I had nothing of essence in common with those around me. With the exception of the Muslim brothers,

I only made friends with two other prisoners at High Desert: the Las Vegas leader of the Crips street gang, who was old school like me with a lengthy criminal history, and O.J. Simpson's codefendant who became my cellmate. The Crips leader and I seemed to bond immediately and appeared to be fighting the same past and present demons. However, O.J. Simpson's codefendant—my cellmate—was a classy highly intelligent brother with no criminal background and had no business being in prison, period. His only crime was guilt by association at a time when state and federal authorities wanted O.J. off the street by any means necessary. My cellmate merely got caught up in what I believe was a vindictive prosecution of O.J. Simpson, and his refusal to testify against O.J. led him to become collateral damage.

Upon my release from High Desert, I was paroled to the State of Nevada with six months left to serve on probation and had no choice but to remain in town during my probation period. I welcomed a change in environment and starting my life over with a new direction and a more positive goal and objective engraved on my heart. I did not mind that I would really be all alone in Las Vegas knowing no one, fresh out of prison, and dead broke. My plan was to start anew all across the board and the natural survivor in me was determined to land on my feet and fully embrace the idea of starting at the bottom once again. My stay in Las Vegas would not only prove to be a pivotal moment in my life, but Las Vegas also became a battlefield where I had to fight to save my life and my soul.

My six-month probation period in Las Vegas would stretch into a three-year stay in Sin City. Not wanting to sit around idle for six months and eager to begin a positive, crime-free life, I enrolled in a junior college to study audio production. With the assistance of a fellow Muslim brother, I got a job managing a 7-11 convenience store on Boulder Highway, one of Las Vegas' main strips for drugs and prostitution. Working full time and being a full-time student kept me busy and, for once in my life, I was doing the right thing and living right. As a Muslim, I had my priorities in order; I was consistent with my daily prayers, maintained all my religious responsibilities, and stayed active in the Las Vegas Muslim community. I even spent my weekends feeding the homeless in

Las Vegas' skid row area, which unfortunately covered an entire neighborhood. Although I lived on a mediocre budget and was no longer living large and carefree, I was finally at peace with myself.

After doing a great deal of soul searching and seeking understanding of the profound question—Why had my life experience taken the path I had traveled?—my Las Vegas experience would reveal to me and firmly convince me that my life had purpose and significance far beyond my control. It seemed to me that I had already been tried and tested by the flames of fire produced by my rebellion over the years, and I had survived it all. Strong and confident, I thought I could handle any situation I faced. Las Vegas turned into a spiritual war zone for me where I felt like I fought the devil on his own grounds and Allah alone saved me. I truly found myself in a real battle for my soul with an enemy who did not play fair and who attacked me from within and from without: an enemy whose sole purpose was to destroy me at all costs before I reached my divine destiny.

I often thought about a time when I was a kid, about seven or eight years old, living in the deep South on my grandparents' small farm in North Carolina. I used to look up into the sky on a clear star-filled night and find myself spellbound and completely mesmerized by the awesome creation I beheld. The sky would be filled with bright shining stars and I remember always getting a distinct feeling that something extraordinary was behind this profound artistry. Long before I had a mature concept of religion, I felt a strong connection with God and all creation, a special connection beyond my comprehension as a mere human being. As a youth, I not only felt connected spiritually with creation, but I also felt like the heavens looked down on me favorably and with approval. I could not identify the source from whence my intrigue manifested during my youth, nor do I claim my personal experience applies solely to me.

In Las Vegas, it would be the bright lights of the hotel casinos and the constant whisper of mischief relentlessly pursuing me that demanded my attention. With both eyes wide open, I began to see clearly all the sin and suffering the world had slipped into and accepted as a normal way of life. Perhaps I was an idealist at heart in search of the impossible dream when thinking I would find the world a perfect place to live once I made the proper adjustments within myself. What I actually discovered was that the world and society itself had grown darkened with an unhealthy appetite for divergent conduct, contrary to the laws of God. The more I strove and persevered to lead a clean and God-fearing life, the more evident it became that the human race was truly in big trouble. As a people, we were going totally against all divine instruction on how to carry and conduct ourselves as God's vicegerents in the world. It did not take a rocket scientist or genius to see how mankind has defaced creation and made lawful that which God has made unlawful and forbidden.

In the solitude of my mind, I saw the world as being in a worse position than a modern-day Babylon or a Sodom and Gomorrah combined. Every problem that confronts us in the world today can trace directly back to our failure to adhere and submit to the guidance of God. This may sound strange coming from an individual with my background and a long history of defiance and outright rebelliousness. Yet who, other than Allah can change or reveal what's in a man's heart? The truth does not change simply because I speak it. Mankind in his finest moment of great accomplishments was living in his darkest hours. I saw the human race spiraling blindly out of control under a diabolical influence that made our sinful behavior seem appealing and socially acceptable. The presence and spiritual light of God were reduced to a mediocre concept that left us enjoying the temporal pleasures of this world's life at the expense of losing our souls.

Disdained and feeling completely disenchanted with life in general, and seeing how the world around me continued to recede into a cesspool of godlessness and lack of respect for the divine order of life, I fell into a purely pathetic state of mind. Many of our social problems would be solved if mankind followed the simple and basic teachings of being his brother's keeper, being fair and just with each other, and wanting for his brother what he wanted for himself. I was not the bad seed; rather, the world we lived in was planting bad seeds by the acres, At the core of my soul, I did not want to be part of the world in which I lived anymore. My personal guilt and shame regarding my own bad deeds of the past would only magnify and confirm the ugliness I saw in the world and in myself while going astray. That was the deep dark hole I found myself in when I decided to commit the cardinal sin and ultimate violation of taking my own life. The decision seemingly popped into my head out of thin air and without a second thought, I immediately embraced the unholy suggestion.

One day while contemplating my place in life and in the world, the belief systems I had subscribed to for most of my life crumbled, exposing all my vulnerabilities. As a street hustler, I made millions and could not find the peace and happiness for which my heart longed. As a man and an ex-convict with a career criminal history who was striving to improve himself, I saw that the more I changed my attitude and behavior, the more I recognized the wickedness in society as a whole. It appeared to me that the environment and the self-righteous society that condemned me and my unlawful conduct was worse than or just as bad as the lifestyle from which I was fleeing. The hypocrisy of it all painted a hopeless picture of despair and the inevitable demise of the entire human race, with the exception of those who put their trust and faith in God and refrained from iniquities and shameful deeds.

I went from dislike and contempt for what I was seeing going on in the world around me to no longer wanting to be part of this world. I wanted to live; I simply did not wish to continue living in a world where the devil's influence was more prominent than God's. With all the adversity I had already faced in my life and the many dark holes I crawled my way out of along the way, the thought of killing myself never occurred to me. I actually abhorred the idea of committing suicide, yet there I saw swallowing down a handful of sleeping pills, determined to end a life I no longer wanted to live.

Going through my cell-phone contacts, I either called or sent colorful messages to friends and family, intentionally being rather ambiguous in saying my good-byes. Knowing what I was about to do and acknowledging the gravity of the unforgivable sin I intended to commit, I turned to God in prayer, pleading for mercy on my soul. With tears in my eyes, I begged for God's infinite forgiveness and mercy, repeating over and over, "I no longer wish to be part of this world," and asking God to forgive me for what I was about to do. Years later, when I looked back on my decision to suddenly end my life, I realized reaching this juncture was more astonishing and irrational than the actual act itself. Nowhere in my DNA did I perceive having suicidal tendencies and always believed my fortitude had me far above contemplating such a thought.

My brother Kelvin would read between the lines of my text message to him and interpret it as a scream for help. Kelvin was the only person to respond to my goodbye texts, and for some reason, he felt compelled to track down my Las Vegas address and promptly sent the police to my house. To my knowledge, no one knew where I lived in Las Vegas except my brother David, who sent me a package soon after my release from prison in Nevada. How Kelvin located my whereabouts and what led him to take the action he took, I have no idea, and the matter has never been discussed between us. Yet true enough, Kelvin's intervention, no doubt, contributed to me still being here today.

The last thing I would remember before the sleeping pills took effect was an overwhelming sense of calmness that came from a place deep within, a sense of calmness I had experienced several time before when death was attempting to lay hands on me and claim my soul. It was the same calmness that enveloped me when Gary, Indiana, homicide detectives were planning to murder me years ago at age 15. Many times, when death approached while living the bad-boy life in prison and in the streets, I would experience this same sense of calmness. I recall thinking to myself as I lost consciousness, "Everything is going to be just fine now."

I was rapidly reaching the point of no return when the police arrived, followed by a team of paramedics. The police voices penetrated the thick layers of darkness enveloping me and temporarily pulled me back to the present moment. The police asked for my identification and when I tried to raise from my bed to get my wallet, I could not move. From that point on and for the next three or four days, I only have vague frames in my memory bank as to what happened.

I experienced no phenomenal visions such as bright shining lights or spiritual sightings, only vast darkness and clouds of nothingness that seemingly stretched into eternity. When my faculties finally returned and I was able to form a coherent thought, I realized I was still among the living. This realization would create a cascade of profound inner confusion, leaving me to ask myself a single question: "Why am I still here?" In that very instant, I felt my life held a significance far greater than anything I could ever conceive. I also strongly felt I had a mission in front of me that I had avoided all my life from which I could no longer run and was now prepared to embrace.

Although I saw no bright lights or spiritual sightings, I did wake up a totally different man. From head to toe, I felt like I had been severely chastised in every way a person could be chastised and I felt empty in every way an individual could feel empty. The experience had humbled me to the core of my very heart and soul, purging my inner being of all the garbage and unhealthy ideas I had accumulated and force fed myself over the years. None of the things I once held to be of high importance carried weight any longer. Power, money, material possessions, and social status all became absolutely meaningless to me. I had a burning desire to save my soul and strive diligently to make amends for my past transgressions. I wanted nothing more than to please God according to my understanding and merge my will with the will of my higher power, Allah.

I did not evolve overnight into a saint; rather, reinventing myself as a man with real substance and true conviction was a gradual process. The realist in me quietly acknowledged I could never reach perfection or overcome all my human faults and shortcomings. My sole objective was simply to pursue the straight path to become the best human being I could produce with what I had to work with. In the beginning, of what I recognized as my new life-long journey, I encountered my share of trials and tribulations as I eradicated the obsolete and the bad-boy tendencies to which I once subscribed to with true loyalty. Moving forward and never entertaining the thought of looking back, I would eliminate people, places, and things that ran contrary to my new direction, removing everything from life that could potentially hinder my progress and surrounding myself with individuals traveling the same path as mine.

Getting the bad conduct and behavior out of my system was the easy part, yet the more serious problem existed within. I had issues with deep psychological roots that I once lived by that went back many years and I had no one-step solution to resolving those issues. It took time to correct my thinking and to rid myself of suggestive thoughts to cut corners and revert to previous lunacy. I also had a deeply rooted anger-management problem that scared me because I knew very well what I was capable of when provoked into violent action. During the early days of my journey to reinvent myself in the spirit of my true self, I would not leave the house out of fear someone would say or do something that caused me to explode. The survival techniques I learned to used when facing a physical altercation were deeply ingrained and designed to really hurt someone. In prison, convicts had no grey areas and every conflict equated to being a matter of life or death. This was not necessarily true in the free world and I had to make the proper adjustments to raise above my anger issues or they would lead to my downfall.

I remained in Las Vegas for perhaps another two or three months following my suicide attempt, during which time that lethal side would manifest itself twice. In both situations, I had murder on my mind and came close to doing just that, stabbing one would-be drug dealer repeatedly and later stopping short of doing the same a second time when confronted by a want-to-be tough guy. Both men made the critical mistake of underestimating me, like many in the past had done, and nearly paid for that mistake with their lives. Following each incident, a nagging feeling haunted me: if I did not flee Las Vegas soon, I would eventually end up dead in the streets or with a life sentence in prison or on death row. This was one of the things I knew with a degree of certainty that I could not deny. I felt it coming close on my heels and only had a small window in time to escape, and that window was closing fast.

My brother David, a kidney-transplant recipient who survived on dialysis for about eighteen years, would pass away, and his death probably saved my life. For a long time, I felt guilty, thinking it took my brother's death to get me out of Las Vegas, Nevada and begin the process of totally reconstructing my entire life from the inside out and from the bottom up. With the passing of David, I not only lost a brother; I lost my best friend and the one person who understood me more than anybody in this world. His death was a devastating blow. In 2012, like an old 59 Chevy on four flat tires, my departure from the Sin City proved laborious, charged with an emotional overload, and filled with a deep hurting pain. All the way to the very end, some unexplainable force seemed to work against me to prevent my leaving Las Vegas where nothing good was promised in my future.

I vividly recall the sense of relief that came over me as I boarded the plane to depart Las Vegas for North Carolina where I was born and partly raised. I remember thinking to myself, "I'm going home where my life began and start all over again." With no desire to any longer seek fortune and fame in this material world, I surrendered to the plan I strongly believed Allah had in store for Abdul-Jameel Taajwar. I no longer wanted a bank account full of dollars and cents. I wanted to accumulate a bank account filled with good deeds and blessings. One day at a time, one step at a time, and addressing one problem at a time, I would fight the good fight, against all odds.

> Say: "Verily, my Lord
> Hath guided me to
> A way that is straight—
> A religion of right—
> The path trod by Abraham
> The true in faith,
> And he certainly
> Joined not gods with Allah."
>
> Say: "Truly, my prayer
> And my service of sacrifice,
> My life and my death,
> Are all for Allah.
> The Cherisher of the Worlds..."
>
> Al-Qur'an Chapter VI verses 161 and 162

Epilogue
(Year 2020)

It was Not a Dream! There I was standing on the coastline of the Atlantic Ocean looking into the past to better understand the present moment and to firmly grasp my new awakening. I had a strange intuitive feeling my life had suddenly come full circle in a very profound way. I was in Ghana, Africa, at the Cape Coast Castle looking across the waters which led to the middle passage for my people. The old ghostly castle itself gave me an eerie feeling I couldn't shake, the surf of the ocean waves seemed more aggressive and told horrific stories of the many lost to its vastness and depth. I felt that if I could tune out the noise from the daily activities, I would hear all the voices of suffering and misery left behind on the castle floors and walls and throughout the building structure. Stubbornly, I refused to pay the required admission to tour the old Castle, saying to myself that there was no way I would pay to relive what I was still living with. I also had a big chip on my shoulder because it appeared that everyone was still capitalizing and profiteering off the vestiges of the slave trade. My refusing to pay the Castle admission fee is how I ended up standing there looking across the ocean waters, my eyes seeing both the past and the present. I experienced many mixed emotions as I stood there where my people were shipped off into enslavement. I thought about how far my forefathers had traveled and all they had to endure, and there I stood where it all begun. The prodigal son had return home after being lost in the wilderness of America.

I first visit Ghana in 2015 and immediately cultivated an extended Ghanaian family; that family continues to grow with my every trip home. I live amongst the people in the villages, not like the visiting tourist. I got to know the people and the people got to know me; it was a beautiful exchange. I would eventually find my Ghanaian Queen and marry her to forever establish my home in Ghana and plant some serious roots. Following my initial trip to Ghana, I returned stateside thinking about how I could use my God-given talents to aid and assist the people of Ghana in building schools.

The idea of building schools in Ghana was planted and the mere thought of my intended plan gave me a head rush I cannot express or explain, but I was left with the impression that I had finally found a purpose in life worth embracing wholeheartedly. There was something highly contagious about this idea, or it had the potential of being contagious once fully developed, and I believed in what I wanted to do. I was totally committed from the moment I conceived the idea. Later I met my Beloved Sister Khadijah and learned about The Toyibul Anfas (Pure Hearts) Foundation, a non-profit Ghana organization in the early stages of forming and establishing itself. Toyibul Anfas and myself were the perfect fit across the board and in every aspect, and I felt my energies could be well used through this organization. The Foundation goals were to build schools and provide housing for orphans, as well as being a service to the community and the underprivileged in Ghana. I attached myself to the Toyibul Anfas cause and was made the U.S. President for the organization. My new mission in life was inspired in that instance and I have never found anything more rewarding and fulfilling than the work I was doing and wanted to do in the land of my forefathers. I saw my first responsibility to be a financial quest to raise the funds to finish work the Foundation had already started, and although we have made some progress, there is much more work still to be done. I have pledged proceeds from the sales of Against All Odds to the Toyibul Anfas (Pure Hearts) Foundation to further our goals and objective to build schools and assist the disadvantage. I also ask all those who read my story to support me in this truly worthy cause and make a donation to our GoFundMe campaign and help us help others.

For more information contact:

Toyibul Anfas Foundation

c/o Abdul-Jameel Taajwar

P.O. Box 430

Goldsboro, NC 27530